## LIFE BEYOND GRADES

This book raises the question of whether or not educators can promote intrinsic motivation among college students when they seem overwhelmingly focused on grades. Indeed, can there be life beyond grades? The answer is "Yes." A love of learning can coexist, even thrive, in the face of competing pressures from grades.

Drawing on recent groundbreaking classroom research, the authors articulate a new understanding of the causes of the stalemate between intrinsic and external motivation, so that a reconciliation between them can be achieved. Then the authors apply a powerful set of motivational and pedagogical principles to lay out a step-by-step blueprint for designing and teaching college courses that promote intrinsic motivation as a primary educational goal in its own right, above and beyond knowledge and skill acquisition. This practical blueprint draws on authentic case study examples from a variety of subject-matter disciplines.

MARTIN V. COVINGTON is Professor of the Graduate School (Psychology Department), University of California, at Berkeley and holds the Berkeley Presidential Chair in Undergraduate Education. He is the author of numerous books and research articles, and a recipient of the Berkeley Distinguished Teaching Award and the Phi Beta Kappa Award for Outstanding University Instructor of the Year in California.

LINDA M. VON HOENE is Assistant Dean for Graduate Student Professional Development and Director of the Graduate Student Instructor (GSI) Teaching & Resource Center at the University of California, Berkeley. She codirects Berkeley's Summer Institute for Preparing Future Faculty and Berkeley's SMART program, a graduate/undergraduate research mentoring program.

DOMINIC J. VOGE is Associate Director of Princeton University's McGraw Center for Teaching and Learning where he leads the undergraduate learning program and conducts faculty development. He was awarded the K. Patricia Cross Leadership Award (American Association of Colleges and Universities) and the TRPP Associates Innovation Award for his project, Principedia.

# Life Beyond Grades

## DESIGNING COLLEGE COURSES TO PROMOTE INTRINSIC MOTIVATION

Martin V. Covington
*University of California, Berkeley*

Linda M. von Hoene
*University of California, Berkeley*

Dominic J. Voge
*Princeton University*

CAMBRIDGE
UNIVERSITY PRESS

# CAMBRIDGE
## UNIVERSITY PRESS

University Printing House, Cambridge CB2 8BS, United Kingdom

One Liberty Plaza, 20th Floor, New York, NY 10006, USA

477 Williamstown Road, Port Melbourne, VIC 3207, Australia

4843/24, 2nd Floor, Ansari Road, Daryaganj, Delhi – 110002, India

79 Anson Road, #06–04/06, Singapore 079906

Cambridge University Press is part of the University of Cambridge.

It furthers the University's mission by disseminating knowledge in the pursuit of education, learning, and research at the highest international levels of excellence.

www.cambridge.org
Information on this title: www.cambridge.org/9780521801379
DOI: 10.1017/9781139032896

First published 2017

Printed in the United States of America by Sheridan Books, Inc.

*A catalogue record for this publication is available from the British Library.*

*Library of Congress Cataloging-in-Publication Data*
NAMES: Covington, Martin V., 1938– author. | Von Hoene, Linda Marie, author. | Voge, Dominic Jon, 1964– author.
TITLE: Life beyond grades : designing college courses to promote intrinsic motivation / Martin Covington, UC Berkeley, Linda von Hoene, UC Berkelely, Dominic Jon Voge, Princeton University.
DESCRIPTION: Cambridge, United Kingdom ; New York, NY, USA : University Printing House, [2017] | Includes bibliographical references and index.
IDENTIFIERS: LCCN 2016056219| ISBN 9780521801379 (Hardback) | ISBN 9780521805230 (Paperback)
SUBJECTS: LCSH: Education, Higher–Curricula. | Education, Higher–Aims and objectives. | Curriculum planning. | Motivation in education.
CLASSIFICATION: LCC LB2361 .C69 2017 | DDC 378.1/99–DC23
LC record available at https://lccn.loc.gov/2016056219

ISBN 978-0-521-80137-9 Hardback
ISBN 978-0-521-80523-0 Paperback

# Contents

# Figures

# Tables

# Preface

In our office hours, we have encountered students anxious about grades who focus on achievement per se, seemingly to the exclusion of all other considerations, and for whom it feels there is no life beyond grades. We have worked with graduate student instructors worried that their authority will be challenged in the classroom and that students (or worse yet, the course professor) will find out that they are imposters with insufficient expertise to teach. We have also facilitated workshops for faculty demoralized by their inability to effectively engage their students and instill in them a deep understanding, fascination, and appreciation of their discipline and who want to be allies in learning but feel at odds with their students over grades and grading.

The common denominator in all of these scenarios is fear – the fear of failure caused by feelings of incompetence, hence worthlessness. Fear of failure obstructs learning by both inhibiting and diverting mental resources that could otherwise be devoted to mastering the knowledge and skills needed to learn and to teach. Students strongly motivated by fear may become grade obsessed, over-engaging with our grading systems, as when particularly insistent students seem to put more creative thought into arguing for a higher grade than learning the material that was examined in the first place. Fear directs students' attention toward grades and may cause them to disengage from learning as a defensive, protective measure. We are much less likely to interact with those students who avoid our office hours. But we nonetheless still see their names on our grade sheets.

For today's students, can there be life – that is, significant, positive motivations for learning – beyond grades? If so, it must be nurtured even in the face of worries about grades and what grades mean for their academic success, for their career plans, and even for their self-respect. For faculty, are there reasons for learning besides for grades that can be cultivated in order to promote deep engagement among their students so that college courses do not become mere opportunities to acquire grade points?

This book considers these questions through the lens of the powerful theoretical framework of self-worth theory that remains largely unknown to many educators. This theory unearths the often counterintuitive reasons for why students disengage from learning and instead strive single-mindedly for high grades. Our analysis reveals a "hidden agenda" present in virtually every classroom and context where high achievement is sought, expected, and evaluated. We also demonstrate how to use core motivational principles derived from our research to design engaging college courses that can redress this negative agenda in favor of learning for the sake of discovery, curiosity, and self-development.

This book is written primarily for instructors who are designing or redesigning courses or for faculty developers or consultants who collaborate with them. Moreover, it can also be integrated in whole or in part into pedagogy seminars designed to benefit graduate student instructors, future faculty, postdocs, and adjunct professors. Additionally, educators and administrators at all school levels as well as parents (especially of college students and those who are college-bound) will find valuable insights in these pages because they illuminate the fundamental dynamics of the motivation to learn, and reveal obstacles to learning, that can be observed in virtually all school settings. Anyone wishing to understand the sometimes perplexing motivational dynamics of students will benefit from an understanding of the self-worth theory of motivation that lies at the heart of this book.

This book is organized in two complimentary parts. The first four chapters that comprise the first half of the book can be read on their own. Chapter 1 articulates a fundamental tension in the college classroom, which is not always fully appreciated, regarding students' motivations to learn and achieve. Chapter 2 introduces a theoretical lens that not only reveals this hidden agenda but also unravels its often perplexing complications. Chapters 3 and 4 explore several additional obstacles to student engagement, including mismatches in the respective roles and responsibilities of instructors and their students.

In the second part of the book, the remaining chapters provide a blueprint or road map for developing college courses that are designed specifically to offset these obstacles to true learning as revealed through self-worth theory, as well as to promote positive motivational dynamics that enhance an appreciation for learning while simultaneously ensuring traditional achievement goals and the mastery of subject matter content. Readers can follow this blueprint, step by step, through several real-life case study examples drawn from a diversity of subject matter domains ranging from neurophysiology to anthropology and the social sciences. Appendices provide resources to guide workshops and seminars in modular form.

Undoubtedly, readers will recognize many of their own students in these pages, and perhaps even themselves in the roles of instructors, and even of parents. But in addition to recognizing such familiarities, we are confident that readers will also come to see issues and problems more fully, and from this new perspective design more motivationally engaging and effective college courses.

# Acknowledgments

A number of individuals and groups have contributed to the birth of this book, and in many cases have continued to shape the evolution of its writing. First and foremost, we are deeply indebted to those Berkeley undergraduates (now numbering in the thousands) who have participated as informants over the years. Their candidly shared personal stories regarding their academic experiences constitute much of the data reported in these pages.

Equally critical, and also greatly appreciated, was the cooperation of those Berkeley faculty members who allowed their classrooms to become real-life, authentic laboratories for our data collection, as well as the welcoming support and endorsement of dozens of graduate student instructors (GSIs) who also participated in data collection and numerous fruitful discussions about the theory and practice of intrinsic motivation. We are also indebted to the staff of Berkeley's GSI Teaching & Resource Center, who contributed to our research and provided inspiration and unfailing support for our work over many years.

The collection of empirical data was followed by a second step of creating practical, real-world applications of our findings. For this task, we were once again blessed, this time by the enthusiastic commitment of some 200 advanced Ph.D. candidates from some 50 different academic departments and programs on campus, who contributed their time and energies as members of a special graduate seminar we offered during 12 different semesters over the previous decade. The purpose of the seminar was to craft the insights gathered from our research into a practical blueprint or road map for designing college courses whose structure is based on motivational principles that engage a love of learning. The challenge for seminar members was to address the question: What would a course in your discipline look like based on motivational principles intended to enhance a love of learning and intrinsic engagement, above and beyond subject matter mastery and performance goals?

For us, the greatest personal and professional satisfaction to emerge from this collaborative experience was that several hundred young, promising scholars who have now launched their academic careers literally throughout the world and across virtually every subject matter discipline are armed with the pedagogical tools that will elevate their teaching horizons to encompass a love and appreciation for learning.

We wish to acknowledge several individuals who deserve special mention for their contributions to the success of these seminars, including Drs. Chris Gade and Matt Gingo for taking charge of various administrative aspects of the seminar and managing the course website. Special recognition goes to Dr. Leah Byrne who deserves our deepest gratitude for her emerging role, beginning initially as a seminar participant herself, to becoming a co-instructor of the seminar over the past five semesters. In addition to being a superb researcher and teacher, Dr. Byrne modeled for us what it means to be a truly supportive colleague. We also would like to extend our gratitude to Dr. Kim Starr-Reid who assisted us in facilitating mock job interviews with seminar participants, the culminating activity of the course, and to Benjamin Krupicka for assisting us with research. Our thanks also go to Dr. Keith Jacoby for his wise counsel, technical expertise, and enthusiastic encouragement from the conception of the project down to the present.

Regarding logistical support for the project, we point to the indispensable contribution of Diana Hillmer for her professional handling of all the technical and logistical challenges involved in producing the prepublication form of the book manuscript. Likewise, our thanks extend to the Cambridge University Press production team, headed by Content Manager Sarah Lambert and Project Manager Divya Mathesh at SPi Global, for their masterful transformation of the manuscript into the book you are now holding in your hands.

Finally, we extend our gratitude and best wishes to those readers who, for benefit of their students, embrace the educational challenges and proposed solutions presented in this book.

# 1

# Introduction and Overview

TEACHER: What did you get out of the class?
STUDENT: I got an A.

## INTRODUCTION

Perhaps nothing frustrates college instructors more than when students forsake learning in the pursuit of grades and in the process fail to appreciate the power of learning for the sake of self-expression, personal growth, and meaningful discovery. Certainly, many college students are grade driven, not to say "grade grubbing." Indeed, we have found that many students rate achieving the highest grade possible as the main reason for undertaking assignments, with such intrinsic reasons as overcoming a personal challenge coming in a distant second (Covington & Wiedenhaupt, 1997). Ironically, we also find that students often accuse instructors of rarely encouraging the same intrinsic aspects of learning that instructors, in their turn, lament that students have come to disregard. From this perspective, instructors and students alike are often caught up in a drama with all the elements of a classic Greek tragedy: an overweening grade focus separates all the parties including faculty and graduate student instructors (GSIs)[1] along with students who fall short of their gifts for learning. This book is about the nature of this potential tragedy, its origins, its consequences, and, above all, how it can be avoided for the mutual benefit of all.

## UNDERSTANDING CAUSES

The first main theme of this book involves understanding the underlying causes of this stalemate. At first glance, the predominant grade focus may

1

seem intractable. Grades are not only sought after by students; they are also feared by students, with the winners being seen as brilliant, hardworking, and personally worthy while the losers are judged to be none of these things. This situation is made worse still by the fact that good grades are often made scarce by competitive pressures, so that many students must struggle to avoid failure rather than aspire to success. The scarcer the good grades become, the greater the importance that grades assume as evidence of superior ability. Faced with this confection of fear, materialism, and a rat race mentality, educators may despair at the prospects of ever encouraging a love of learning among their students. Can intrinsic educational goals such as subject matter appreciation coexist to any degree, let alone flourish, in the face of a performance ethic based on school grades? Indeed, is there life beyond grades?

## PROMOTING ACADEMIC ENGAGEMENT

The second main purpose of this book is to provide answers to these questions. To anticipate our response, the answer is *yes*; intrinsic engagement and a love of learning can coexist with the competing pressure of grades, but often only barely. And thriving, not just surviving, is quite another matter. In order to encourage a vibrant intellectual life of the mind, we must overhaul the ways we teach largely in an effort to offset the divisive dynamics that drive a preoccupation with grades. Even if grades were to be eliminated – a most improbable scenario in any event – it would do little to ease the situation. This is because grades per se are less the problem than is the distorted meaning of grades as indices of personal worth. Thus, the task before educators is to teach in ways that encourage students to alter the meaning of grades and accord them a more positive role in the learning process. To the extent that classrooms can become a safe haven from the threatening formula that equates good grades with one's worth as a person, curiosity and a sense of wonder will emerge naturally and flourish spontaneously. Also, on the positive side of the ledger, not only can curiosity arise spontaneously as part of a natural process, but there are teaching strategies available that can directly reawaken and strengthen these intrinsic impulses.

Our ambitious objective is nothing less than elevating positive task engagement to the level of a preeminent teaching goal, coequal with traditional achievement and performance objectives. But before there is any real hope of achieving this goal, we need to understand more about the psychological nature of task engagement itself – what factors sustain it and what circumstances act to undermine it. We also need to appreciate more fully the relationship between intrinsic engagement and tangible, extrinsic rewards like grades. It is an uneasy relationship. For example, there is some evidence to suggest that the connection is an antagonistic one. It is thought that grades may tarnish, if not destroy, the value of learning for its own sake (Kohn, 1993). This is because learning may simply become a way to acquire these rewards, and when they are no longer available, learning and its appreciation will wane. Yet, to the contrary, there are countless everyday examples of people redoubling their personal interest when given the tangible means to pursue these rewards further. Rewarding aspiring young actors with a financial scholarship that allows them to attend a summer theater group comes to mind here.

In order to understand these complexities better, we will appeal to the empirical research that has emerged from the decades-long scientific study of human motivation as it applies to achievement goals and to the phenomenon of intellectual commitment and task engagement. This is not to suggest that our understanding of the nature and nurturing of academic engagement is complete. Far from it. Much is yet to be learned, but we now know enough to recognize gaps in our knowledge and what research steps need to be taken next. But above all – and this is the important point – we know enough presently to make a difference for the better in real-world classrooms.

### BLUEPRINT FOR CHANGE

The third, and arguably the most important, aspect of this book involves the matter of solutions. We will provide a blueprint or road map for developing college courses whose highest priority is to encourage the twin goals of content mastery and the will to learn over a lifetime. This blueprint has been developed to accompany a graduate seminar co-taught by the authors over the past decade. The seminar challenge reads as follows: "What would a course in your discipline look like based on motivational principles intended to enhance a love of learning and intrinsic engagement, above and beyond subject matter mastery and performance goals?" Seminar participants are advanced graduate students who will be going on the Ph.D. job market within a year. Typically, the participants choose to develop a course they will likely teach in their first year as new instructors.

This blueprint takes the form of a series of instructional steps that form the structure of this book, chapter by chapter, with the content of each chapter providing both theoretical and practical guidance to assist readers in designing courses. (The blueprint is found in Appendix A.) This book offers several important features. First, it is suitable for several purposes for a diverse range of audiences. For instance, this book can form the basis of a curriculum for a graduate seminar similar to the one described in this book. It will also serve equally well as an advanced upper-division social science or education course. Alternatively, readers can work through this curriculum on their own, perhaps receiving independent study credit. Also, readers can employ this book as a reference source for the art and science of course design and redesign from the unique perspective of achievement motivation.

A second feature allows readers to follow the step-by-step development of three case studies, one drawn from the social sciences, another from the biological sciences, and the third from the humanities. These case studies illustrate the diversity of approaches and pathways that the course design process can take, while providing some degree of continuity and order in a creative process, which is typically nonlinear in nature. Additionally, the fact that these case studies represent three decidedly different academic domains, each with its own assumptions and conventions for what constitutes scientific and scholarly evidence, its preferred methodologies of inquiry, and its unique intellectual histories and traditions, strengthens our claim to the generalizability of our approach to college course development.

In overall summary, then, this book is intended to function variously: first, as a scientific inquiry into the nature and nurturing of *intrinsic task engagement*, and the crafting of arguments favoring the will to learn as a legitimate, attainable educational objective; second, as a bridge between psychological theory and educational practice; and, third, as a principled blueprint for creating educational change in the college classroom.

## SPOTTING THE MIRACLE

Everyone knows what it is like to be fully immersed in the pursuit of one's studies. And we can easily recognize the fruits of such engagement in others when, for example, a student suddenly brightens with radiant excitement that says, "Oh, now I get it!" And as teachers will tell us, this process is reciprocal. We have this assurance directly from teachers themselves. As it has been remarked, "Few things can compete with the teaching of eager, talented, well-prepared and demanding students that crave, in fact, demand, precision and excellence ... how lucky I really am," and "Teachers live for such moments, when realization glows like a cartoon light bulb over a student's head." In moments like these, task engagement becomes a living event. It actually assumes a rhythm and cadence of its own, so that at one moment the collective energies of the classroom are in step with students eager to learn more, leaning forward in the lecture hall expectantly; and at other times, this headlong exuberance is tempered only by the need to consolidate past lessons learned. There is nothing static here. This is why the concept of intrinsic task engagement is so elusive. It is a moving target. In sports, such engagement is referred to as momentum; in business circles, it is called teamwork; in education, unfortunately, it is all too often called rare.

There are significant reasons for this scarcity. The process of task engagement is made elusive by the fact that if students join in a collective commitment to learning, they do so to different degrees and at different times depending on their reasons for learning. Some students will remain tentative travelers, isolated from the group, content simply to accumulate grade credits. Other students, hobbled by the fear of failing, will hover at the margins of involvement, and may eventually implode and simply stop coming to class. Then there are those students who are committed to learning from the outset, and gain strength and resolve as they proceed.

What can be said more specifically about the nature of intrinsic task engagement? What is it? How is it manifest? At one level – on the surface – there is an easy answer: "We know it when we see it!" So what is there to see? More often than not, the casual observer sees a deep, abiding level of concentration and commitment as attested to by various comments from our undergraduates when asked to give examples of what it means to be task engaged. One student put it this way: "Students in Italian 1 going to watch films in Italian without subtitles week after week and not minding the fact they only understand 1% of what is being said on the screen." Equally compelling examples were offered by two other students: "In my Economic History of Europe class, I sit next to a girl who is on the edge of her seat during every lecture. I look over at her and think that she must be listening to a different lecture," and "Celebrating out loud during lab section when you manage to recreate the reaction that the professor was talking about all week and you feel that it is the most beautiful thing ever produced in a test tube."

Naturally, there are additional characteristics of all task-engaged persons, besides concentration and commitment. Task engagement also involves an appreciation for what is being learned, along with an admiration for the intellectual processes involved and a respect for the personal sacrifices of individuals that is the basis of all artistic creativity as well as significant scientific and social discoveries. Engagement also means being invested in the processes of discovery and inquiry for one's self, and the application of these insights to problems and challenges worthy of great commitment. In effect, when students are task engaged, they become practitioners in the creation and use of knowledge, not just academic bystanders content merely to absorb predigested information.

But so far, we have only given voice to anecdotal definitions of task engagement and described some of its outward but still largely surface manifestations. What about the underlying psychological nature of the processes at work? To pursue this question, we asked members of our graduate seminar to describe a time or event in their own college experience involving an academic, school-related task of relatively long duration in which they were fully engaged. We also asked that they share what feelings and emotions prevailed; what was going through their minds at the time; and what were the circumstances in which they found themselves. Out of the many dozens of responses, we selected the following personal stories as representative:

"I remember studying for an exam during Washington DC's 'snow-mageddon' that dropped several feet of snow for which the city was unprepared. Consequently, I was trapped in my apartment with nothing to do but study. I posted large poster-sized pieces of blank paper all over the walls and drew visual representations of chemistry concepts. I would draw electron configurations, quantum states, and periodic trends using different colored markers. The excitement was because the material itself was interesting to me, and turning study into a coloring activity made me naturally more engaged. Lots of fun! I'd enjoy doing this no matter what I was drawing!"

"During my junior year, I took a seminar on James Joyce's Ulysses. I was a little nervous about undertaking this notoriously challenging text. We were expected to come fully prepared, but not expected to have "correct" answers – just thoughtful, well-articulated ones. My reading of the text was motivated by a desire to actually understand what was happening and appreciate the beautiful language. Even though it would sometimes take an hour and flipping through four other books to read and understand two pages."

"During my senior year, I was involved in a documentary film class which required making our own film. The idea of making films is inherently interesting to me. My dominant feelings were both excitement and trepidation – excitement that I would be able to produce work in a medium that interested me and showcase it to my peers; trepidation in that I did not want to fail. But the fact that I had an idea for what I thought would be a good film excited me."

To aid in our analysis of these and other stories, we have divided the concept of task engagement into four different psychological strands of what is widely believed to be a multifaceted process (Covington, 2009; Covington & Elliot, 2001). First and foremost, it seems clear that engagement is the result of a motivational process. By motivation we mean, simply put, the *reasons* individuals have for learning. And there are as many reasons for learning as there are learners. The influential German composer Robert Schumann put this point best regarding the complex landscape of motivation when he observed that "[p]eople compose for many reasons: to become immortal; because the piano forte happens to be open; because they want to become a millionaire; because of the praise of friends; because they have looked into a pair of beautiful eyes; or for no reason at all!"

Similarly, in the academic sphere, the reasons for being task engaged are also numerous and diverse, as reflected in the essays of our seminar members. In the case of these three examples, the motives were all constructive in one way or another, namely either wanting to become the best one could be, turning work into play, or pursuing a personal interest. Other essayists add to this list. They tell of striving for public recognition: "I wanted to prove to my Professor that I could solve the problems on my own," or striving for the sake of career advancement, "I wanted a good grade because I was in the process of applying to graduate school." Others recall striving to acquire a deeper understanding of events: "I hoped to string together all the facts which had previously seemed disjointed," and "I got to thinking about how this new knowledge could be a springboard to combine some of my interests." Also, essayists unexpectedly recognized themselves in a new light: "Being able to work through these problems may have been the first time I really began to see myself as a chemist." Yet others aspired simply for the sake of personal satisfaction and enjoyment.

From these observations, it is easy to appreciate that the quality of task engagement – its purposes, duration, and consequences – depends largely on what reasons for engagement dominate. Some reasons are potentially liberating and constructive, as in the examples presented earlier, while – as we shall see shortly – other reasons can be profoundly self-destructive.

Second, task engagement is also a cognitive or mental process. In the vanguard of motives are one's intellectual skills, unique ways of thinking, and those planning strategies that give substance and direction to one's reasons for learning. One of the most intriguing aspects of this mental realm is that our informants frequently reported reconfiguring or even altering the task facing them, as illustrated by our snowbound chemist's strategy (in the first example listed), when she converted abstract constructs – electron configurations and quantum states – into visual representations using children's crayons for ease of learning and also to have fun to boot. It is not unusual to find a sense of playfulness and feelings of joy as companions to task engagement. Other essayists cast their work in metaphorical terms, thereby simplifying their understanding of the problem at hand: "The facts in my head were the puzzle pieces, and the models and rules became the guidelines for fitting those pieces together." Our essayists also proved adept at personalizing tasks by bending them to their interests in order to guarantee personal satisfaction. This meant taking personal ownership of problems, issues, and ideas – of being playful with them, even enlisting levity in the face of serious problems, and of reducing reluctant problems to their simplest forms.

Third comes an emotional strand in which task engagement expresses itself through a variety of feelings, including simply being curious: "I didn't have to take this class. I did it just because I was interested," and "My feeling was a sense of intrigue about what I was going to learn next." Then there are feelings of being committed to a personally meaningful project with a readiness to be inspired to further effort by one's discoveries: "I was excited to be working in an area that was completely new to me. There was so much to discover that would push my mind in new directions." Emotions are also noteworthy sometimes for their apparent absence, but only because they are overshadowed by an all-consuming intellectual fascination with a problem. Nonetheless, apparent or not, in the view of our essayists, feelings and emotions remain part of the driving, motivational force that animates task engagement.

Perhaps the most revealing aspect of these stories was the characterization in emotional terms of what was, in effect, a profound approach/avoidance conflict: "I was a little nervous about undertaking the notoriously challenging text, but curiosity about the novel outweighed my fear." Despite these implied risks, our essayists nonetheless took up the challenges they recounted in their stories, but not before they had hedged their bets against failure: "What moderated my anxiety was the fact that I was working with a friend whom I deeply respected and I was confident that together our skill sets could make a solid project." The task-engaged individual is attracted to risk, but reasonable, surmountable risk that resides just beyond the outer bounds of their talents and knowledge: "I felt excited about solving a problem that was truly just beyond my grasp." Yet even with these qualified protections, sometimes risk overwhelms. Indeed, some of these personal stories ended in failure. But even in these cases, setbacks and disappointment were seen as temporary. Commitment and sometimes dogged persistence are the strong suits of the task-engaged person, as poetically reflected in the self-description of one essayist: "I am a tumbleweed when it comes to learning. It is true that obstacles come along every once in a while, but I push on, keep trying, and finally rise above those obstacles and just fly over them!"

Fourth, and finally, task engagement is also a social process. Virtually every essayist endorsed this proposition in one way or another. We were impressed by the variety of social relationships mentioned as well as the wide range of benefits and benefactors. Consider the following:

"Knowing that my work would be shown publicly, I was motivated to do my best."

"Helping others to improve their projects was fulfilling in that I felt like a 'real' researcher."

"Those interactions [with co-workers] were beneficial for all of us because in explaining our work to one another, we had to process again what we already knew."

"I think that the Prof got a lot of satisfaction out of my interest and commitment to the class."

"The instructor received the satisfaction of seeing me eventually shift my trajectory toward graduate school as the result of my positive experience doing research."

"Even if I am not doing well grade-wise, if I have an instructor who cares about what I am doing, I am motivated to work harder because I want to make her proud of me."

In short, task engagement is a socially defined event. The social implications of many of the synonyms of engagement make this point convincingly. For example, to whom and for what reason would one "*pledge* himself," or "*promise*," or "*agree to serve*," or be "*persuaded* by?" Indeed, we will argue that the quality of academic engagement for everyone – instructors, teaching staff, and students alike – depends on a series of relationships, or as they say in "pop" psychology circles, "it's in the relationship" – in this case "it" being the quality of reasons for learning and teaching. When these relationships are positive and uplifting, we will call them, collectively, an alliance.

Each of these four components of task engagement is beyond debate. But taken singly, each is incomplete. They must be considered as a whole. Nonetheless, they can be prioritized as to their overarching theoretical importance. It is our position that, at its core, task engagement is fundamentally a motivational phenomenon. All other propositions flow from this vantage point. Yet motivation and engagement are not synonymous, nor can they be treated interchangeably. Task engagement is best thought of as an outward manifestation of the reasons or motives that prevail at any point in time. This means that any effort by teachers to enhance the will to learn needs to be directed ultimately to the task of strengthening, or even repairing, the underlying reasons for learning.

One final observation brings the notion of task engagement in contact with the central theme of this book.

## Intrinsic Motivation

Our inquiries focus on a special distinction between *intrinsic* and *extrinsic* motivation (Covington, 2000b). When we speak of task engagement as a valued teaching goal, our attention will be given primarily to intrinsic motivation. Here the rewards for learning reside in the benefits and satisfactions to the individual derived, for example, from becoming a more effective person: "I not only improved my understanding of botany, but also trained my ability to reason," or from simply satisfying one's curiosity: "I was inherently interested in the material so I just enjoyed learning it." The rewards in these examples are intrinsic to the actions taken to complete the task – that is, the actions are their own reinforcement. Intrinsically engaged students seek out these rewards, which become, in turn, the reasons (motives) for learning more: "I felt like I was finally doing 'serious' work for the first time in college and felt like I had made intellectual progress." In short, "engagement begets engagement." It is this process that gives meaning to the notion of lifelong learning. Learning can be defined by horizons, but there is nothing inherent in horizons that limit progress. To move toward one horizon is simply to create another horizon, and the act of moving from one to another is the reward.

## Extrinsic Motivation

By contrast, extrinsic motivation is said to involve the performance of an action, not necessarily out of any intrinsic satisfaction derived from the action itself, but for the sake of extrinsic payoffs such as gold stars, social recognition, and grades. These rewards are considered extrinsic because they are unrelated to the task itself. This is not to say that these kinds of rewards do not motivate; obviously they do. Nor are they necessarily counterproductive to learning. The offer of money or the promise of social recognition can usually mobilize individuals and sometimes to their best efforts. The problem is that extrinsic rewards do little to sustain the educational goals we espouse. The effects of extrinsic rewards tend to be short-lived, since extrinsic reasons are largely unrelated to the act of learning itself. When tangible rewards such as social recognition or monetary prizes are no longer available, extrinsically driven motivation will fade. Our hope is to encourage sustainability in learning that ultimately must come primarily from intrinsic reinforcements. These benefits are always available.

However, if the withdrawal of tangible rewards makes for instability in learning – a sufficient reason, in any event, not to rely too heavily on extrinsic payoffs – there is potentially worse to come. According to a widely held view, the mere presence of tangible rewards – leaving aside their absence – can subvert intrinsic reasons for learning (Lepper, Greene, & Nisbett 1973). This is because of the possibility that offering rewards to students for doing what already interests them may undercut that interest! This kind of reasoning implies that intrinsic goals are simply incompatible in a world dominated by extrinsic inducements, and in particular by school grades. And, grades are not just any tangible payoff; they possess enormous influence. Grades are widely regarded as an index of ability, and in our society the primary determinant of one's status and worth depends on the ability to perform successfully. This message is deeply embedded in the minds of many of the undergraduates we have interviewed, as reflected in these painful observations: "Everyone knows the students who struggle in class. You come to pity them and think to yourself they should not be here, that they just aren't smart enough. I don't want to be one of these sad people who fail publicly, so I never stop preparing for tests and start research papers way early," and a more succinct version of this same sentiment, "When a grade comes in, it defines me as a person."

If high marks in school become increasingly more important as students grow older, not only for the tangible future benefits they bestow, such as eventual entry into prestigious occupations, but also as an indication of one's personal worth, then what becomes of the value of learning for its own sake? Is caring about learning always to be marginalized? It is this question – and our answers – that constitutes the underlying theme of this book, particularly in light of the fact that intrinsic goals, if they are to thrive at all, must do so surrounded, if not overmatched at times, by a host of extrinsic induce-ments and payoffs, few of which are as powerful as school grades.

Not content to pause on a negative note, we can anticipate in advance that the odds are not as heavily loaded against intrinsic engagement as implied so far. We are only pointing here to the difficulties to be overcome. Balances can be sought in which extrinsic payoffs can actively support intrinsic values – precarious balances to be sure, but potentially capable of offsetting an otherwise potentially antagonist relationship. The promise held out for such a positive reframing of this relationship can be found amid many of the reassuring remarks of our undergraduate informants:

> "The process of doing the work – apart from my grade in the course – was rewarding in itself."

> "Rather than being material that I dutifully forced myself to study for a grade, the concepts became potential tools that could help me solve the problems I wanted to solve."

> "I remember the point at which I succeed in the task and feeling accomplished, which is a distinct feeling from doing well on a test for a grade."

> "I try hard in all my classes, and when I see that my work is acknow-ledged by a good grade or positive recognition, I feel confident in my abilities to learn even more."

By now, with all these complications in mind, the mere task of spotting the miracle of intrinsic task engagement, let alone probing its underlying dynamics, is not quite as easy as may have been thought at first. But by making one additional try, perhaps we can sharpen our target right from the start by offering several negative examples – that is, indicating what intrinsic task engagement is not!

First, intrinsic task engagement is more than merely participating. Participation in classroom life is often measured by the extent to which students concentrate, attend lectures, and submit assignments. These actions are the most obvious behavioral, or outward, manifestations of engagement. But effort expenditure per se – whatever form it takes, is an incomplete view of task engagement because the particular reason for participating is left unspecified. And we know that reasons are everything when it comes to the quality of participating. For example, although compliance with authority is clearly a reason to participate, it is not among the best of reasons because it can easily harbor resentment and antagonisms.

Second, neither is engagement simply being involved. Being involved is part of what we mean. But involved in what and for what purpose? Engagement, as we have said, exists fundamentally in the form of relationships, and not only among individuals, but also involves a working relationship with such intangibles as ideas, theories, and conjectures, or the contemplation of puzzles and possibilities – any innovative product of the mind. Involvement per se can be counted superficially in terms of numerical units such as the frequency of contacts between faculty and students over coffee or during office hours. But simply counting the number of incidents reveals nothing about the circumstances of the contact and, most importantly, once again, the reasons for these contacts. And sometimes even the reasons are suspect. Our informants often express doubts about the real purposes of many of these contacts. As one student explains it, "Students speaking up in class where participation in discussion is part of the grade is not necessarily indicative of engagement." And, an equally jaundiced observation: "Students going beyond what is required in order to receive extra credit is not true engagement."

From our perspective, then, the most challenging and expansive view of intrinsic task engagement involves a deeper, sustainable, and personally more profound matter than merely mobilizing one's efforts temporarily or the arousal of enthusiasm momentarily for a passing interest. While these fleeting aspects of engagement are part of the picture, so are the processes by which individuals become deeply absorbed in a lifelong commitment to the pursuit and active exploration of ideas, arguments, and of philosophical positions as well. Engagement also means being devoted to the processes by which intellectual and artistic products are created, and, most importantly, for the right reasons. And not only is it student engagement we seek to encourage, but also to reinforce the dedication and joyful commitment on the part of the teaching staff. When the reasons for learning and teaching are constructive and synchronized, for the mutual sake of curiosity, for the altruistic purpose of seeking a more just society, or simply to help students better understand, then the quality of the relationship among all the parties is healthy and uplifting. The feelings that flow from this positive confluence become self-sustaining for teachers as well as for learners. And behind it all is the quality of the motives or reasons for teaching and learning. Clearly, then, our motivational target goes well beyond merely ensuring student compliance or students simply becoming more polite or patient, or even forgiving of their instructors. We have set a far more ambitious motivational agenda: a vision of encouraging the will to learn for a lifetime.

## SPOTTING TROUBLE

Our brief introductory tour of the nature of intrinsic task engagement would not be complete without addressing the shadowy, troublesome flip side of engagement – disengagement! At one level, disengagement is easy to spot and painful to observe. Yet, other forms of disengagement are harder to detect. They can pass unnoticed – a kind of moribund, plodding "business as usual" in which instructors are on autopilot lecturing from decade-old notes, while students pretend to listen. Everyone is sleepwalking through the school term. It can be a joyless existence. To the casual observer, disengagement means passivity and mental, if not emotional, withdrawal often reflected as sullenness, indifference, or inaction. Once again, we have only a description here, not necessarily an explanation. There is a deeper psychological reality at play behind these surface manifestations of inaction and withdrawal. The appearance of indifference can mask the fact that disengagement is, ironically, often a highly motivated state. Our research (Covington, 2001; 2014) suggests that the motive most likely operating here is the need to avoid failure. For example, one defensive tactic involves students choosing not to try (hence the appearance of indifference) or to try so little, that failure – although a highly likely prospect in this case – at least cannot necessarily be attributed to incompetence.

Just to complicate matters further, the fear of failure that drives some students to withdraw can also drive others to extraordinary effort. These students – whom we refer to as *overstrivers* (Beery 1975) – have learned that the best way to avoid failure is to succeed! They study incessantly, take meticulous notes, are well prepared for discussion sections, and rarely miss a lecture. These students may, on your campus as they do on ours, call this "grinding" and themselves "grinders," a term that evokes joyless overwork. But even with all their efforts they nonetheless worry secretly that they are ill prepared or even imposters, fearing that they know far less than their good grades would indicate. Despite all the successes that overstrivers enjoy, self-doubts and even self-loathing can persist because error-free perfection is their unattainable goal. It is only at a motivational level, typically well hidden and strongly defended, that the true cost of such negative engagement can be glimpsed.

Thus, any educator hoping to promote positive task engagement must take into account a variety of puzzling dynamics, including the observations that a state of disengagement can be just as surely motivated as is engagement, or that a noteworthy GPA may be masking a fear of failing, or that the reasons for learning may be in conflict with one another.

Sorting out these dynamics and their implications for educational practice is no easy task, but neither is it impossible. The broad solutions we propose make both theoretical and practical sense once the complexities of this motivational state-of-affairs are more fully understood. These solutions have been well documented as to their effectiveness both in research laboratories and in classrooms, including our own.

## A SCENARIO: AFLOAT BUT BARELY

There are so many psychological subtleties operating in the college classroom that they are likely best appreciated when put in the form of real-life events that are within reach of our own personal experiences. We do not want our arguments to die a slow death from abstractions. Let's start our journey together literally on the same page by grounding ourselves squarely in the midst of an actual college classroom – well, almost an actual classroom; in point of fact, in the midst of a realistic scenario, a pastiche of reality composed of actual experiences reported to us by students and the teaching staff.

We intend this scenario as a touchstone for identifying and explaining many of the troublesome dynamics that instructors and students often face. We will return frequently to this scenario – and to its fictional protagonist, Professor Jones, along with various other usual suspects as guides to our deliberations.

But first what should be our starting point? For starters, we need to know something about how those who inherit such classrooms – real teachers and students alike – struggle to make sense of the turmoil and tensions portrayed here. What assumptions do they bring to the table? What conclusions do they draw? How do they unravel, if at all, the many crosscutting dynamics that until now may have gone unexplored or even undetected by them? Addressing these questions is the first step in planning solutions.

We begin all our graduate seminars and workshops by presenting participants with the following scenario accompanied by two questions: (1) What are the dilemmas, frustrations, and obstacles to learning and teaching facing the individuals and groups portrayed in this scenario? (2) What are the causes of these frustrations and obstacles? Readers may also wish to ponder these questions along with seminar members. Afterwards, we will comment on the ways that students, staff, and instructors typically go about answering these questions and identify the assumptions they make as well as evaluate the conclusions they draw, some of which are helpful in understanding the dynamics involved, while others are decidedly not.

For the past 10 years Professor Jones has taught a large course with 300 or more students. This term Professor Jones is teaching the course with five GSIs.

Professor Jones meets with his GSIs weekly for an hour to go over course logistics. For example, he uses some of the time to distribute the lesson plan that he expects his GSIs to follow closely in their teaching of sections.
The head GSI, Chris, appears somewhat bored and impatient with this process. He is an experienced teacher who has taught the course before with Professor Jones who is also in charge of Chris's Ph.D. dissertation research. Pat, another GSI, is teaching for the first time. She attended the fall orientation conference sponsored by the GSI Teaching and Resource Center and is eager to utilize the ideas that were presented at the conference to keep students motivated in section. Pat is having difficulty, however, integrating the techniques she learned at the conference with Professor Jones's lesson plans, and she does not have enough time in section to do both.

Jan is a freshman in Professor Jones's course. Jan sometimes finds it difficult to follow along in lecture and to stay awake. In Jan's opinion, Professor Jones drones on and on about meaningless things. This irritates her because, she believes, "it's up to the professor to motivate students." But she likes section meetings because of the small class size. Yet she often goes to section without having done the readings, assuming her GSI will cover the readings and summarize lectures when necessary to help students succeed on the exams. Jan studies just enough to pass the tests, but not so much that she will feel she wasted her time if she does poorly. Not surprisingly, so far Jan has not done very well on the first two exams. Though she had planned on majoring in this field, her C grade so far is causing her some doubts about that, and even about her ability to compete for a top grade. She finds it increasingly difficult to concentrate on her studies and has begun putting off preparing for tests until the last minute.

In Jan's section, some students are extremely upset about the last test and complain bitterly to Chris, but to no avail. Chris explains that he has no authority to change grades. The test was graded on a curve by Professor Jones with the cutoff for an A grade reserved arbitrarily only for the top 10% of the students. And Professor Jones later increased the requirement for an A even more because, retrospectively, in his view there were still too many A grades. Chris tells his students that he understands their anger and also thinks that grading on the curve is unfair, but laments that nothing can be done to correct the situation. "Just study harder next time," he advises, "maybe you can break the curve."

After the exam, Pat decides to do a midterm evaluation and asks her students for feedback on what types of activities they should be doing in section to improve their learning. Pat is frustrated to find that students mainly wanted a summary of the lectures and when necessary, clarification of some of Professor Jones's sketchy remarks. Nor do they want to do activities such as group work or analyzing case studies anymore because those things would not help them on tests. Also, some students mentioned that other GSIs do a lot more to prepare their students for exams, and they think it is unfair that she does not do the same.

Professor Jones is relatively pleased with how the course is going, though he always feels a sense of isolation in lecturing for an hour without any direct interaction with the audience. Yet, he is somewhat relieved because he has never felt comfortable trying to answer questions on the spur of the moment without advanced warning. Students seem to be attending lecture regularly, but Professor Jones is concerned that many students do not seem engaged as he looks out at them from the podium. He is also concerned that his office hours go largely unused by students. But at least the first test went well as evidenced by the grade distribution he finally imposed. Professor Jones feels confident that the rest of the term will go smoothly.

So much is unremarkable about this scenario, at least on the surface. Sure, there are tensions here. But aren't there always frustrations in teaching, and certainly when teaching on such a huge scale, where students' feelings of isolation and loneliness are an ever-present danger? But behind the scene, below the surface lurk deeper more troubling dynamics which make the best that can be said about this course is that it is "afloat, but barely" (Beery, 1975). Suffice it to say that things are about to take a turn for the worse. Student complaints heard now only in whispers can quickly escalate to a volume and intensity that can no longer be ignored.

Our analysis of the reactions to this scenario is based on input from several hundred individuals, including members of our seminar, attendees from dozens of faculty workshops, numerous GSI mentoring workshops, and a variety of undergraduate focus groups.

First, let's turn to the scorecard regarding Question #1: What are the obstacles to learning and teaching? Basically, each group of respondents – faculty, teaching staff, and students – receive high marks. Virtually everyone proved quite adept at identifying the many frustrations and obstacles to learning and teaching embedded in the scenario – similar perhaps to playing the childhood game of searching for Waldo! Waldo can be found anywhere and everywhere in his picture puzzle. In some instances, respondents identified even more issues than we had in mind! Besides the outpouring of responses, our analysis also revealed several "mindsets" when it came to identifying troubles in the scenario. The distribution of fault finding as well as the perceived severity of the infractions depended on group affiliation. Student respondents more often found fault with Professor Jones than did faculty respondents, and conversely, faculty tended to take sides more often by picking on students. No surprises here. Nonetheless, this finding illustrates just how pronounced and deep-seated such biases can be if they are so easily elicited in the relatively benign context of a hypothetical example. Clearly, students and teachers occupy different worlds defined by their respective perceptions. But must these differences be as adversarial as suggested by these findings? We will have more to say about this as we proceed.

While the ability of respondents to ferret out interpersonal conflict was impressive (Question #1), when it came to speculating about the causes of these troubling events (Question #2), things tend to fall short for two reasons. The first concern involves the nature of these alleged faults. For both students and faculty respondents, there was a pronounced tendency to interpret faults in moral terms – that is, assuming that problems arise not so much because individuals are victims of circumstance, but rather because of some inherent flaw within individuals, rendering them undeserving or even unworthy. Hence, Jan is pronounced "lazy" and Professor Jones is considered by many to be "unethical." This tendency, too, is not surprising, given the enormous satisfaction derived from unburdening one's frustrations on others. But it also can be employed to absolve teachers of their responsibilities: "Who feels obligated to teach 'lazy' students anyway?" is the remark sometimes overheard in faculty workshops. And, of course, it is equally easy for moralistic accusations to be hurled at teachers by students. Any self-serving benefit of framing issues in moral terms is offset by the fact that they are unhelpful in crafting solutions. This is because there are compelling examples suggesting that circumstances *are* as important as alleged personality flaws in causing trouble. These examples included the fact that when faculty are put in awkward circumstances similar to those in which students often find themselves, faculty exhibit the same unattractive behaviors that they abhor in their students. More details regarding these examples shortly.

The second concern involves the assumption made by many respondents that each individual problem or frustration has a different, unrelated cause. For example, consider two students in the course, Diana and Sam. Respondents might say that Sam behaves disrespectfully because he resents having to take the course, while they also reason that Diana is indifferent to her studies because she is bored. Whether any particular explanation is true or not, is not our concern right now. Rather, our concern is that the search for causes is often pursued as a kind of "laundry list" exercise ending with nearly as many separate explanations as there are identified problems – in a word, "piecemeal." But in this example, is it not possible that these two seemingly unrelated incidents – Sam's disrespect and Diana's indifference – share a single, more basic cause? The danger in not entertaining this question is that we risk becoming uneconomical in our reasoning. Having so many seemingly unrelated causes implies the need to consider an equal number of basically uncorrelated solutions, an essentially impossible burden on any instructor – again the term "piecemeal" comes to mind.

We believe that the proper analytic strategy is to consider the possibility that many of the flashpoints portrayed in this scenario reflect a single underlying root cause whose explanatory reach is essentially universal, and is basically motivational in nature. In our experience, the root cause is *fear*, and more specifically the fear of failure. How then does fear link together Sam's resentment and Diana's inaction? For Sam, the fear of failing the class causes him to react with anger whenever he risks falling short in the eyes of others. For Diana, the fear of failure causes her inaction because, according to her self-protective logic, if she does not try, then she cannot fail!

But what is it about failure that can be so threatening? After all, falling short is a natural companion to learning. It is part of the "feedback loop" that signals the need to take corrective action. Falling short is an ever-present certainty in all our lives, or as it has been so wisely put, "If you don't succeed at first, then you are about average!" However, while falling short is par for the course, nonetheless, individuals may not be able to bear the burden of failure with its implication that they are unworthy as persons.

But if fear is the root cause of all the troubles highlighted in the scenario, then Professor Jones is likely fearful, too. But fearful of what? Why should individuals in authority be fearful, especially those whose academic reputations are built on a bedrock of proven brilliance and a capacity for extraordinary intellectual contributions? If it is fear for Professor Jones, is his fear really driven by self-doubts about his worth?

Like students, instructors also define their worth around evidence of competency, and like students, they too are also evaluated, even graded by their students as well as by their academic colleagues. One's competency as a teacher is always on public display, and sometimes actually on the line when it comes to promotions, even retention within the Academy. We will also soon find that GSIs labor under similar pressures.

## OVERVIEW AND RATIONALE

This book is divided into two main sections. Chapters 2, 3, and 4 address the causes of the discordant voices echoing throughout Professor Jones's class, namely fear and the fear of failing. The causes of these fears are found in what we will refer to as a *hidden agenda*. This agenda is made up of three elements. First, comes the negative motivation whose purpose is to avoid failure that can become self-destructive. Second, there are the beliefs of students and instructors regarding their respective roles and responsibilities that are often misaligned. The third element of the hidden agenda is student resentment over what they perceive to be the unfairness of some grading policies.

This three-part agenda is hidden for many reasons. It is often eclipsed by other more immediate, pressing logistical concerns as instructors rush to prepare their classes. Also, the workings of this agenda often remain shielded by their apparent defiance of common sense. For example, who would think after years of schooling that college students would still not be clear about their roles as learners? And, finally, this divisive agenda remains hidden because bringing it to light may challenge often entrenched, misguided beliefs about the nature of teaching and learning. Sometimes it is more comfortable and certainly easier not to know. Yet, for all this resistance, the hidden agenda is not inaccessible.

### Self-Worth and the Fear of Failure

In Chapter 2, we consider the first aspect of the hidden agenda that deals with the fear of failure. To anticipate briefly, these doubts have a common origin for all members of the teaching staff as well as for students, although they are expressed differently among the players due to their different roles. For everyone, however, these self-doubts and fears arise out of a Herculean, life-long struggle to establish and maintain the conviction that we are worthy of the approval of others. This is the essential proposition of *self-worth theory* that will guide our inquiries (Beery, 1975; Covington & Beery, 1976).

Self-worth theory proposes that individuals strive to gain the approval of others by achieving goals as varied as the death-defying conquest of a Mt. Everest or gaining sufficient respect of street gangs in order to join them. Within the academic sphere, the essence of the self-worth struggle is best captured by our colleague, Richard Beery (1975), in his seminal observation that the protection of one's reputation for competence, and particularly the ability to compete with others for academic rewards, is paramount – or as translated in personal terms by an undergraduate, "Students begin the term with one goal in mind: to achieve the best grades, and so to prove to everyone they know that they are smart enough." Ironically, this need is felt both by those with stellar academic histories and by those students who are struggling. The need to be perceived as able accounts for the fear students have of failure, not necessarily the event of failure itself, but the *implication* of failure that individuals are incompetent, hence unworthy. In effect, students come to believe that they are only as worthy as their ability to achieve competitively. This is why schooling can become so threatening. The odds for failing increase whenever there are fewer rewards (high grades) than there are contestants.

Students have proven themselves highly creative when it comes to inventing ways to avoid the implications of failure should it occur (Birney, Burdick, & Teevan, 1969). Ironically, these self-protective strategies created to deflect the implication that they are unworthy are just as likely to cause the very failures they are attempting to avoid. For example, when individuals jeopardize their academic standing by taking too heavy a course load or by procrastinating, they virtually ensure failure, but at least it is failure "with honor" – failure that reflects little on their ability, because no one else could be expected to do very well when academic burdens are so great, time is so short, or the opportunities to study so few. For such failure-avoiding students, their reasons for achieving are less concerned with the intrinsic value of learning than with the survival of psychological well-being. Joyful learning has little place in this threatening world.

## MISMATCH OF ROLES AND RESPONSIBILITIES

If the dynamics of fear are bad enough – and they certainly are – things are likely to worsen. The effects of a fear-of-failure mentality are intensified by the simultaneous operation of a mismatch between instructors and students regarding perceptions of their respective roles and responsibilities. What, briefly stated, is this mismatch as revealed by our research (Covington, 2001; 2004)? When asked to describe their role as learners,

undergraduates typically respond with essentially shallow, passive interpretations. Their role, they argue, is essentially that of dutiful absorbers of
subject matter material presented by the instructor. This passive absorption of information often involves the mindless ritual of memorizing
material without much understanding. This is largely the product of fear.
The fear of failure drives many students desperately at times to simplify
and curtail the demand of learning and reduce it to its simplest denominator and its narrowest, most manageable scope. But no matter the source of
such behavior, it all adds to a picture of students as passive, even indifferent, in their approach to learning.

At the same time, students often assign the responsibility for animating
the learning process to instructors. Not only are instructors expected to
deliver information in easily understood, pre-digested forms, but they are
also held responsible for making it all palatable, if not fun and even
entertaining. Too few students see themselves as having a central role in
the process of bringing material to life or transforming it for their own
purposes. In short, it is instructors who are expected to motivate students
to learn. For their part, at least, instructors get it right. As a group, the
instructors we have interviewed maintain that the responsibility for learning ultimately resides with students. However, having expressed this,
the fact is that instructors sometimes unwittingly teach in ways that
compromise their contention that students should be the primary creators
of their own futures. There are several ways that instructors may needlessly
contribute to student docility, each of which will be considered in coming
chapters.

In summary, students often act passively – a posture that, although
abhorred by instructors, is often unwittingly reinforced by them – while at
the same time, both parties often clash over who is to provide the motivational impetus for learning, with the result that one group can easily pass
the buck to the other.

## FEAR AND LOATHING OF GRADES

If, metaphorically speaking, there is a vortex that most captures the
resentment and frustration of students, it swirls around the issue of grading
policy. The very strength of these emotions suggests deep abiding dynamics. We have already highlighted what is at stake for students. Grades carry
excess meaning that cuts to the heart of their struggle for self-approval.
Doing well, grade-wise, discharges one's sense of obligation to family
and friends whose sacrifices may have made higher education possible.

High grades are also passports to graduate and professional schools and to prestigious careers, and failure to qualify for admission to advanced training can be demoralizing.

Grading can also be an agonizing ordeal for instructors and GSIs who appreciate the high stakes involved but who struggle nonetheless to maintain rigorous academic standards. Sometimes, however, GSIs are left to sort out these grading demands whenever instructors retreat from this responsibility, comforting themselves in the truism that GSIs "know their students best." But although they are acquainted with their students, GSIs may not have sufficient authority to deal effectively with grading issues on their own. Often the result is the spectacle of an instructor's office hours being turned into a battle zone in which faculty feel required to defend their grading policies to students who likely care less about philosophical nuances than about the points they missed on a test.

The greatest source of discontent over grading is reserved for policies that measure the quality of student work by comparing the performances of individuals against the aggregate performance of their group. What this amounts to is grade rationing or a quota system, or as students more typically refer to it, "grading on the curve." Cynics use a fancier, if somewhat sarcastic, turn of phrase: "grading as a market economy" (Campbell, 1974). This practice typically amounts to relying on an arbitrary rank ordering, by which the performances at the top of the scoring heap – typically the upper 10% – are pegged in the A range without necessarily considering the actual quality of this or any other lesser performances. Perhaps these A students deserve a top grade, but then maybe not. Perhaps their performances are just the best of a flock of mediocre performances. A statistical distribution is a poor proxy for judgments of excellence. What of those cases in which a student performs credibly but nonetheless receives a demoralizing signal in the form of an unjustified low grade owing to the fact that the performances of others against which her efforts are compared were truly outstanding? In these circumstances, students are often left with little, if any, rationale for why they received the grade they did other than through a comparison with fellow students. But this is precisely the time when students deserve clear and candid appraisals of their strengths and shortcomings, judged against absolute standards derived from the professional experience and wisdom of an instructor. One student's comment conveys his legitimate anger toward the perversity of "grade rationing" in as succinct and eloquent a fashion as we have ever seen: "I hate feeling cheated out of understanding my grade. The curve really does not tell me anything meaningful about my performance.

To improve, I need to hear what my score implies in terms of preparation for future exams, and a score relative to others does not give me that kind of feedback."

To be balanced in this critique, it is important to remember that in some professional fields, college graduates far outnumber the openings for postgraduate training, as in the case of medicine law. Given this reality, it may be argued that, in fact, students are already competing with one another, and that competitively based grading policies serve a necessary sorting and selection function in society. We will discuss this assertion in more detail in Chapter 8. In the meantime, we will conclude that the true function of grading is to serve as feedback to students regarding their progress and, only incidentally, should it operate as an occupational sorting device, with the important proviso that it is students themselves who need take primary responsibility for weighing their future prospects, including making occupational judgments by means of self-selection and personal decision-making, not primarily on the basis of test scores.

### BLUEPRINT FOR CHANGE

In the second half of this book, beginning with Chapter 5, we offer a working blueprint for developing college courses designed to promote intrinsic task engagement, and in the process also to dismantle the hidden agenda. Dismantling involves confronting the fear-of-failure dynamics that are typically driven by perceived – and sometimes actual – inequities in grading policy. Second, dismantling also involves tackling the mistrust between instructors and students born out of a clash of beliefs, expectations, and goals. The players in this drama are not always on the same page, nor do they always play by the same rules. But assuming for the moment that all these negative forces could be magically swept away, what positive policies would replace them? Replacement involves helping students trade up from the struggle to avoid failure and taking on the positive challenges implied by the motive to approach success. But what kinds of success? Our answer is success at solving problems of significance within a given academic discipline whose solutions as well as the experience of achieving them become the ultimate goal of any course.

By adopting a problem-oriented approach to teaching, all aspects of student work is coordinated around a seminal *capstone* problem on which students work for a significant amount of time, if not through an entire school term. Everything is drawn in harness with one end in mind, if not yet in sight: *solutions*. In short, solutions to teachable problems become the course goal. To these ends, we will propose that problem-focused courses be designed around four broad principles, all independent of any particular subject matter discipline, and each intended to reverse or at least moderate some aspect of the hidden agenda: (1) ensuring coherence and transparency; (2) ensuring grading equity; (3) encouraging alliance-building and inclusion; and (4) providing inherently challenging problem-solving tasks.

## Ensuring Coherence and Transparency

The fear of failing arises in part from confusion about the intended destination of a course and the lack of a road map for getting there. The traditional course syllabus often falls short on this score. Course objectives often tend to remain abstractions, with little justification for why what students must learn serves these larger purposes. For this reason, course work may appear disconnected without a unifying rationale. As a result, students report becoming confused and bewildered, even disoriented, and worst of all uncertain about their ability to cope – all states of mind that trigger anxiety, particularly for failure-oriented students who count heavily on the safety and security of knowing the purpose of their efforts.

In the problem-solving approach we advocate, all aspects of student work are coordinated around the steps necessary to solve a central problem. Introduction of the problem initially, if not from the very outset of a course, provides students with an "early warning" target. It is the nature of the problem itself that determines the content of the curriculum by informing students about *what* they must learn and *why*; *when* they must learn it, and *how well*. This adds clarity for the journey ahead and in the process reduces confusion and uncertainty.

## Ensuring Grading Equity

We have briefly outlined the case against competitive grading practices that judge academic excellence of the individual in relative terms against group performances. These policies tend to create a scarcity of deserving rewards, which exacerbates the fear of failing as well as promotes a cutthroat scramble for grades to the detriment of intrinsic task engagement.

By contrast, in a problem-focused approach, the problem itself becomes the final arbiter of excellence. The quality of student contributions can now be tied more objectively to the question of how effective their work is in creating progress toward solutions judged against such merit-based criteria as practicality or utility. Defined in these ways, excellence is potentially attainable by all students who meet or surpass the prevailing standards set by instructors, thereby establishing an equity goal when it comes to grading.

## Alliance-Building and Inclusion

Assuming that classroom dynamics have been repositioned in accordance with the first two principles, the way is paved for achieving a basis for compatibility among all the players. For us, alliance-building means establishing a partnership in which instructors and students together dedicate themselves to tackling meaningful problems or issues of significance, and challenging enough to command the best that each has to offer. Naturally, this is not a partnership of equals. The differences in the respective roles and responsibilities of instructors and students remain, but at least they are compatible. For one thing, the motive to achieve success is shared by instructors and students alike. Additionally, instructors are no longer viewed as gatekeepers to success for the few. There also are no more expectations that it is the instructor alone who is responsible for animating the learning process. Also gone is the passive stance of students, replaced by active engagement. Instructors become mentors of students, and can inspire them indirectly through the example of their own involvement in a task that they find professionally or personally meaningful. Here is the ideal opportunity for an instructor's love of learning to shine through. A short philosophy of teaching might be, "Love your subject and convey that love; all else is secondary." This is mentoring at its best – infectious and beguiling, with students sustained by the realization that they are thought well enough of by their mentors to be entrusted with an important challenge.

## Inherently Challenging Tasks

The theme of problem solving exudes a sense of mystery and intrigue. It is said that everyone loves a mystery, and for this reason problem solving is potentially "reward rich" in intrinsic payoffs that sustain task engagement. There is the pleasure of satisfying one's curiosity, of feeling part of a team, and of making discoveries in the service of achieving something worthwhile. It is the anticipation of intrinsic rewards such as these that sustains the student's continuing search for personal excellence. At the same time, a problem-solving theme also provides instructors with an ideal vehicle to promote the ultimate purpose of schooling, which is to prepare for the transfer of these thinking skills to an unknowable future.

## ACADEMIC ENGAGEMENT AS AN EDUCATIONAL GOAL

Before proceeding, it seems only right, and perhaps even necessary, to present the case for elevating the notion of intrinsic task engagement to the level of a preeminent educational objective. After all, considerable rethinking may lie ahead for any teacher who entertains such an objective. So it behooves us to clarify the benefits of such an undertaking and doing so without exaggerating its claims. Too many arguments for educational change have ended ignobly following overestimates of the positive payoffs.

To be frank, our basic message that the motivation to learn should be a critical educational goal in its own right has until recently gone largely underappreciated, and to a great extent flies in the face of conventional interpretations of the role of motivation in the learning process. For the better part of the past century, at least in academic circles, motivation was conceived of as a drive – a power, a need, or force, issuing from within the individual, which impels people to action (Atkinson, 1957; McClelland, 1961). This *motive-as-drive* notion typically views motivation as an enabling factor – the means to an end, with the end being better performance, improved status, or perhaps an increased sense of security. This perspective dominates whenever schools are admonished to motivate students to do better scholastically. The underlying assumption is that if we can deliver the right rewards and enough of them, or threaten sufficient punishments, we can arouse (drive) otherwise lazy, dispirited students to higher levels of achievement. Then there is the virtually inevitable corollary that arousal is maximized when these rewards (grades) are distributed on a competitive basis, that is, the greater number of rewards going to those who perform best or quickest.

A second perspective on motivation, the one we adopt here, is a relative newcomer to the academic research scene. This perspective considers motives in terms of goals or incentives that draw, not drive, individuals toward action (Covington, 2005; Elliot & Dweck, 2005; Locke & Latham, 1984). Researchers in this tradition assume that all actions are given meaning, direction, and purpose by the goals that people choose, and that the quality and intensity of their actions will change as their goals change. Seen from this perspective, motivation is a unique human resource to be cultivated for its own sake, not merely the means to a short-term payoff such as improved scholastic performance. By this analysis, fostering the right reasons (or goals) for learning becomes part of the ultimate purpose of schooling at all levels. We, like other *motive-as-goal* theorists, focus on noncompetitive, intrinsic reasons for learning that by their very nature entice students as well as instructors into action rather than push or drive them, and generally for ennobling reasons. In short, engagement is the product of positive goals and the rewards that follow from pursuing these goals, which in turn, become self-sustaining instigators of continuing engagement.

Having said this, it can be argued that there is nothing new here. Or worse yet, that our recommendations are rendered unnecessary by the fact that these values are already on the books. However, although it is true that these values are honored, they are honored more often in theory than in practice, and for several reasons. First, teachers sometimes view concepts like motivation as unnecessarily elusive and mysterious, and hence unlikely to contribute significantly to tangible performance goals. Second, it is often argued that because of the highly selected nature of many undergraduate populations, everyone is already motivated to learn, and if not, they will soon be replaced by an eager set of new recruits who *are* sufficiently motivated. Third, there is the belief that intrinsic engagement is itself largely the by-product of succeeding academically, and therefore contributes little directly to the pursuit of achievement goals. Fourth, some teachers feel it is beyond their expertise, even beyond their responsibility, to encourage these motivational goals.

Each of these arguments will be addressed as we proceed. We will demonstrate that the principles that control the motivational climate of classrooms are scarcely elusive, but rather are lawful, well understood, and, above all, accessible to all teachers, irrespective of their subject matter discipline or teaching style. Moreover, we will provide evidence that being intrinsically engaged is not simply a by-product of successful learning, but in a circular fashion is also an instigator of the willingness to learn more.

But does our interpretation of motivation as goal-driven really add anything new or important to traditional interpretations of motivation as a drive? Yes, at least three things.

First, the available evidence (Covington, 2000a) demonstrates that the task-engaged learner acquires subject matter information more quickly, retains more of what is learned, and internalizes information in ways that expands one's capacity to learn more, and at deeper levels of understanding. This notion of deep level processing will take on considerable importance as we proceed.

Second, the task-engaged learner is always alert to the as yet undiscovered problem, to the incisive question yet to be asked, and sensitive to the unrecognized, hence unmet, need or to the potentially troublesome situation gone undetected. The fundamental nature of this discovery process is the readiness of individuals to find problems everywhere, to be puzzled by the obvious, to see the extraordinary in the ordinary, and the willingness to turn the familiar, prosaic event into a provocative revelation. This is all part of the capacity to apply one's knowledge to recognizing and solving a wider arc of problems than the few teaching problems on which a student was trained. This ability to transfer knowledge is key when it comes to preparing for the future with all its unknown contingencies, and is as important, if not more so, than a high GPA.

Third, the capacity to become absorbed in learning has realworld implications for occupational success. Of all the career fields studied by Spence & Helmreich (1983), including that of corporate executives, businesspersons, and research scientists, the most significant predictors of success were a willingness to explore ideas and to master new skills for the sake of self-improvement. Success was measured by yearly income for the executives and businesspersons, and for scientists by the number of times their research was cited in the literature. What counts in the march toward career prominence is being task-engaged and striving to become more skillful. Incidentally, the same correlation also held for college students where the measure of success was a high GPA!

## CONCLUSION

Much has been offered in this opening chapter regarding the value to students of being intrinsically task-engaged. Now we begin the challenging task of designing college courses that hold promise for promoting these values as a central educational goal. As already remarked, our first step is to become fully aware of the negative dynamics that must be offset and of those positive features of instruction and assessment that must take their place. These are the main themes of the next three chapters.

# 2

## The Sum of All Doubts

What we seek to know is our knowledge of reality, not reality.
– *Anne E. Berthoff*

### THE CONSTRUCTED WORLD OF SUCCESS AND FAILURE

It is critical that educators realize that events such as *success* and *failure* and states of mind like *expectations* or feelings of *self-confidence* are all creatures of a subjective world of the individual's own creation. This is the essence of a *constructionist* view of human nature. Truth and falsity aside, reality often has little standing for humans. What counts more are beliefs, appearances, myths, and magical thinking that, for instance, can minimize the importance of a failed task or shift the blame for failure to events beyond one's control. Moreover, by shifting one's aspirations upward in unrealistic directions, one can unwittingly create an irreversible, downward spiral of repeated failures. In contrast, by adopting more attainable goals – say, targets slightly beyond one's current reach – individuals can initiate a positive, uplifting, and mutually reinforcing cycle of repeated successes and growing self-confidence. But then, as we will see, the individual may have little choice in the matter of goal setting. In competitive environments, there is continuous pressure to raise one's aspirations to keep pace with others sometimes beyond the limits of one's present abilities, and severe self-recriminations may be in store for not doing so.

In this chapter we will explore the dimensions of this subjective world from a motivational perspective, and spotlight the first of the three basic forces that animate the hidden agenda: self-worth and the fear of failure. Chapter 3 explores the beliefs of students and instructors regarding their respective roles and responsibilities that are often misaligned. The third element of the hidden agenda – the perceived inequities and unfairness of some grading policies – is considered in Chapter 8.

## SELF-WORTH AND THE FEAR OF FAILURE

What is so fearsome about failure? After all, failure is an inevitable part of the learning process. Moreover, there is no evidence that the act of learning itself is inherently threatening, but rather is a natural, adaptive process. The short answer is that failure is threatening because it implies that one is not worthy as a person. This interpretation of fear and its ultimate meaning is the basic premise of self-worth theory (Beery 1975; Covington & Beery, 1976) whose essence has never been better put than by Oscar Hammerstein: "The biggest and truest and most significant line in all nursery rhymes is a line in Little Jack Horner – 'what a good boy am I!' – that is what everybody wants to say to himself, but he can have little assurance of his belief unless it is endorsed by other members of his group. Everyone has this desire for approval."

And, an even more celebrated voice, that of Abraham Lincoln: "Every man is said to have his peculiar ambition. I have no other so great as that of being truly esteemed of my fellow men, by rendering myself worthy of their esteem. How far I shall succeed in gratifying this ambition, is yet to be developed."

Self-worth theory assumes that the search for approval and self-acceptance is the highest human priority. As a consequence, all individuals are motivated to establish and maintain a sense of personal worth based on approval and acceptance by others. Ideally, in schools, this process involves a decidedly positive quest in which both teachers and students are drawn together for enriching reasons. For teachers, the search for acceptance involves payoffs in the form of personal and professional satisfactions, including feelings of being needed by others, of having made a difference in the lives of students, and of being admired and respected as a knowledge-able authority. By the same token, students seek personal satisfactions based on having learned one's lessons well and on being valued by their mentors as competent and hardworking, and hence worthy of the trust placed in them by their teachers. College students put it this way: "If the professor makes me feel like an expert on the subject-matter even for a moment it makes it all worthwhile"; "I am motivated to work hard to make the teacher proud."

These mutual, interlocking satisfactions for both teachers and students are positive sources of self-worth. Yet, this supportive relationship implies an extraordinary psychological burden. It also carries the threat of not being satisfied, and with dissatisfaction comes the potential loss of a sense of personal worth for one party, or the other, or both. And the more one's sense of worth depends on being acknowledged as a competent authority, the more devastating, proportionally, to one's sense of well-being will be any perceived loss of authority. It is this perceived loss or rebuff that is the root of fear. One of the most threatening psychological risks associated with being an expert is the fear of being unmasked as a fraud – essentially, persons who feel they do not really know anything but who have somehow convinced others of their expertise.

Let's now extend this motivational analysis, first to learners and then to teachers, and explore how these dynamics can interact between both parties in ways harmful to the love of learning and of teaching.

### The Hidden Motivational Landscape of Learning

How do these self-worth dynamics apply specifically to students? For many students, if not the vast majority, doing well in one's studies is a major benchmark against which they are judged worthy or not by themselves and by others. The universal measure of how well one is doing in school is grades, which means that one's sense of self-identity and respect can easily become linked to the quality of one's grades. Indeed, there is a general tendency in Western society to equate achievement with human worth.

The processes by which one's sense of worth becomes linked to one's achievements start early in the life of students, as seen by the fact that beginning in the primary years, researchers find that no single thing contributes as much to the student's sense of esteem as does a good report card, nor shatters it so profoundly as do poor grades (Rosenberg, 1965). Additionally, a preoccupation with ability, as the handmaiden of good grades, also begins surprisingly early. Most five-year-olds can already identify those they perceive to be brightest and dullest among their peers and often point out the differences with relish. Moreover, these youngsters are convinced that ability is the main ingredient in achieving academic success and that inability is the likely cause of failure. And according to the harsh logic of childhood morality, it is also widely held that success is the only legitimate basis for giving rewards, and simply having tried hard is no special virtue and should go unrewarded. Although this severe attitude toward one's efforts mellows somewhat with age, success, especially defined competitively, remains predominant as the supreme virtue right into adulthood (Covington, 2006; Harari & Covington, 1981). Given all this, it is understandable that ability, and by extension one's performances, can become confused with one's worth.

## Avoiding Failure

At a critical juncture in the lives of some children, the praiseworthy desire to "do well" devolves into an ominous variant: "doing well" becomes "doing better than others!" Although our understanding of this troubling process remains incomplete, it is clear that various questionable child-rearing practices are implicated. These practices promote the anchoring of one's worth in the ability to surpass others. This is an inherently risky gamble because it means entering into a competitive arena where there are few winners and many losers. In short, to be able is to be worthy, but to do poorly is evidence of inability and reason to despair of one's worth. This proposition is endorsed through the candid confessions of students: "I study my hardest for every class, because you are only as good as your place in the grade distribution"; "My only reason for learning is not wanting to receive a bad grade."

By the time youngsters reach college age, the legacy of this competitive gamble undertaken earlier in life can be seen among students in the fear, anger, and apprehension expressed in the ways they describe their lives: "I am angry at how hard I have to try just to keep up with the smart students"; "I am trying to maintain a gram of sanity while chasing the grade and trying to outperform 400 other students"; "I always study on my own and do not join a study group that might help some student who may later turn out to do better than me on the test and steal my grade"; "If you can not compete and win in college, you won't be able to do so in the real world"; "College just like life is a competition. If your grades are not better than other people's you will not have the better life."

These pressures force many youngsters into a fateful decision often made unconsciously, certainly unwittingly, and without apparent appreciation for its consequences. They reason that if they cannot be certain of success, they can protect their dignity by avoiding failure, or at least avoiding the implications of failure that they lack ability. For example, one can avoid failure entirely by simply not entering into the competitive fray. However, nonparticipation is scarcely a viable strategy, not only because teachers penalize students for not trying but also because from the student's perspective trying hard and the successes that sometimes follow do have their benefits such as teacher praise and recognition. As a result, some effort is called for, at least, just enough to avoid punishment, yet not enough to risk the prospects of feeling shameful should one fail (Covington & Omelich, 1979).

This strategy describes the behavior of Ralph, one of the undergraduates in Professor Jones's class. Although Ralph is only a hypothetical figure, readers will recognize his behaviors as typical of many college-age students. Ralph's high school academic career can be characterized as checkered at best. It consisted of weeks of neglect and indifference toward his studies and apathy toward school in general, punctuated by bursts of energy to make up for lost time. Ralph relied on his superior ability to save him from crises of his own making. But these crises brought on largely by procrastinating served a vital purpose, even though by postponing his studies Ralph risked creating the very failures he was attempting to avoid. But, at least from his view, these failures would be rendered harmless, so to speak (Beery, 1975) – that is, failures that did not necessarily reflect badly on his ability, because, as his reasoning went, "no one else could have done any better given so little time." Besides, when Ralph did do well, despite postponing his studies, his reputation for brilliance was assured because he had spent so little time preparing!

Yet there is a price to pay for such self-sabotage, not the least of which is feelings of self-deprecation that result from these excuses. If insufficient effort is Ralph's salvation, it nonetheless makes him "lazy" and shiftless in the eyes of others (Covington, Spratt, & Omelich, 1990). The doggedness of some students to endure such social and personal stigma indicates something of the overwhelming need to be perceived as more capable than others. For instance, we found that among most college students a reputation for brilliance was the most important contributor to feelings of personal well-being, far more important, astonishingly, than one's overall GPA, and that being seen as a hard worker contributed only marginally to these positive feelings (Covington, 2001).

Ironically, even Ralph's cliff-hanging successes did little to offset his secret worry that he was not really as accomplished or as smart as his record of occasional brilliance suggested, and that surely someday he would be found out.

Considering how little Ralph was intellectually engaged in high school, he did well enough to earn a place in the freshman class at a prestigious university beginning in September. In the summer following high school graduation, Ralph decided to become a physician, a career choice that pleased his parents and impressed his friends. Unfortunately, Ralph had not taken the advanced high school courses needed to prepare him for the rigors of a premed major in college. As a result, he started his course work in chemistry, physics, and biology at a disadvantage. Just to make things even more problematic, Ralph's habit of procrastinating, which protected him through high school – but just barely – was totally overmatched by the more stringent pace and demands of the college curriculum. Ralph could no longer put things off until the last moment, especially since the studying of scientific disciplines is typically a cumulative affair, not to be delayed until next week. As a result, he began to fail his classes. But he was determined to succeed. Ralph's pride was now on the line; he would still show everyone that he could succeed. He vowed to work twice as hard next term. However, such resolve is just a manifestation of Ralph's erratic achievement pattern, swinging from inaction to a last-minute explosion of activity. Besides, even if he should fail, it is better, he argued – in his twisted reasoning – to flunk premed than to flunk a less prestigious major!

As a strategy, Ralph's use of procrastination was of a far different order than those tactics used occasionally by everyone to avoid exposing one's ignorance, because students do not always prepare for class in advance, nor always listen when directions are given. Everyone can recall those desperate moments when classmates scrunched down in their seats, trying to become the smallest target as their GSI scanned a room of faces searching for the latest victim in the game of "question and answer." Another self-protective strategy in this case is to respond to the GSI's question in as vague and noncommittal a manner as possible, vague enough to avoid revealing that one simply does not know the answer but forthright enough to be given the benefit of the bluff.

In Ralph's case, however, instead of merely avoiding being seen as unprepared, the struggle was to escape being seen as stupid. To avoid the implication that one is stupid, riskier strategies are called for – riskier because they can hinder the individual's chances for any meaningful successes as well as undermine the will to learn by causing the very failures that are so threatening.

### Failure-Prone Strategies

Self-protective, defensive ploys are virtually endless (Birney, Burdick, & Teevan, 1969; Snyder, 1984; Thompson, 1993). The several tactics described in this section are only a partial listing, but will serve to illustrate the range of devious possibilities. Some of the tactics typically adopted by failure-threatened students are collectively referred to as *self-handicapping* strategies, which involve establishing some impediment to one's performance – either imagined or real – so that individuals have an excuse for failure other than incompetence. Such strategies include procrastination and erratic goal setting.

PROCRASTINATION. As already noted, Ralph's self-handicapping ploy of choice was *procrastination*. This comes as no surprise, since procrastination is one of the most universally adopted of all defensive strategies. Some experts believe that at the college level for a near-majority of students, procrastination is a way of life (Rothblum, Solomon, & Murakami, 1986). Other more pessimistic estimates go as high as 95% (Ellis & Kraus, 1977). By studying only at the last minute, procrastinators like Ralph can hardly be blamed for failure, and had he not been so busy with other things, he explains, he could have done much better. Moreover, although Ralph's work might be mediocre, at least it was pursued with energy. Actually, never dismiss the benefits of mediocrity, since mediocre individuals are always at their best! And being too busy gives one an added sense of importance.

A subtle variation on the procrastination theme involves apparently genuine attempts to keep busy, very busy – in fact, too busy and with little to show for it. The student who spends endless hours collecting references for a term paper so that in the end nothing ever gets written illustrates this strategy. So, too, does the student who can never get beyond rewriting the introduction for a term paper in an endless succession of polishing and tinkering. The illogical uses of one's time and resources allows for a variety of explanations for eventual failure, including the argument that "I ran out of time." This same explanation is also available to the individual who takes on so many jobs that she can never devote sufficient time to any one task, which neatly explains her inadequate work.

ERRATIC GOAL SETTING. Failure-threatened students tend to set their learning goals erratically, either by setting them far beyond their current capabilities or by setting their goals so low that success is always guaranteed. In the first instance, pursuing unattainable goals makes perfect sense from a self-worth perspective. Failure at an exceedingly difficult task reveals little about one's ability, since in this case success is beyond the reach of everyone but the few most capable and energetic students. If almost everyone else fails, too, then the problem resides in the choice of goals or in the difficulty of the task, not in the individual. The old adage, "misery loves company," says it all, because the collective failure of the many obscures the individual failures of a few.

In the second instance, by setting one's academic goals low enough, there is little chance of failure. This strategy cushions students against the debilitating effects of anxiety in their preparation for upcoming tests. The student who publicly announces before an exam that he will be satisfied with just a passing grade is taking crafty advantage of what is referred to as *defensive pessimism* (Norem & Cantor, 1986). Naturally, however, there are trade-offs. Chronic low-goal setting eventually leads to poor performance and boredom. Moreover, guaranteed successes become completely predictable and lose any intrinsic value associated with uncertainty and challenge. Success without risk is not success at all. Here success simply means not losing. These victories are hollow and do nothing to increase a sense of student self-confidence, nor does it engender pride in accomplishment.

ANXIETY AS A PLOY. Test anxiety has all the elements of the ideal excuse for performing badly. In this and other similar ploys, the individual admits to a minor personal weakness or handicap in order to avoid disclosing the greater shortcoming, in this case being intellectually lacking. Attributing one's failure to an anxiety attack neatly deflects inability as the culprit. And it is the perfect victimless crime; no one can be blamed for being anxious, and often that person is a figure of sympathy. Moreover, anxiety is difficult to control, hence outside one's responsibility. Besides, anxiety is real enough; it is difficult to fake, and everyone knows what it feels like. Indeed, there is evidence that anxiety as a defensive ploy is too good to pass up when issues of self-protection are at stake. For example, the evidence suggests that anxiety symptoms of highly anxious college students may or may not be reported, depending on the availability of other kinds of excuse making (Smith, Snyder, & Handelsman, 1982).

Yet, at the same time, there is no doubt that anxiety is more than a self-protective convenience (Hill, 1984; Zeidner & Matthews, 2005). Its effects are real as well as widespread and profoundly debilitating. Conservative estimates indicate that from one-third to one-half of all public school youngsters suffer from test anxiety, and profound because this means that for at least a substantial minority of students, anxiety has caused invalid estimates of what they have learned or are capable of learning. Many students likely know more, reason better, and think more creatively than they can tell us through conventional, anxiety-prone testing. More on this point in Chapter 7.

## The Collapse of Defenses

Ralph is well aware that he is blaming his poor performances on getting started too late to do his best, yet without necessarily recognizing that this excuse is the product of a fear of failing. In short, he is aware of his actions, but not necessarily the reasons behind them. To this extent, Ralph has succeeded in deceiving himself. But a second round of deceptions must also succeed if his defensive tactics are to allay the threat of failure. His explanations for failure must also appear credible in the eyes of others. Or, as Fritz Heider (1958) put it, excuses maintain their self-serving value only for as long as they "fit the constraints of reason." This balancing act is illustrated by the fact that individuals are constantly altering their public persona to their advantage depending on circumstances. In the case of schooling, we (Covington & Omelich, 1981) found that following a disappointing grade, undergraduates demoted their self-perceptions of ability only slightly as long as non-ability explanations for failure were available. Moreover, they also believed that outside observers would accept these still inflated self-views, thus closing the circle of self-deception – that is, fooling themselves as well as others. At the same time, when low ability was a compelling explanation for failure – for example, when students had studied hard and failed anyway – they readjusted their self-estimates of ability significantly downward to meet the demands of credibility.

Yet, students do not always act like weathervanes, constantly shifting their efforts at impression management in opportunistic, self-serving ways. Powerful forces are also at work to narrow one's field of maneuvering and in some cases ultimately to endanger their self-image of competency, and with it the psychological resilience needed to continue striving. The most corrosive factor in this process is the occurrence of repeated failures when students are doing poorly in several classes at once, or are falling progressively behind in the same class. In these situations, self-serving explanations progressively lose their credibility, and initially vague fears regarding one's ability can crystallize into a certainty, a process we see repeated in college each fall among scores of previously high-achieving high school students.

We have tracked the collapse of these defenses in cases where students are falling short of their personal grade goals on each of several successive tests in a single class (Covington & Omelich, 1981; 1990). The data suggest that with each of several initial disappointments, self-estimates of ability diminish. This is because the available non-ability explanations for failure, such as the alleged unfairness of a test, become increasingly implausible because of repeated use. As a result, feelings of shame and self-loathing intensify. At the same time, these same students increase their estimates of the importance of ability for succeeding. In effect, this places them in the vise of a double jeopardy: as failures mount, they increasingly believe themselves deficient in the very factor – ability – that they increasingly consider the most important ingredient for success. This demoralizing process was most apparent among students who initially felt themselves the least able. As colleges and universities recruit and admit students who have not had the benefit of adequate education, the frequency of this cycle is likely to increase.

## Approaching Success

Fortunately, there are healthier interpretations for "doing well" than for "winning over others." "Doing well" can mean becoming the "best one can be." Pliny the Elder put the point best centuries ago when he urged young people "to become who you are," implying that the quest for selfhood means to grow into one's talents and emerging abilities that may otherwise remain hidden from view unless discovered and exercised. This is the mantra of success-oriented individuals contrasted to that of failure-avoiding students. This is not to suggest that perceptions of ability are no less important to success-oriented students. It is only that for this group, ability is considered the means to desired ends, not an end in itself as a talisman of one's worth, and that the desired end-goal is learning! One student put it this way: "Grades do not matter that much to me, and as long as I do my best, I will be satisfied with the result."

Yet grades are not simply dismissed by success-oriented students. Grades are still recognized as important gatekeepers to further education and eventually to entry into desired careers. But grades are viewed as by-products of learning, and learning for the right reasons – for the sake of self-improvement, to better prepare oneself to help others, and for the satisfying of curiosities. In this alternative formulation, grades are seen as derivative of learning rather than trumping learning. This attitude benefits students in at least three ways. First, it increases the likelihood that students will attain even better grades than might otherwise be expected because now learning occurs in an atmosphere of reduced anxiety and fear. We will shortly come to appreciate more fully just how critical an anxiety-free climate can be for the pedagogical goals we seek. Second, as a result of their altered status for the better, grades can assume their rightful, more constructive role as feedback for how students can improve their future performances. Third, the focus on learning for positive reasons carries with it a host of intrinsic rewards, which are essentially unlimited, not a commodity made scarce by competitive rules.

In contrast, by "trying to win over others," the defining reward involves *power*. But only one person can be the most powerful. However, when this divisive version of the self-worth formula is transformed, the prevailing value becomes one of *strength* – strength of will, of persuasion, and of endurance, qualities that can be possessed by everyone. Moreover, because of the motivational benefits of measuring excellence in personal terms, success-oriented students expect to succeed. This is because they effectively manage the risks of failure and its threats to their worth. They do this by setting their learning goals at or only slightly beyond their current capabilities. This means not only that the chances of succeeding are maximized but that any failure to reach their goal – should it occur – is robbed of much of its potential threat. This is because when judging success as realistically within their grasp and only requiring the application of diligent effort, failure for these students is unlikely to be attributed to incompetence. When success-oriented students fail to meet their goals, they believe they have fallen short on effort, not fallen short as a person.

Not only do success-oriented students view the role of ability quite differently in self-worth terms, but their perceptions of the essential nature of ability are also fundamentally at odds with those of failure-threatened students. For success-oriented students, ability is viewed as a resource – actually a means to an end that is learning (Dweck & Bempechat, 1983). This perspective suggests that ability functions in an executive capacity whose purpose is to plan and execute strategies for purposes of data gathering, decision-making, and problem solving. This plastic, flexible view of ability has been referred to as *incremental* in perspective, that is, ability considered as a repertory of skills that can be improved incrementally and expanded through experience and practice. Students who hold an incremental view of ability are more likely to concentrate on the task at hand, show greater involvement, and are less concerned with ability as a test of their worth (Dweck & Bempechat, 1983). These attributes are an essential part of being success-oriented. By contrast, failure-threatened individuals perceive ability as a stable, fixed entity, akin to an amount, not a process, that is basically unchangeable either by experience or by practice. No wonder that holding an *entity theory* of ability is potentially so devastating in the face of repeated failures.

By highlighting these two kinds of students – success-strivers and failure-avoiders – and magnifying their differences for expository purposes, we do not mean to suggest that these distinctions are easily maintained in reality. In actuality, there are countless variations within the psychological boundaries described here. But despite the many complexities involved, these defensive dynamics ultimately reflect a primordial search for self-acceptance and, when necessary, a retreat for the sake of self-protection. This process is so elemental that some students are prepared even to sacrifice good grades for the sake of appearing worthy by reason of ability. Experienced instructors have all observed the perplexing behaviors of students who are highly motivated, even anxious, to achieve yet make obviously maladaptive choices.

## Overstrivers: A Variation on the Theme

Overstrivers are failure-threatened students who make a frontal assault on failure (Beery, 1975). They attempt to avoid failure by succeeding! Overstrivers embody both an overweening desire to do well, grade-wise, and an overwhelming fear of failing. In effect, they are a hybrid. On the positive side of the ledger, overstrivers describe themselves as highly qualified intellectually; and indeed, they often have the scholastic record to prove it. However, on the negative side, they secretly worry that they are not really as smart as their outstanding record of accomplishments would suggest. In actuality, they can never be smart enough, since their private test of success is to achieve perfection. Perfection is sometimes measured in terms of competing successfully, head-to-head, with the best and the brightest students in class, or by competing with one's own personal, idiosyncratic standards whose demands are likely to continue spiraling upward, unchecked by reality. Yet, ironically, in the short run, overstrivers can become *too* effective in evading failure because over time the burden of maintaining an ever-increasing upward spiral of successes becomes intolerable. No one can avoid failure forever, despite Herculean study efforts, especially in the face of increasingly unrealistic self-demands. As a result, overstrivers become victims of the most damning kind of self-entrapment in that one success demands another, and greater than the last.

The fact that overstrivers must prepare slavishly for each testing ordeal, disqualifies them from taking refuge in the defensive strategies available to most other failure-threatened students. For instance, overstrivers cannot afford to procrastinate given the level of excellence they must achieve. They are the first to start studying for an upcoming test, and the last to stop, often just as the exam is being passed out. Sometimes their study notes must be literally ripped from their hands! Nor can overstrivers blame failure on their having had too many distractions to permit adequate study before a test. Excused failures are insufficient. Unadulterated success is the only acceptable way to prove their worth. Moreover, the fact that they have studied relentlessly makes failure all the more horrifying because, as already noted, having failed after studying hard is clear evidence of incompetence. The resourcefulness with which overstrivers attempt to avoid this conundrum – indeed, the desperation that drives them – is well illustrated by the actions of those individuals referred to as *closet achievers* (Beery, 1975). Closet achievers study secretly, usually in the bowels of the library or off-campus, and have been known to study under their blankets using a flashlight after hours so as not to reveal their subterfuge to roommates! Thus, if they do poorly on the test, explanations of not having studied adequately have the ring of authenticity; and best of all, should they succeed, having done so presumably with little or no study is unimpeachable evidence of brilliance!

The phenomenon of overstriving helps us understand two puzzles regarding achievement behavior of students everywhere. First, why is it that high grades do not necessarily lead to a sense of student pride and expanding self-confidence? Actually, personal satisfaction depends as much on the reasons for learning as it does on grades themselves. Because the praiseworthy academic records of overstrivers are the product of the fear of failure driven by self-doubts, their achievements do little to enhance their feelings of confidence in facing future challenges. It is for this reason that teachers need to pay as much attention to the underlying motives that sustain student achievement as to the quality of the achievements themselves.

Second, if positive self-regard is the result of an accumulation of successful achievements over the years, then why is it that one's sense of confidence can be shattered after only one failure? Should not all those past successes offset that one failure? Again, motives are everything. In these cases, failure, even a single one, simply confirms what overstrivers have feared all along, that they are less capable than perfection demands. Once again, we see that it is the meaning of success and failure, not necessarily their occurrence or frequency, that controls the motivation to achieve and the quality of one's achievements.

## Test Anxiety

Clearly, fear can rouse individuals to action. But fear can also interfere with learning and disrupt one's ability to demonstrate what *has* been learned. In this regard, fear typically makes its most visceral appearance in the form of test anxiety. For this reason it is critical that we understand something of the nature of test anxiety before proceeding.

The study of test anxiety is said to have the longest sustained history of scientific inquiry of any topic in the field of psychology, starting back in the last decades of the 19th century (Spielberger, personal communication,

1982). As a result, vast amounts of research have been generated over the years, and numerous theories have been proposed regarding the mechanisms responsible for the devastating effects of anxiety on learning and memory. All these converging lines of evidence and conjecture forge a powerful argument for viewing test anxiety in self-worth terms. In effect, test anxiety is a multiheaded reaction to the threat of failure: that one is incompetent, hence unworthy.

As a culprit, anxiety takes at least three forms, all of which are known to interfere with the retrieval of information stored in memory and to disrupt the higher-order mental processes that transform this stored information to useful purpose (Covington, 1985b). The first form of anxiety is physiological in nature. This is basically the "butterflies-in-the-stomach" phenomenon, typically consisting of a racing heart, sweating, and heightened blood pressure. Second, comes an emotional strand consisting of feelings of tension and stress, which also interfere with the recall of previously learned material. Then there is the third strand, picturesquely referred to by Jeri Wine (1980) as "a reverberating circuit of worry," which consists of all those distracting thoughts during testing that can interfere with recall. Students worry that there is not enough time to finish, and then they cannot think of anything more to say; they worry that others might be watching, so they appear to be thinking; and they recall other similar situations that ended disastrously. Needless to say, these students rarely get around to concentrating on the task at hand.

Consider a fourth and the most provocative of all the possible explanations for the mechanisms involved in test anxiety. Rather than being a *retrieval-deficit theory* (Spielberger, 1972) like all of the three factors just mentioned – that is, factors that interfere with already stored memories – this additional notion is a *skill-deficit theory* (Culler & Holahan, 1980). It holds that neither worrisome thoughts, nor physical upset, nor bad feelings are necessarily responsible for poor test performance, and that the real culprit is a lack of proper study. From this perspective, emotional, physical, and even self-defeating thoughts are simply by-products of students recognizing that they are unprepared and likely to fail. This notion has been marvelously conveyed by the remark of Dean Inge that "Anxiety is the interest paid on trouble before it is due." By this reckoning, poor test performance occurs not because anxiety interferes with what students know, but because students cannot retrieve what they never learned!

What is important to take away from this brief overview is that all these different factors are additive to our fuller understanding of the nature and causes of test anxiety. For example, these factors are not always equally disruptive, and each factor exerts its influence at different points in the study-test cycle. Moreover, they impose their impact differently depending on whether the individual student is an overstriver, a failure avoider, or success oriented.

It is worthwhile to explore briefly just how all this plays out within the larger perspective of self-worth theory. To do this, we will continue to follow the misadventures of Ralph, our failure-avoiding freshman. Ralph puts a human face on the countless students who wrestle with test anxiety, a substantial sample of whom we found among some 400 undergraduates we tracked through an actual study-test cycle (Covington & Omelich, 1988; 1990). We subdivided this cycle into three successive stages. First came the test appraisal stage in which the upcoming exam was judged by students to be either a challenge or a threat. Second came the test preparation stage in which students begin studying while experiencing various feelings and thoughts regarding the likelihood of succeeding or failing. This point in the process is the focus of skill-deficit notions of anxiety. Third came test taking itself, with the efforts of students to recall what they had learned, sometimes amid great tension. This stage is the site of all retrieval-deficit hypotheses.

As will be recalled, we left Ralph at a point where his poor performances in several courses prompted him to vow to work harder next term. Here was his chance to make good on his promise.

### Appraisal Stage

As Ralph listened attentively to Professor Jones explain the course requirements during the first class meeting, a sense of dread washed over him, as was actually reported in real time by many of the students in our sample. These formless feelings of foreboding took specific, tangible form in worries that they might not do well enough to stay in school, that they might lose scholarships, or that they would not have enough time for study, but most of all that failure might unmask them as incompetent. Try as he might to rid himself of these worries, Ralph remained so preoccupied that any inclination to study was driven from his mind.

### Preparation Stage

The test is in two days! Time to start studying! But Ralph's efforts remained largely ineffective because of what we have called the "pivot of fear" (Covington & Omelich, 1988). Fear turns on this pivot, reaching out in three interlocking directions. First, reoccurring worries about his ability broke Ralph's study concentration. Whenever he failed immediately to grasp a point in the readings, he wondered again if he really was smart enough to be a physician. Second, fear triggered a host of defensive thoughts, all of which, according to our data, acted to disrupt Ralph's attempts to study even further. Ralph indulged in wishful thinking (e.g., "I wish the test would somehow be over") and projected blame on others (e.g., "If I had a better teacher, I might do better"). And just to close this ring of fear, mounting feelings of tension and one bout with nausea destroyed his concentration completely, at least for the moment. Not surprisingly, Ralph never really settled into serious study (but later he will recall having spent a lot of time studying). He quit working as soon as he started, but promised himself to begin again when he felt better. In the meantime, he attempted to add company to his misery by derailing the study efforts of his roommates by suggesting a movie.

## Test-Taking Stage

Now Ralph entered the examination room and took a seat. The exam began. Halfway through the hour another wave of worries washed over him because as Ralph looked around nervously, he wondered why so many students were leaving already. Maybe the test was easier than he thought – "I must really be dumb!" Ralph found himself unable to think straight and he could not remember the basic facts he had memorized just minutes before he entered the exam room. Worse yet, he didn't even understand several of the questions on the test. In the words of William Manchester (1983), "it is as if the mind seems fathoms down, like some poor land creature entangled in the weeds of the sea." Sadly, in Ralph's case, both the retrieval-deficit and the skill-deficit hypotheses seem alive and well. At the end of the hour, some minutes after a GSI collected his work, Ralph uncoiled himself from a semi-fetal position in his chair and slowly made his way outside.

We have seen just how invasive the effects of self-doubts about one's ability can be as they reverberate throughout the entire study-test sequence. Initially, the doubts aroused in the appraisal stage permeate successive study sessions, cascading forward in time in the form of defensive, avoidance-oriented thoughts that easily transform themselves into physical manifestations of stress and tension, and finally trigger delayed worries during testing itself. In Ralph's case, he is at a double disadvantage. Like other failure-avoiding students, he learned too little to begin with, thus creating a massive skill deficit, rendered more deadly still by defensive posturing and procrastination. Then what little he did learn could only be retrieved imperfectly because of the intrusion of worries and stress during testing.

These findings yielded several important insights for our purposes. One is that the specific mechanisms responsible for Ralph's poor performance as a failure avoider were quite different than the dynamics we observed for overstrivers. Overstrivers tend to control their fears sufficiently during test preparation so that tension actually acts positively to mobilize and sustain their enormous appetite for study. There is no evidence here of haphazard, inadequate test preparation – what we have called a "skill deficit." Unfortunately for overstrivers, however, learning and performance are not the same thing. The very tension that aroused the overstriver's great gifts for learning in the first place reasserts itself in a far more virulent form at test time. At this point, overstrivers appear to suffer a massive failure to retrieve what they have overlearned! Worries about falling short of perfection could not have occurred at a worse time. The student who laments, "but I knew it cold before the exam," is likely an overstriver (Covington & Omelich, 1987a).

The pattern of anxiety data for success-oriented students is different still. Interestingly, success-oriented students also reported experiencing anxiety at various points in the study-test cycle just like other students, although generally to a lesser degree. Apparently, no one is entirely immune from the fear of failing. But what was most intriguing is that variations in the degree of anxiety experienced by success-oriented individuals were essentially unrelated either to the quality and length of their study or to test performance itself. In effect, while traces of anxiety were present, they were not particularly disruptive. These findings are consistent with our earlier conclusion that because of the more positive ways success-oriented students define their worth, they have moved beyond concerns about their ability status and the more conventional competitive definitions of success and failure.

The fact that anxiety strikes students in different ways and at different points in the study-test cycle confronts instructors with a clear dilemma: How can they accommodate so many differences in motivational patterns and learning approaches, especially in large classes that may exceed hundreds of students? And the complications do not stop here. It turns out that no one kind of anxiety reduction technique benefits everyone equally. This point was demonstrated neatly by Moshe Naveh-Benjamin (1985) who administered relaxation therapy to one group of anxious students who had good study skills, akin to our overstrivers. Another group of equally anxious students, but with poor study skills, akin to our failure avoiders, was given training in good study techniques. Both groups increased their performances on subsequent tests because the respective interventions addressed their particular weakness. However, when Naveh-Benjamin reversed the order of treatment for two more groups in order to provide a base-line control, neither of these latter two groups benefited because their weakness went uncompensated.

Our research efforts, too, confirm the rather narrow range of effectiveness for anxiety reduction strategies, depending on the kinds of deficits treated (Covington & Omelich, 1987b). For example, one of the most intriguing ideas for optimizing test performance is to arrange items within a test so that the easier items come first, on the theory that a few early successes will increase a student's confidence to tackle harder items later. As it turned out, we discovered that failure-avoiding students performed at their best under this condition, but performed at their worst when the item order was reversed. However, overstrivers revealed just the opposite pattern. They performed best when harder items appeared first, presumably because failure, if it occurs on especially difficult tasks, holds fewer negative implications for ability, since so few other students would have succeeded either, thereby freeing these conflicted students to do their best. Not surprisingly, success-oriented students not only outperformed the other groups overall but did equally well under both item orders.

Clearly, findings such as these hold more theoretical implications than practical significance. Instructors cannot be expected routinely to prepare and administer various forms of a test depending on the individual motivational characteristics of their students. However, with the advent of *customized testing*, instructors can consider this possibility. More on customized testing in Chapter 7.

Finally, we are left with the larger question of just how effective any kind of intervention techniques can be by themselves as long as competitive, ability-focused values dominate the classroom. Putting this point differently: we now know a great deal about the learning dynamics of failure-threatened students because researchers have studied them in environments that are peculiarly hostile to their vulnerabilities. But what will be the positive consequences, if any, for these students if they find themselves in less threatening, more supportive learning environments of the kinds we will propose? This is the central question addressed in the concluding chapter.

## SUMMING UP

Meanwhile, what are the most important observations made so far regarding the motivational dynamics of learners from a self-worth perspective? Two points stand out.

## Motivation of the Wrong Kind

First, it now seems clear that we must be careful about blaming the failure of students to learn on a lack of motivation. Actually, indifference, docility, and passivity are just as motivated as is lively, animated behavior, but for different reasons. According to self-worth theory, inaction born of anxiety and avoidance is driven by the need to protect one's sense of ability. Thus, the problem facing instructors may be less a lack of student motivation as it is motivation driven by fear. By the same token, we need remain wary of highly engaged, positively appearing states of mind that in actuality may harbor fear as the stimulant to action. This suggests that in rethinking our educational goals, we should strive to alter these destructive reasons for learning rather than simply raising the stakes that further threaten one's identity as a worthy person. Indeed, all students hold some amount of both approach and avoidance motivations. Instructors can help tip the balance by virtue of the course design choices we will describe in later chapters.

## The Threat of Effort

Second, we are now also in a position to appreciate why effort and ability are potential adversaries in the quest for self-affirmation for some students. Cannot students achieve personal satisfaction via hard work and in the process also increase their sense of competency? Yes, they can, and we will soon consider some possibilities for achieving such a symbiosis. Otherwise, it is an unlikely proposition, since studying hard or exerting thoughtful effort is a potential threat to one's worth because if a student tries hard and fails anyway, then attributions are likely to go to low ability. How, then, can instructors successfully motivate their students if trying hard is a potential threat?

In important ways this question confronts educators with the ultimate irony. We have investigated this paradox in some detail. In one study (Covington & Omelich, 1979), we asked a large sample of undergraduates to indicate how they would feel had they received a disappointing score on a test for which most of their classmates had done well. Students reported that if they had studied only a little, if at all, they would experience little diminution in their ability status. By contrast, had they studied hard and failed, they would anticipate feeling considerably less able, and quite ashamed because of the implication of their being incompetent. In another phase of this study, a second sample of students from the same class was asked to assume the role of college instructors and reprimand students in the first group, depending on whether these failing students had studied hard or little at all. These proxy teachers were highly critical when students had not studied, yet they greatly moderated their negative reactions when told that other students had studied hard. Incidentally, this is essentially the same reaction that we have found among real teachers at all educational levels beginning in the elementary years (Omelich, 1974).

Here is clear evidence of a clash of values. Teachers value and reward effort. But, as already noted, for many failure-prone students when "push comes to shove," maintaining one's ability status trumps a reputation as hard workers. Ironically, then, our proxy teachers moderated their criticism of failure in precisely those situations that triggered the greatest shame for students should they fail. Conversely, the proxy teachers most strongly discouraged those conditions (not trying) that provide students the greatest cover from the negative implications of failure!

However, the final greatest irony was reserved for the results of a third failure condition, not yet mentioned. The proxy teachers were also told that some of the hypothetical students had studied hard, but this time had a plausible excuse for their failure, for example that, "just by chance, the test emphasized different topics than those the students had studied the most." Not only was teacher criticism reduced to its minimum in this situation, but now that students had a plausible explanation for their failures other than incompetence, their burden of shame was greatly reduced as well. Thus, there emerges from this final pattern of data, ironically enough, an optimal survival formula for fear-prone students at risk for failure: "Try, or at least appear to try, but not too energetically, and always with excuses available!" It is difficult to imagine a strategy better designed to derail the pursuit of academic excellence and sabotage true engagement in learning.

These findings indicate why merely raising the academic stakes by requiring more effort from students is potentially disastrous. It assumes that instructors can encourage achievement by rewarding hard workers and punishing the indifferent. Yet what is most important to many students are not rewards for hard work, but finding ways to avoid the implications of having expended too much effort when risking failure.

This impasse is best sidestepped by rethinking the role of effort expenditure in achievement dynamics. Effort is a threat when it becomes implicated in an *ability game* in which schooling is seen as a contest among students for limited rewards. The fewer the rewards available, the more ability is believed by students to be the main factor in attaining rewards, and in the process the more valuable these rewards become, too, because if only a few can win, then success becomes all the more convincing as evidence of great ability. In this circumstance, defensive ploys kick in and effort becomes problematic in the equation for the protection of a sense of worth.

What is needed is a paradigm shift in thinking about the possibilities of transforming ability games into equity games – equity in the sense that all players have an equal opportunity to succeed as long as prevailing academic standards are met. Depending on the nature of the work required and the levels of competence demanded, ability will always play its part in learning. But now one's efforts can be more effectively organized and profitably focus on overcoming the difficulties of the task, and less attention given to worrying about one's own ability status and that of others. Instructors can also encourage their students to entertain alternative, more constructive interpretations in the event of their falling short other than having insufficient ability. No longer should effort expenditure serve a predominantly defensive function. Rather, students can exert effort as required by the task. In effect, they can become task-engaged, and with it more likely to discover the intrinsic benefits of learning. If equity games and their presumed benefits are to become a reality, then we must ask if there are any circumstances in which expending effort – even asking for help to correct mistakes – will not necessarily trigger suspicions about one's ability, but rather will enhance one's reputation as being a dedicated, thoughtful, and persistent student. The answer to this question is yes, as we will discover in subsequent chapters.

## The Hidden Motivational Landscape of Teaching

The search for self-worth that animates the achievement dynamics of students also reflects similar struggles facing teachers. The sources of personal worth for teachers and students are essentially a mirror image of one another. For many students, feelings of worth are tied to performance goals. For the teaching staff, worth is tied to the effectiveness of their teaching to these goals. A fundamental revelation of self-worth theory, as it applies to schooling, is that teachers and students alike are linked, cheek-to-jowl, around a common need to be appreciated by one another in their interlocking roles. For this reason, teachers are equally subject to the fear-evoking risks of rejection. Here the fallback position in the struggle for approval is to not lose; in the case of teachers, to not lose authority, and for students, to not fail. Teachers worry that they may have lost the momentum for teaching whenever they must give conversational CPR to moribund students who remain unresponsive to entreaties to participate in class. And teachers fear that they may be incompetent (or viewed so) and unworthy as instructors following a class meeting that goes badly. It is these self-doubts that can pave the way for a defensive posturing in much the same ways these negative dynamics work with students. Teachers are particularly vulnerable because their professional identities are tied to their impact on students as well as their disciplinary expertise. This is why the dismissive gestures of students can cut so deeply, and why instructors complain so bitterly about students' disregard for the gifts of learning, replaced by a short-sighted focus on grades.

But the waters run deeper still. For example, why would renowned academics, such as Professor Jones, lecture over the heads of their students, employ arcane vocabulary to excess, or make obscure references in their lectures that go unexplained? Clearly these are not good teaching practices. Instructors risk confusing and alienating the very students on which they rely as a major source of their own approval. Professor Jane Tompkins (1990) explains this apparent paradox as efforts by instructors to impress students with their brilliance, not necessarily with their ability as teachers, but rather as experts and authority figures in their field – in effect, to demonstrate how smart and knowledgeable they are. According to Tompkins, and consistent with self-worth considerations, this is the essential cockpit of fear for teachers: "Fear of being shown up for what you are: a fraud, stupid, ignorant, a clod, a dolt, a sap, a weakling, someone who cannot cut the mustard." (Tompkins, 1990, p. 654) But why would ability be at issue for instructors whose reputation for competence, if not brilliance, is already confirmed by the very fact of their high-status position? Tompkins suggests an answer in terms of a *performance model* that shares much in common with self-worth theory. Simply put, she argues that instructors continue to perform for the teachers who previously taught *them* – to prove oneself able and intellectually promising enough to be worthy of the attention and respect of their former mentors, even though it is no longer necessary to offer such proof.

If we assume that in their high school years and earlier, future college instructors also experienced developmental dynamics similar to those we have already reported for current undergraduates, then this all makes a certain kind of sense. Because of converging societal and family pressures, the ability to achieve, especially by competitive means, comes to rival, if not exceed, in importance all other personal attributes for those aspiring to academic careers. In short, instructors were students once, too. And because scholastic success rests so heavily on intellectual ability – often of a rare, arcane variety – then so much more would ability considerations dominate the lives of these young academics.

By this reckoning, then, there exists in college classrooms another audience besides the sea of upturned undergraduate faces – an imagined, phantom audience to which instructors often, but unwittingly, direct their remarks. This audience includes an idealized self, based on the possession of those attributes thought to be most needed for scholarly acceptance. At other times, this imagined audience may also consist of a jury of one's current peers. According to Tompkins, these kinds of juries will always be out! This palpable, if invisible, presence helps us understand why lecturers sometimes direct their remarks literally at their assembled GSIs sitting in the front row of the auditorium, remarks that easily go over the heads of everyone else in the room. Typically, it is only the GSIs who chuckle appreciatively at the humorous asides of lecturers, and it is lecturers who take their cues from the nods and body language of their graduate students. This is "insider trading" of information and ritual at its most exclusive, much to the detriment of the clueless undergraduates who merely stand witness to this privileged spectacle.

There are also other related risks for instructors associated with their need for approval besides the fear of being unmasked as intellectually limited. These fears include losing one's power of authority over students that is derived from one's formidable status as an expert. This involves the unsavory prospect of having one's cherished theories or opinions not only challenged by lowly undergraduates but also perhaps even refuted. Indeed, it is sometimes true that in the process of explaining one's position publicly, certain flaws in reasoning that would otherwise have remained undetected or unchallenged can come to light. For all the advantages of such encounters for clarifying issues, it can nonetheless be embarrassing, especially so because many undergraduates expect instructors to be, as one student put it, "walking and talking encyclopedias," with the not-too-subtle implication that if they are not, they must be less than able. Such an assumption reveals a grossly distorted view of the nature of knowledge and what it means to be an expert. However, graduate students do seem to get it right. Their respect goes to the instructor who may not know the answer immediately but knows how to figure it out. Nonetheless, among undergraduates, the damage may already be done. Parker Palmer (1998) has referred to this as fear of the judgments of the young!

## The Destructive Cycle

When the sum of all the self-doubts of both instructors and students are put in play, they can easily magnify exponentially into a destructive, self-perpetuating cycle. Although this cycle has many variants, it is essentially a drama in three acts.

### Act One

The belligerent behaviors of some students go unappreciated by instructors for what they may really represent – not necessarily the defiance of instructor authority or the willful disregard of scholastic values, but rather fear-driven strategies to avoid the implications of failure.

### Act Two

It is easy, and quite human, for instructors to attribute such troubling belligerent behaviors to the moral lapses of undeserving students, and blame them, rather than considering the cause to be the product of fear.

### Act Three

These reactions of instructors simply confirm what students have feared all along – that some instructors are insensitive and disinterested in their welfare. As a result, both parties can find themselves caught in an uneasy truce, what Richard H. Herh, a former college president calls a "mutual non-aggression pact" (Merrow, 2005), simply going through the motions of teaching and learning.

This dynamic has all the features of a *self-fulfilling prophecy*, which has been defined as "a false definition of a situation that evokes a behavior which makes the original false conception come true" (Merton, 1949, p. 423). This dynamic can be unpacked more specifically by recalling those fears that initially washed over Ralph, our failure-avoiding student, in his first day of class. Ralph's initial perception was that Professor Jones was unreasonable, even unfair, in his course requirements, an attribution doubtless due in part to the threatening lens through which Ralph views the academic world. As the course proceeds, this fear-driven judgment triggers defensive behaviors on Ralph's part, such as indifference to the topic or unguarded resentment to which Professor Jones responds with exasperation, thus confirming Ralph's original judgment of Professor Jones as uncaring.

These troubling dynamics can develop more quickly, are triggered more easily, and potentially made much worse in large lecture courses where many students already tend to feel isolated and anonymous, and where instructors may stand remote from students emotionally as well as administratively, and even spatially, literally "above and beyond the fray" – out of the psychological contact zone, shielded behind a lectern on an elevated stage in the front of the auditorium.

## Self-Justification Strategies

Self-worth theory holds that teachers, too, attempt to protect themselves against the various threats of rejection and failure implied in our three-act drama. It is these defensive strategies adopted by teachers and misperceived by students as to their actual causes that fuel the dynamics of a self-fulfilling prophecy. Several of the most frequently observed of these strategies are briefly mentioned here.

### *Delayed Vindication*

A clever strategy adopted by Professor Jones is to attribute the causes of his slumping teaching ratings and the increasingly vociferous nature of student complaints to the unwillingness of students to take responsibility for their own learning. Here he fancies himself as the defender of rigorous academic standards to which, if students are unwilling to submit, are not worthy of his support or special consideration. The unprecedented number of students who withdraw from his course just prior to administrative dropout deadlines becomes convincing evidence for Professor Jones that his uncompromising stance is working; only the most able, dedicated and serious students remain. From this perspective, it can be argued that student unrest is the price that sometimes must be paid for knowing that an instructor has not surrendered his standards for the sake of simply being popular. Moreover, it is also suggested in some academic circles that teachers cannot always be liked by their students, at least not in the short run, but hopefully respected over the long haul by a remnant of hard-working, dedicated students. Actually, this hope has little support in reality. Retrospective nominations by former undergraduates for their most influential college instructors did, in fact, identify those mentors who maintained high standards, but only when these demands occurred in the midst of a caring outreach, and a clear enthusiasm for teaching. In describing a universally beloved teacher on our campus, one of our fellow colleagues put it this way: "She doesn't let students off, but neither does she let them down." Even if frustrated instructors believe that their spotty teaching record will eventually be exonerated by history, there is scarcely any near-term satisfaction from drawing self-serving explanations through the eye of the needle of self-justification. These actions provide dubious salve for their discontent.

## Discounting Teaching

Another fallback strategy for instructor self-protection is to discount the importance of teaching altogether, not unlike the ploy favored by some students when they minimize the importance of a failed task. One potential ally for legitimizing this tactic is the academic community itself in which reputations for good teaching are sometimes undervalued compared to the prestige and professional recognition associated with excellence in research and scholarship. Within such a community, one need not feel particularly threatened by lackluster teaching, a function that is often airily dismissed as only tangential to one's central job description of scholar and researcher.

Not only is teaching often discounted in some academic circles; there may also exist a view that the educational mission itself is essentially exclusionary by nature. According to this argument, instructors teach, and when students do not learn, it is either because they did not study enough, or not in the right ways, or because they are simply not smart enough (Stevens, 1988). By this logic, there is little or no fault to be found with the instructor, and besides, as the companion argument runs, "some students are destined to fail anyway, no matter how helpful the instructor might be." Another such belief is that an instructor's responsibilities are limited to encouraging only the few most talented or most promising students, while the remainder must fend for themselves. Of course, such pedagogical philosophies actually create the very failures they predict, whenever they operate as justifications for ineffective teaching practices. These self-serving rationalizations are especially easy to maintain in those prestigious institutions where there is always an eager cohort of new freshman recruits waiting in the wings, willing to replace those hapless students who lack the "right stuff." Here again we see the mechanisms associated with self-fulfilling prophecies at work, but this time at the hands of teachers, not students. In this case, teachers can blame supposedly craven students, as the cause of what in reality may well be their own failures to teach effectively.

Sometimes even teaching well, as reflected by superior student ratings, can be harmful to one's professional standing! Laudatory student ratings can arouse suspicions that they are the result of an easy course, or that an instructor has succumbed to the temptation of currying favor with students by giving them what they want – better grades, in return for being liked by them. However, more often than not, the correlation between good grades and instructor approval is not the result of pandering, but of good teaching practices when, for example, instructors prepare special or additional study guides or hold extra office hours. This additional support leads both to improved student performance and higher instructor ratings. Of course, extra help in any form may be disapproved of by those who argue that students ought to struggle on their own to gain the most benefit from their education. By this logic, the struggle itself is thought to justify the rigors of a difficult course by making students stronger. However, if the rigors have less to do with responding well to intellectual challenges and more with battling confusion, uncertainty, and feelings of unfair treatment, then these struggles are unlikely to make students stronger – certainly not more self-confident or motivationally resolute in the face of academic challenges.

### TEACHERS IN THE MIDDLE: GSIs

GSIs are the players in the middle. They stand uneasily between being defenders and interpreters of the instructor's policies and buffeted by their students' needs. As to their flock of students, GSIs are confronted with issues far from the initially welcoming prospects of guiding eager, young minds. Instead, they often must deal with frightened, combative, and suspicious individuals, an ordeal that can tax the resolve of even veteran teachers. At the same time, GSIs are often viewed by instructors as their surrogates when it comes to administering course policy and maintaining the infrastructure of week-by-week teaching. This dual responsibility is made particularly challenging by the fact that GSIs typically are very much students themselves – often only one or two years beyond their own undergraduate careers, and unlikely to have mastered all the intricacies of their chosen field of study. Yet they are considered to be subject matter experts by their students. Moreover, GSIs, as apprentices learning how to teach, begin their appointments as novices in the art of teaching. The bleakness of this combined inexperience was characterized by one GSI informant as "not knowing enough content to teach, and not knowing how to teach it." Little wonder, then, that GSIs are often fearful of having their as yet relatively unsure grasp of their field challenged by mere undergraduates as well as fearful of losing control over their classroom. These initial experiences of GSIs with college teaching may in turn contribute to defensive postures that limit their ability and willingness to teach. This largely functional analysis of the roles and responsibilities of GSIs serves as a backdrop against which we can now briefly explore the self-worth needs of GSIs.

GSIs are particularly vulnerable to the results of student evaluations as a referendum on their teaching effectiveness because of their relative inexperience. Novice teachers have yet to develop a stable reference point against which to gauge the validity of these evaluations. And since their identity as teachers is still in flux, they may have little in the way of pedagogical conviction about the correctness of their teaching decisions. By contrast, veteran instructors can rely on their own seasoned perspective as a counterweight to student evaluations, expressed in the faintly condescending observation of taking these ratings "with a grain of salt." Meanwhile, for the inexperienced GSI, the salt, granular or not, is more likely than not to worsen their wounded pride!

Our GSI informants have provided a list of those interchanges with students that are particularly likely to threaten their sense of ability as teachers. At the top of this list is that dreaded moment when students ask a content question for which the GSI has no knowledge, let alone an answer. Sometimes, GSIs duck such questions in ways that would do veteran politicians proud. At other times, however, they may fudge answers or spin stories that have the veneer of plausibility. But the aftertaste is often one of deceit as well as feeling stupid. Then there are those strategies designed to avoid these embarrassing moments altogether. For example, GSIs may find that nonstop lecturing is a safer strategy than using an open forum that is more conducive to student questioning. And sometimes they may even go so far as to wrap themselves in a mantle of unapproachable academic superiority in order to discourage genuine discussion.

GSIs have good reason to be horrified at the prospects of being unable to field every question with professional authority. Students often expect their GSIs always to know the answers; otherwise, as one individual put it, "I would lose respect for teachers who don't know. They must be incompetent." As we will argue in Chapter 3, this statement reflects a basic misunderstanding of what it means to be an expert, and is largely the result of a parochial view of education as the simple transmission of fact-based information from the teacher to the learner; or as the argument runs: if knowledge is facts, then the knowledgeable teacher knows the facts, and the incompetent ones do not. The self-recriminations of GSIs as somehow having failed in their teaching responsibilities can cut deep, carrying with them feelings of shame and guilt – shame at presumably being found out as incompetent, and guilt by reason of not having prepared for every contingency.

Inexperience is not the only problem for GSIs. If students are absolutely powerless, then GSIs are relatively so. The very nature of the role of GSIs as a supporting cast makes their power over teaching decisions tenuous and uncertain. GSIs serve at the behest of the instructor. Rarely are GSIs the co-architects of class policy, nor are they consulted by instructors in these matters. Yet they are expected to administer policy. This hierarchical arrangement with descending degrees of power and authority can provoke tensions between GSIs and instructors, when, for example, GSIs are expected by default to apply grading policies created unilaterally by instructors with which GSIs may philosophically disagree, or are required to make difficult grading decisions without sufficient guidance, or are faced with the ordeal of attempting to explain to students why there are substantial differences in the grading done by GSIs in other sections.

### CONCLUSIONS

So far, the view of classroom life according to self-worth theory portrays a world populated by conflicted, vulnerable players whose sense of well-being depends precariously on the actions and expectations of one another. As difficult as a positive resolution is to achieve, even under the best of circumstances, the hope for a successful rapprochement dims considerably when it is assumed that the problems described in this chapter arise largely because bad or undeserving people are involved. Although it is easy enough to ascribe moral lapses to someone else, actually the problems described here more often than not arise out of legitimate human needs gone astray. The causes owe more to the unhealthy context in which the players find themselves and to the mismatched roles they unwittingly assume. The wrong-headedness of blaming people rather than situations is perfectly revealed by a comic incident recently witnessed by the authors. A group of college faculty attending a regional conference on teaching effectiveness was being lectured by a guest presenter. Midway through the lengthy, somewhat tedious monologue, several members of the audience began exhibiting precisely the same behaviors as those exhibited by students, which earn fierce faculty rebuke. One attendee began reading a newspaper and several others began to fall into a sleep-like trance, while yet another began some paperwork – akin to students in the lecture hall doing homework for another class! When instructors are placed in the role of students, they tend to behave as students do. Blameworthy here are not necessarily the players, but rather the circumstances in which they find themselves.

One more example will suffice to make the point. Instructors often complain that students shamelessly manipulate the grading system in ways worthy of Machiavelli. They do only the assignments they judge will be covered on exams; they probe GSIs incessantly for clues to exam coverage; and they become incensed when they feel they were misled. Our observations suggest that these efforts to control the vagaries of testing are less the result of students being craven exploiters of the system and more the product of the circumstances in which they find themselves. Whenever grading criteria are uncertain, when it is unclear what is required to do well, and when these criteria are not stable, but rather arbitrarily set and subject to change without notice – all potential characteristics of grade rationing systems – students will make plans and choices to create some measure of predictability.

Nearly identical dynamics can be observed among college faculty members when they are faced with limited and unpredictably distributed rewards in the struggle to gain tenure, according to Allan Stam (quoted in Piper Fogg, 2004). When Stam looked at the impressive academic qualifications of his fellow colleagues who had not made tenure, he reasoned that, "If I can't predict who they're picking [for tenure] and why, then I got to get out of here!" By his fourth year, Stam was already making choices, such as turning down a request that he direct part of an international studies program. This decision was based on his plan to depart for a tenured job elsewhere. When rewards are unpredictable and not necessarily linked to the quality of one's performances, individuals focus on actions that will more directly lead to desired results (which for faculty likely involves doing research and publishing as the most reliable route to advancement). Thus, in unpredictable, often threatening environments where the criteria of excellence are inexplicit (at least to the one being judged) professors adopt self-protective, defensive, avoidant (escape) strategies as a rational response. We should expect no less from students working under similar inexplicit, unpredictable, and limited reward systems.

Fear of Failure

# 3

# Roles and Responsibilities

Well, to me, it is up to the professor to motivate me. I mean, I want to learn and all, but sometimes the material is so boring and the professor just loves it and they go on and on about meaningless things.
– College student

Our biggest problem here is that students are just not motivated. They just don't seem to care, they are not interested in learning. I can't teach students like this.
– Faculty member

In this chapter we take up the second aspect of the hidden agenda. It involves a mismatch between instructors and students regarding their perceived roles and responsibilities. Simply put, students too often uncritically accept their role as merely absorbers of information. Moreover, they expect instructors to motivate them to this task. Not only is this passive posture one-sided and overbalanced; it is also misaligned because the expectations of most instructors, on the other side of this relationship, assume a quite different contractual arrangement. The teaching goals of virtually every college instructor we have interviewed requires students to become the active agents in the process of transforming information for their own purposes in imaginative and creative ways. For instructors, learning is not a spectator sport.

Yet, some of the teaching methods adopted unwittingly by instructors not only give insufficient support for the challenging goals of creativity and independence but, ironically, may actually reinforce the passive role of students as mere storage bins for information. This puts instructors in the role of codependents in this drama. Speaking of drama, we now fast-forward to any number of college and university classrooms on the first day of the term.

## THE SHIFT

Members of the new freshman class are opening their notebooks and laptops ready to record the "received wisdom" of their instructors, respectful of authority, and eager to learn. So far but potentially not so good, for the long haul. Actually, trouble is waiting in the wings, all part of the hidden agenda. The reality is that the learning strategies that worked so well in high school for the majority of these students will prove inadequate for the tasks ahead in college. As one student put it, "not only is college more than high school, but it is different." What is meant by different? And what happens when the learning strategies that brought success in high school become insufficient or even counterproductive in college?

## Achievement by Conformance

The answers to these questions lie in a single set of telltale statistics. One of the most robust predictors of an outstanding high school GPA is the extent to which students are willing to follow directions carefully, and to do what they are told, although not always understanding why. This work style is referred to as *achievement by conformance* (Gough, 1966). Typically, the kinds of academic tasks found in high school are solved by students conforming to a relatively clear and straightforward plan of action that is well specified in advance. The task here is simply to reproduce known solution procedures. Moreover, typically all the information needed to solve these problems is readily available – no more than needed, and no less (Covington, 2001).

This is not to suggest that the kinds of thinking involved here are simple, uncomplicated, or even unimportant. Quite to the contrary. Confirming a geometric proof can be anything but simple or uncomplicated. Nonetheless, the procedures for conformation, although sometimes quite complex, still rest on the application of a well-known set of steps that follow invariant patterns and that can be memorized without much understanding. This is also true of taking accurate transit readings on a construction site for building a skyscraper. This activity is anything but unimportant, given its bedrock significance. But again, with practice, the procedures involved can become habitual and merely need to be reproduced with accuracy. Although internalizing unswerving protocols, theorems, or formulae has the benefit of producing reliable, accurate outcomes, the very habitual nature of such thinking can also blindside the problem solver when previously successful solution strategies become counterproductive for solving similarly appearing but quite different current problems. More on this point shortly.

*Student Roles*

By this analysis, the self-perceived role of many high school students is to acquire information in ways that conform to, or serve, relatively invariant problem-solving applications (Hativa, 1998; Hativa & Birenbaum, 2000). A particularly telling example – akin to a rote ritual – involves memorizing facts from a textbook chapter and then recalling them on tests in a form little altered from the way they were first rehearsed. Here the emphasis is on accuracy of recall, not necessarily understanding the function or purpose of what is to be remembered. High school students are prone to the mental recording of information without giving it much thought prior to being stored in memory for some as yet unspecified future use. And because it is unspecified, such information becomes "warehoused" as something to be shelved, and as a result, likely rendered inert. Metaphorically speaking, many high school students act largely as mere vessels or receptacles for information – or, at test time, become sponges to be rung dry of information. The most dismaying aspect of these passive interpretations of learning is the absence of ideas about the dynamic purposes served by accumulating information, save for the occasional vagary offered by high school students that learners are "to do something with the facts" which it turns out on further probing has more to do with efforts to ensure accuracy of recall than with any productive use to which the facts might be put (Covington, 1998). Any traces of managing their learning for active purpose are reflected in only a handful of metaphors that, sadly, at their best, simply imply the mere sorting or arranging of information into different categories presumably for ease of recall (e.g., filters or storage bins). For many high school students, knowledge is simply the sum total of isolated facts, undigested commonsense beliefs, and fragments of data that can be conjured up. When coupled with a worldview of the role of students as receptacles of information, a sterile interpretation of knowledge emerges as a pervasive, deep-seated belief system that is quite contrary to true inquiry and scholarship.

We have found that these unfortunate tendencies are also alive and well among college populations (Covington & Dray, 2002). However, giving credit where credit is due, some of our college informants did recognize the error of their passive ways, particularly when preparing for tests: "Having to know all the little details forces students to memorize – dump large amounts of information into their minds hoping it will stick long enough to take the test"; or "going through a review sheet by simply defining every term, but disregarding connections between concepts and not attempting to create a larger picture is pointless." Unfortunately, too often such indictments go unappreciated by the majority of students for what they revealed about the shortcomings of an atomized approach to learning.

### Student Responsibilities

If the self-perceived role of college students is simply that of being guardians of information, not primarily transformers of information, what then are their self-perceived responsibilities in this lackluster process? These responsibilities, students argue, are limited largely to housekeeping duties – attending class faithfully, remaining conscious during lectures, and coming to class having prepared by doing any assigned readings in advance. While such resolutions are admirable, they may nonetheless serve only the aims of passive absorption. There is little expectation here that what is acquired deserves critical attention. This passive mindset also extends to student beliefs about how they can more fully appreciate and value what they are learning. The most frequently mentioned strategy of our undergraduate informants is to "keep an open mind." But as can be deduced from our previous observations, it may only be a mind ready to be filled by someone else!

### Instructor Responsibilities

Now, finally, what is the expectation of our student informants regarding the role that instructors should play in this docile process of information absorption? Basically, instructors are expected to deliver information in a predigested form, a point made quite plain by one informant: "I can't always tell what is important information, and what isn't. To sort this out, I want GSIs and instructors to tell me what I should know right off the bat!" Or, according to the even more insistent demands of another student, "It irritates me when instructors put together a review sheet that has terms like Freud, Adler, behaviorism, prejudice, and other major topics. I've read the text and know that it has 100 pages on Freud, now which of those 100 do instructors want me know?" If instructors do not comply, they are marked down. Indeed, the only thing valued more about instructors than their being engaging lecturers is their willingness to help with getting good grades.

## Achievement by Independence

While students expect instructors to take charge and provide help in mastering their lessons – actually, not a totally unreasonable expectation, especially for the novice – instructors nonetheless have a fundamentally different agenda in mind. Instructors expect students to take an active role in bringing subject matter material to life, of acting as interpreters as well as questioners of the status quo, and not being content with just cataloging information. In short, students are expected to become independent thinkers. These expectations are clearly reflected in the intellectual skill set that best predicts college GPA that is referred to as *achievement by independence* (Gough, 1968). In college, conformance thinking is no longer correlated positively with GPA; if anything, it becomes a negative weight. College assignments require that students take charge of problem solving that previously was largely formulaic and sometimes repetitive in nature. Students can no longer rely solely on the retrieval of unaltered information. They must also go beyond the information given. No longer is the immediately available information always sufficient to solve problems. Students not only need to know where to find additional information but also must be able to detect any gaps in information that must be filled before they can proceed. Moreover, college students must reconcile multiple sources of information and judge which data is most relevant and which is only marginally so. Furthermore, information is no longer packaged in a prearranged form. Also, problems may be amenable to multiple solutions and subject to alternative options that require casting them in ways that reveal the best path ahead.

Requirements for innovating thinking may be encountered for the first time when students enter college, including the art of problem finding (Dillon, 1982). One component of this discovery process involves the ability to detect inconsistencies, incongruities, or oddities that violate the expected. Training for such sensitivities is in short supply in the typical high school curricula; hence, students often come to college ill prepared to meet the challenges of innovative, creative thought.

## Failure to Shift

In summary, a wholly new set of cognitive skills is required to thrive in college, which is not typically promoted in earlier grades. Yet, this necessary shift in academic demands is not always apparent to college students, many of whom now persist in trying to make due with outdated but previously successful thinking strategies. This losing struggle is illustrated by those students in first-year college physics classes who continue to apply simplistic, inappropriate formulae learned in high school to problems that now demand entirely new approaches and ways of thinking.

Our research shows just how problematic this transition from old "tried-and-true" strategies to new and often foreign ways of thinking can be (Covington & Dray, 2002). The dynamics leading up to this critical shift in the intellectual life of students has an extensive developmental history, as revealed by students themselves, starting long before entering college. We asked a large cohort of undergraduates to track, retrospectively, those events in school they recall as having been especially influential in shaping their motivation to achieve, and in particular caring about what they were learning. These memories were prompted through a self-report survey covering three different time periods beginning with the elementary school years, continuing through middle school, and ending with ratings regarding their high school experiences.

A complex picture emerged from these data. Feelings of intellectual competency were recalled as slowly but steadily declining from a maximum in the late elementary years to their lowest point in the high school years. Over the same time span, our informants also rated the pressure to prove themselves via good grades as steadily increasing, and simultaneously competition for grades was perceived as intensifying as well. As we have seen, this confluence of factors is a potential witch's brew: as the pressure to prove one's worth via achievement intensifies, students became less certain of their ability to compete successfully. However, instead of becoming demoralized, our informants continued to thrive, grade-wise, throughout the high school years. Why should this be, especially in light of decreases in a sense of intellectual competency? For one thing, these students reported experiencing increased teacher support and encouragement as the high school years progressed, which likely acted as a partial buffer against the negative elements of this overall motivational picture. By far, however, the most important factor in sustaining an increasingly enviable academic record was success itself. While most other less successful peers in the same age cohort were losing interest in school due to mounting academic disappointments, our informants were enjoying the fruits of successful academic self-sorting. By surviving the gauntlet of academic elimination beginning years before, and despite lingering self-doubts about competency, these students had at last arrived at a pinnacle of academic success defined by GPA on the eve of college entrance.

A second related study tracked an additional sample of undergraduate students regarding their recollections of the transition to college (Covington & Dray, 2002). The data gathered at this juncture revealed a precipitous decline in feelings of academic competency even more rapid and ending far below that reported at the high school level. The first year of college entrance marked the low ebb in this regard. What was the cause? For one thing, teacher support, which was among the most positive, sustaining factors in high school, was reported on the decline in college. It was this withdrawal of support and guidance that our college sample regretted the most. The importance students attribute to teacher guidance is underscored by the many different ways it shows its value as reflected in various student observations: "If I don't know what instructors expect of me, then I can't live up to their expectations." Or: "Verbal feedback from GSIs keeps me motivated and make me feel acknowledged." And: "If I don't know if the professor takes my opinion seriously, there is no reason even to formulate one; then I take the class for what it is worth, which is a letter grade."

For another thing, increasing self-doubts of ability were caused by the unanticipated intrusion of failure experiences into the previously unblemished records of academic success enjoyed by these students. Moreover, college entry ratcheted up a new round of competition within an even smaller, more able cohort of elite students for what seemed before to be an unlimited supply of noteworthy grades. Ironically, these were usually not failures in any absolute sense such as risking academic probation or of being threatened by the loss of scholarship support, but rather of falling just short of lofty goals, as illustrated by the devastated student who received a disappointing B+ on a term paper instead of adding the usual grade of A to an already impressive string of top-notch grades.

Once again, we can question why relatively few failure experiences cannot be offset by a previously overwhelming legacy of successes. As we now know, for some students their successes are only apparent, and, in actuality, often mask the fear of failure. For this reason, such successes provide little counterweight to feelings of self-doubt. Failure underscores what these students have feared all along, that they were simply masquerading as competent. In effect, impressive past accomplishments do not always inspire confidence in one's ability to continue succeeding, especially when the demands of the learning game suddenly shift from conformance to achievement by independence.

The likelihood of failure is a constant presence owing to a basic human shortcoming. It is the tendency to rely on strategies that worked in the past without detecting their insufficiency for dealing with new challenges, a condition that calls to mind the pop-psychology definition of insanity: "The tendency to do the same thing over and over despite the fact that it never works, but always hoping for the best!" This kind of mindless action is less a matter of mental instability than it is the result of individuals being caught up in a rigid mental set. Such repeated mistakes can be particularly devastating. They will not yield to redoubled effort because the ways of thinking are simply inappropriate to the task at hand. Trying harder simply makes these outdated mental furrows deeper and more unyielding to correction. Moreover, there are few safe fallback explanations for failing. If the subject matter had been new or unfamiliar, then initial mistakes and early missteps would make sense. But many of these problems involve the very topics at which students excelled only a few months earlier in high school. The scramble to excuse such failures will likely provide little relief from feelings of shame, or of the humiliation that accompanies self-recriminations, particularly among students whose earlier successes were motivated by efforts to avoid failure.

The will to learn is the first casualty of such repeated failures, which set in motion an avalanche of devastating consequences as documented by laboratory research. For example, following a string of failures, caused by students working on a series of problems that, unbeknownst to them, were actually unsolvable, they were then unable to solve much simpler problems they had thoroughly mastered in an earlier study session (Diener & Dweck, 1978). In effect, repeated failure disrupts otherwise perfectly sound, well-established problem-solving approaches that are fully within the capability of the individual. Also, failure distorts past memories of emotions to the detriment of effective problem solving. After a group of students had experienced repeated failures, they were asked to reflect back on their earlier success experiences (Diener & Dweck, 1980). Due to the intervening failures, these students revised their recollections of earlier successes, which initially had been quite positive, so that now, in retrospect, they no longer remember feeling satisfied with themselves or with their work. Moreover, the negative emotional consequences of failure were more pronounced among failure-avoiding students.

Such dislocations and distortions caused by failure can easily lead to the phenomenon referred to as *learned helplessness* described as a state of depression or loss of hope that accompanies a belief that no matter how hard or how well one tries, failure is the inevitable outcome (Diener & Dweck, 1980). Little wonder, then, that many of our college informants registered far less hope of ever achieving their grade goals now that they were in college compared to their more optimistic assessments in high school.

THE CULT OF EFFICIENCY

What other factors lock students into reproductive modes of thinking besides the tyranny of a mental set? At least one factor in particular. Students are done a disservice by what can be called the *cult of efficiency*. This is the expectation of students that the job of learning should be accomplished as quickly as possible with an economy of time and motion. This expectation is reinforced by a factory model of education in which all schools, even institutions of higher learning, are likened to the workplace (Marshall, 1988). Here time is of the essence and productivity is the byword.

If knowledge is construed – as it is, by many students, as the sum total of dispensed information – then the transmission and use of information should be a straightforward, efficient matter. From this perspective, making errors, committing mistakes, and misremembering are the enemies of efficiency because correcting them wastes precious time. This is undoubtedly why students often cry foul when they spend time following a line of mathematical proofs that ultimately leads to a dead end, only to find to their annoyance that had instructors cared to, they could have pointed out in advance potential pitfalls in their thinking that would have saved time in the correcting. As one student lamented, "After all, isn't that an instructor's responsibility? It seems at times instructors are deliberately trying to deceive us." What this student has failed to appreciate is that the assignment in question likely required students to cross over a mental divide from the mere acquisition of facts to their application – in effect, the difference between learning and thinking. After all, it is not instructors who are necessarily tricking students. It is nature's infinite complexity that defies revealing its inner workings, whether it concern the study of human nature, plumbing the depths of the physical universe, or understanding the process of history itself. However, to be generous, perhaps in this particular example the instructor had not paved the way sufficiently by alerting his students to the altered nature of thinking necessary to solve the problem, nor acknowledged the special frustrations that invariably attend all complex problem solving. These are the communications that often go unspoken, and what makes this aspect of the hidden agenda so corrosive.

Presumed inefficiencies like failure are often thought by students to have few consequences other than to humiliate, to demoralize, or to waste time. However, failure can convey much more in the form of positive, invaluable lessons. As Max Bierbohm commented, "There is much to be said for failure. It is more interesting than success." By this he surely meant that many successes are merely the product of properly applying already over-rehearsed strategies, which is scarcely an opportunity for new insights. But the missteps that cause failure, if properly appreciated, may spark new ways of thinking, which means that one is wiser today than yesterday. But the requirement for wisdom is the courage to risk failure, or as Robert Redford has remarked, "You are only as good as you dare to be bad [risk mistakes]."

However, having put the best face on failure, we know that failure is still a frightening proposition. Here, once again, we confront perhaps the most frustrating of all teaching paradoxes. The essence of successful intellectual encounters that involve mobilizing one's resources to the utmost, yet at times failing anyway, can both attract and threaten students. The question becomes what kinds of teaching/learning alliances can be forged that put failure in the proper perspective as a natural, often necessary precursor to success.

## INSTRUCTOR AS CODEPENDENT

Much of what has been said so far implies an incongruity of sorts. From the outset, we have argued that despite the fact that independent thinking remains a priority teaching goal of college instructors, some of the teaching methods often adopted by them may not only give insufficient support for this objective but, ironically, may actually reinforce the very kinds of reproductive thinking that can undercut the exercise of independent thought! How can this be? Three reasons come to mind. First, there is the obligation felt by instructors to cover all the subject matter material in the course with the result that little time may be left for cognitive instruction in learning to think. Second, there is a de-emphasis on higher-level cognitive objectives in lieu of other subject matter material, which is easier and more efficiently measured. Third, there is a misunderstanding regarding the nature of productive thinking and the best strategies for promoting it as a trainable skill.

## COVERAGE OF COURSE MATERIAL

The first reason that instruction in higher-order thinking often gets short-changed involves a sense of urgency among instructors to "cover all the material." The imperative to touch all the bases is especially compelling in the case of introductory or survey courses where the emphasis typically is on a broad-brushstroke exposure to an entire discipline. The risk in attempting omnibus coverage is to turn courses into a hurried, superficial, and sometimes disjointed gloss. This is not conducive for helping students make sense of subject matter complexities, thus reinforcing shallow processing of information that risks turning students into mere stenographers and narrowing their attention to ensure the factual accuracy of what they are recording. With this mindset, there is little inclination to question the meaning of what they are inscribing in their notebooks or on their laptops, and probably little or no time to pause and reflect. And what may be even worse than encouraging such thoughtless processing, students may conclude that knowing a little about a lot of things is better than a deeper understanding of a few central concepts that have great traction in their application to problems of widely differing characteristics. The loss here is a lack of training on those skills needed to support independent thought.

Complicit with the danger of superficial coverage is the lecture method. It is widely believed that lecturing is the most efficient way to convey information, thus ensuring the greatest amount of coverage in the time available. Actually, lecturing is no more efficient in dispensing information than is reading textbook assignments on one's own or attending discussion sections (Freeman et al., 2014). However, the point here is not that lecturing per se is necessarily bad. It all depends on the purposes to which lecturing is put in the service of course objectives, which is not always to disseminate large amounts of information efficiently. Nor is lecturing necessarily bad simply because it typically involves large audiences. Most often lecturing is less effective than it might otherwise be because its advantages are not properly exploited. For example, the meeting of an entire class, even numbering into the hundreds, can uniquely serve important motivational and pedagogical purposes in ways that are not as well served by smaller groupings. Sometimes it is only the sheer size of a group that can convey a proportional sense of scale or even a sense of urgency regarding a variety of issues. Consider this example. As some 500 psychology students entered a lecture hall, each was given a colored card on a random basis. The number of cards of a given color reflected the proportion of Americans who during their lifetime would suffer from various mental illnesses in the population at large. After a few introductory remarks by the instructor, students holding a given colored card were asked to stand, card-by-card – red for acute depression, green for schizophrenia, and so on, until roughly half of the students were on their feet. Then in the same fashion, the remainder of students in the role of those relatives, loved ones, and close friends who would be impacted directly by mental illness rose from their seats. Everyone was standing, except for one person out of the 500 who represented roughly the ratio of trained mental health workers to those in need of professional help. The power of sheer size can create appreciations that no disembodied statistic can possibly convey. And such demonstrations are not limited by subject matter discipline. The vastness of the universe or the incidence of child slavery worldwide, as well as the microscopic world of brain cells, can take on enhanced meaning. As always, the fault lies not with the method – in this case lecturing – but with its uses, or rather it misuses, that is, not taking advantage of its strengths.

Subject matter coverage is always a problematic issue. No course can be expected to cover everything – at least not well – and sometimes even the most important material can be given no more than a "once-over-lightly" treatment. We believe that covering as much as possible in the time available, often by means of the lecture method, is the wrong way to frame the issue. More compatible with our thinking, as we will argue shortly, is the notion of coverage as a matter of teaching for the transfer of broadly applicable concepts and principles to new and often unforeseen problems. Clearly, factual content is important, but facts tend to have a relatively brief half-life. Adequate coverage can only be approached by stressing the universality of enduring problem-solving strategies. We will have more thoughts in Chapter 6 regarding achieving a proper instructional balance between the tactical role played by local information (e.g., facts) and larger, general strategic considerations.

## Efficiency of Testing

A second reason for an overemphasis on the atomized components of subject-matter material is because learning facts, conventions, and simple definitions is the easiest to assess. It is true that tests need be as efficiently administered and scored as possible, especially in those cases of the often burdensome workload of large enrollment classes. However, the downside of atomized testing is that it is typically limited only to providing evidence of the mastery of material at a recognition level of learning, that is, students recognizing the right or best answer from among a list of distracters, as is frequently the case with multiple-choice testing. Here success largely depends on memorization and on the repetitive rehearsal of material, which reflects the kinds of uninspired, passive ways students often approach their studies. To put it bluntly, this amounts to preparing like the proverbial sponge to be wrung out at test time, or as described in even less kindly terms by Samuel Coleridge who once remarked that students are like "strain-bags (of tea), who retain merely the dregs of what they read."

Even so, an acquaintance with subject matter concepts, if only at a simple recognition level, is sometimes a necessary initial step in the process of becoming a productive thinker. Thus, a recognition mode of learning is not necessarily the problem, nor is multiple-choice testing, nor lecturing for that matter. Again, it all depends on course goals and objectives. The larger problem is the shortsighted strategy of students studying narrowly to pass the test, not mastering the concepts and information that lie behind the test. Sophisticated students know that to do well on tests, they must learn the material in ways that it will be assessed. Thus, if the mere recognition of terms and definitions is the requirement for doing well, out come the "flash cards," and little else.

But cannot the tendency of students to study material in ways that it will be tested be employed for higher purpose, that is, requiring students to contemplate the larger meaning of the facts they are rehearsing, and still take advantage of the cost-effectiveness of multiple-choice testing? Actually, yes. Consider the various functions of factual information in problem solving. First, there is an *anticipation* mode for testing in which students would be required to judge which fact among a set of distractors would likely be most critical for solving an upcoming problem. Second, the usefulness of facts can be assessed *during* a problem-solving scenario, even at the critical moment of decision-making, in which students would need to select the fact that favors the better decision from among several lesser options. Third, tests can *retrospectively* probe failed efforts at problem solving by way of a postmortem review in which students must judge which one among several proffered facts, had it been available earlier, would have led to an otherwise successful outcome. Ultimately, the value of testing of facts in these ways as part of a meaningful, inherently interesting endeavor is that facts transcend their traditional purpose as only things to think *about*; facts now become things to think *with*. When students encounter such test questions as these, their preparation will be quite different than when the demands of assessment are limited to memorizing definitions of glossary terms.

### Learning versus Thinking

Third, although the promotion of productive thinking is a seminal goal among college instructors, there is a widely held belief that direct instruction in higher-order thinking is largely unnecessary because, as the argument runs, productive thought is primarily the result of acquiring sufficient information, and that once all the facts and figures are in hand, solutions will emerge almost spontaneously. This misbegotten proposition fits well with the view that the role of instructors is that of disseminators of information. In effect, instructors need only present information smoothly, in a predigested, understandable form – for more difficult material, perhaps repeated twice – and then the teaching act is complete. From this perspective, the instructor-student relationship is satisfied when a sufficient quantity of information has changed hands.

The belief that the accumulation of information per se is a necessary and sufficient condition for the spontaneous emergence of productive thought is flawed because it fails to recognize that learning and thinking are not the same thing (Covington, 1998). As Emily Dickenson once observed, "He has all the facts, but not the phosphorescence of thought." Learning and thinking differ because they embody broadly different goals. In the first instance, the goal of learning is to acquire information and then recall what is memorable; in the second instance, the goal of thinking is to make meaningful what is remembered. These goals require distinctively different mental operations. Learning places a premium on the skills of precise rehearsal and accurate recall, whereas thinking with what one has learned requires openness, flexibility, and a spontaneous play of the mind. Facts are the grist for the thinking mill, not necessarily the instigator of thought. But we must not be mistaken. While information is not thinking, thinking is not possible without information. Yet it does not necessarily follow that enough information induces productive thought.

And there is more to this misguided view. If productive thinking arises spontaneously without guidance or direction, then it may also be assumed that the shedding of dependency on authority requires little more of teachers than to stand aside with permission given students to proceed on their own. However, freedom is one thing, but undisciplined freedom is another. It is akin to abandonment, especially for the novice. This observation reminds us of the advice given by Getzels (1975): "Find an important problem and then solve it." As admirable a challenge as this is, replete with risk and opportunity, it remains only a challenge. It does not include the playbook necessary to meet the challenge. Students cannot simply be left to their own devices. A creative, independent mindset consists of a complex network of self-regulatory, cognitive processes that amount to internalized rules and regulations that require close and consistent guidance from instructors (Covington, 1998). More on this point in Chapter 6.

## A SLICE OF REALITY

Let's now portray the struggle of students to deal with the stresses of unaccustomed failure in the larger reality of actual classroom dynamics. It is not a pretty picture. Go back to those heady moments, at the beginning of the school term. The scenes of action are those section meetings and laboratory sessions in which students meet weekly in small groups under the tutelage of their GSI.

The teaching staff views section meetings in idealized terms as a special opportunity to create small-scale communities of shared inquiry and learning within an otherwise potentially anonymous and sometimes daunting lecture course, often with a total enrollment in the hundreds. It is hoped that the values that will be fostered in this academic sanctuary include student cooperation, teamwork, and, above all, active learning and inquiry. Here the teaching emphasis is to be placed on what and how students think about what they are learning. The spirited discussions, debates, and sharing of ideas necessary for such personal meaning to emerge are best conducted in small, trusting, and intellectually protected surroundings.

Students, too, generally give these learning objectives the highest rankings, at least at the start of the school term. No accusations of grade grubbing here, only eager, idealistic learners. However, typically after the first midterm exam, and sometimes as early as a first quiz, students' priorities shift decidedly toward a concern over grades. Students begin increasingly to endorse the role of sections as a place to prepare for upcoming exams. They readily backpedal from their initial idealistic stance by insisting that for the moment the first priority must be given to keeping up with the lectures, clearing up unexplained digressions from the lecturer, or giving more extended explanations of concepts than those provided in the textbook.

What happened to the noble learning goals endorsed by all the players in the beginning? And what will become of those carefully crafted lesson plans developed by GSIs designed to enhance creativity and stimulate independent thought? All too often they are destined to be undelivered at least this time around, a point made with justifiable irritation by one GSI: "[I'm] spending a lot of effort preparing for section meetings, and then my effort goes to waste or yields no positive results." This shift in student priorities includes not only those who are falling behind but also those students who are actually ahead of the curve. These latter individuals are most likely overstrivers who see being extra diligent early in the achievement game as a form of insurance against potential shortfalls as the game is played out. Being in competition for a limited number of good grades adds a further note of urgency and a reminder of the high stakes involved as students simply struggle with the basic task of trying to master the course material.

## Help Seeking

Novices need and deserve guidance. Yet, as we have indicated, they are often disappointed by a lack of staff support, which can easily lead to a sense of abandonment. A primary reason for the dwindling staff support comes from the complaint borne out of the disillusionment of instructors when they find that students are less interested in learning than in the grades they hope to receive, or feel they deserve, or of being fearful of the grades they might get. One instructor expressed this frustration in the simplest of terms: "Students are no longer here to learn; they are here to get an A."

As a consequence, instructors may become dismissive of grades, which they argue get in the way of real scholarship. But such minimizing by instructors, far from relegating grading to the sidelines, simply intensifies student anxiety. The advice faculty often give students out of exasperation goes something like this: "Don't worry about grades; grades will take care of themselves as long as you study hard." But grades do not always take care of themselves, even with concentrated study. In their defense, students tell us that what drives their anxiety as well as resentment regarding the reluctance of instructors to help is not so much grades per se, but simply wanting to know the rules by which they will be judged, but not always getting clear answers. Consider this barrage of indictments: "Sometimes it is obvious that the professor has not thought about how grades will be assigned and refuses to talk about it because he is simply not prepared"; "Being in a class taught by a professor who is winging it when it comes to grading makes me very uncomfortable"; and "We can't afford not to know where we stand. Everything in college rides on our grades. It makes me mad when a professor says that I should not try to translate my test score into a letter grade because 'it's too early to tell.' Am I expected to be OK with that?"

Students complain that the search for clarity is virtually an endless task, and often punctuated with nasty surprises. These surprises include the reversal or suspension of previously stated grading policies without prior notification, and all without an opportunity for student or even GSI input.

As one student described it, "It is unfair when the instructor changes the weight of a project after it has already been completed. If we were counting on it being only 5% of our grade, doubling its weight may have a negative effect on those who spent a small amount of time on it due to its relatively small initial weight."

Also, according to students, their questioning the rules of the grading game is driven not only by a grade focus per se, but by the need to minimize the amount and scope of work necessary to do well given the time pressures on students. Our informants were particularly anxious to make sure their instructors took this reality into account: "College is all about time management and prioritizing, and I only have so much time to spend on one class before I have to move on and do something for another class"; "Sometimes I think professors believe that we only have their class to study for. I hate to break it to them, but we do have obligations outside of their classroom;" and, "Professors sometimes guard the details of the grading policy as if it is top secret. In order to do well, we need to know how we will be graded, and it is the job of a good student to inquire about it."

Some instructors are genuinely oblivious to this grade-driven drama. Recall Professor Jones who believes his course is going smoothly despite clear signs that trouble is brewing. GSIs also often react to such studied indifference by instructors with blistering comments, one of which is particularly striking: "Faculty have no idea what their GSIs are doing in sections, what works, what doesn't, what struggles GSIs face, and what issues arise in the classroom." Other instructors are quite aware of the situation, and for this reason may studiously avoid becoming embroiled in the often-cantankerous administrative and policy issues involved in assessing students and the assigning of grades. The success of this evasive, distancing strategy is aided by the general reputation of instructors as Olympian masters of their subject matter field. By reason of this elevated status, they attempt to stand above the fray.

## Help Giving

To the extent that some instructors abdicate their teaching responsibilities, it is left up to GSIs – once again, standing in the breach – to take up the slack. Because GSIs were once undergraduates themselves, often only a year or two before, they sympathize with the plight of their students. GSIs rally to aid their students by preparing extra study sheets and holding additional review sessions. However, the futility of this kind of support can only be appreciated by recognizing the differences in the kinds of help that students are often seeking and what GSIs are willing to offer. Many students are disinterested in taking the lead in consolidating or expanding their own knowledge, as clearly reflected in the following student pronouncement: "Students should not be held responsible for coming up with their own intellectual extrapolations." According to some student informants, it is the responsibility of the teaching staff to make sense of everything. Given these expectations, it is not surprising that GSIs find that students expect them to provide in a predigested form the very information they themselves should be learning on their own. It is one thing for GSIs to create study reviews for what students should be doing themselves. This is abdication enough. But matters are made worse when students abandon even the pretext of learning by focusing exclusively on what specifically they need to know for an upcoming test ("I want the GSI to tell me clearly and straightforwardly what the answer is, without telling me to go look it up").

However, as troubling as it is, this preoccupation with testing rather than with learning is understandable. Students operate in the thrall of an efficiency mode. They often learn just what is necessary to pass the test, and little more. As we know, this strategy is in part the result of time pressures and the accumulation of academic demands, not to mention other responsibilities such as outside work commitments. The following student remark legitimizes their position in so far as possible: "A typical student takes at least four classes each semester. These include major prerequisites and also upper division classes, and we have to do well in them. We do not have time to go through everything that may possibly show up on a test."

GSIs realize that these demands are a perversion of the goals of true learning. And for GSIs to give in to their students' entreaties about what will be on the test makes them complicit in the deceit. What is sure to follow, if GSIs comply with these requests to any degree, is an uneven patchwork of student preparation. Students overlearn a concept here and disregard a theorem there – all decisions driven by the presumed test content, typically without any appreciation for how all these details fit into a larger intellectual schema. Even so, the guarded, sketchy summaries provided by GSIs for what is likely to be covered on the test seldom provides enough detail to satisfy students. As a result, conversations often devolve into an unsavory game of "cat and mouse" with students seeking to trap the GSI into answering directly the perennial question: "Will this be on the test?" Of course, the GSI may have no idea what the instructor intends, since in some cases, like that of Professor Jones, instructors prepare tests privately in order to protect their GSIs from just this kind of student pressure. But even this precaution may backfire. The fact that GSIs plead ignorance regarding test content, even if true, may simply be interpreted by students as the "end-game" move of the mouse. Ignorance of test content can also put GSIs on the spot later when they have to defend a test for which they had little or no input.

GSI reactions vary in such litigious situations. One seemingly reasonable strategy often remarked on by GSIs is to limit students' questions about grading based on the presumption that eventually, continuing to talk about grading becomes counterproductive. It simply creates more anxiety rather than less. Increased anxiety can translate into a sullen unresponsiveness on the part of students whenever GSIs attempt to shift the topic from grades to learning activities, which students are likely to see as irrelevant to their real concerns. Naturally, such seeming indifference by students to the carefully crafted teaching plans of GSIs only deepens the view of students as being disinterested in learning.

## Teaching to the Test

So far, we have been exploring ways students attempt to outwit the test-maker by anticipating what will be covered on the test. But what about taking the remaining excitement out of this cat-and-mouse game by insisting that instructors teach directly to the test? The expectation that learning should be fitted to tests, that is, learning only what will be tested, rather than the other way around – testing what should be learned – arises in part from a misunderstanding by students about the requirements for true learning. This involves the critical role of testing. Effective learning depends on detecting faulty or incomplete reasoning, on pinpointing gaps in knowledge, and on the constant reinforcement of lessons learned. These are the goals of testing at its best.

However, if, as some students reason, learning is essentially a matter of absorbing information, then once sufficient information is conveyed to learners, it is only logical that tests be limited narrowly to the recall of this information. This not only seems fair to students; it is also efficient of their study efforts as well. Obviously, the cost of learning in terms of study time required is minimized by the disclosure of test content. And another advantage is that pre-announced targets ensure higher test scores! In this worldview of what counts as fairness, presumably everyone wins, except for the value of learning.

The notion that tests should narrowly reflect what is taught often approaches an article of faith for students. As one student put it, "No question should appear on the test that has not been covered in class, otherwise the test is unfair." Conversely, unless material is covered on a test, it is thought to be unfair to assign it for study in the first place. Indignity, even outrage, runs high when this requirement is ignored, as reflected by the following outburst: "GSIs often waste time in section reviews by going over things that they know will not show up on the test. It is so counterproductive. It is almost evil since we could be reviewing something that we truly need to know." Presumably, by this reasoning, there is no payoff for unnecessary extraneous preparation, like (heaven forbid) having incidentally learned something of value. At least this appears to be the logic of such criticisms as represented in this student comment: "The lack of lecture material on tests is unfair to those who attend lecture without fail"; or, "There is little incentive to come to class, since all the necessary information should be found in the textbook."

Again, we see the operation of an "efficiency" mentality. Why should students be required to jump through extra hoops if it doesn't count? Also, since time is an essential commodity, it seems only right to students that the amount of time devoted to one's study should be a factor in calculating grades, and in some instances given equal weight to the quality of actual performances! Also, students generally consider it only fair that those topics demanding the most study be given the greatest weight and coverage on exams. And, as a corollary, students assume that the more time instructors devote to a concept in a lecture, the more important it is, and therefore should be given greater weighting on tests. Disregarding these expectations receives great rebuke such as, "It's frustrating to feel like you need to put in a lot of effort for something that is not as recognized in the grade as it should be." All these complaints stem from the misbegotten metaphor of schools as a factory, an argument that can be paraphrased in the slogan: "A fair day's wage (grade) for a full day's work (study)."

Fairness has already emerged as a key concept in our deliberations, certainly from a motivational perspective, and especially in matters of testing and grading. So important, in fact, that it will prove helpful to pause briefly and consider some of the facets of the concept of fairness arising largely from the fact that all the players hold various interpretations of fairness, with complex cross-currents hidden within this deceptively simple concept.

Once again, Professor Jones pays the price for this example. Basically, the story is this: Professor Jones prides himself for having made fairness the centerpiece of his testing philosophy. To make things absolutely fair, he keeps everyone in the dark about the content of his tests, even his GSIs. He alone prepares the tests. This way GSIs cannot inadvertently tip the exam during test review sessions or be tempted to give away more information than they should. This procedure does, in fact, ensure what we can refer to as *horizontal fairness*. In effect, Professor Jones is distributing ignorance about test content equally across all students. Everyone starts on an even footing. What could be fairer? Professor Jones's single-minded insistence on this kind of fairness may impress his colleagues and look good on paper. Indeed, it is admirable as far as it goes. However, as a single, overarching basis for ensuring equity in testing, this particular notion of fairness is decidedly limited. For one thing, it does not acknowledge the fact that there is more than one kind of test unfairness to be considered, which can jeopardize learning goals. Students typically hold a "top-down" or vertical view of fairness, which amounts to an implied contract between an instructor and each student individually that requires tests be valid. Validity requires that tests reflect a close connection between the course goals at the *top*, or the essential priorities, and descending *downward*, testing for those specific mental skills needed to attain these goals. When tests have little to do with evaluating the skills needed to achieve course goals, they become *vertically* unfair.

A related aspect of unfairness to students involves test difficulty. Test difficulty needs to be commensurate with student skill levels. Otherwise, when tests are too easy, there is no challenge, and when tests are too far beyond the present capabilities of students, they cannot profit from their mistakes. These requirements seem reasonable. In fact, they are part of sound test development. Without these characteristics, tests are unfair to students, neither being helpful as feedback for improving their abilities nor providing sufficient motivation to improve. Such test characteristics as these are difficult enough to satisfy, especially among beginning students whose prior preparation and knowledge, as well as their rates of progress as learners, can be enormously different. Maintaining a compact of vertical fairness is particularly problematic for Professor Jones who, by creating tests unilaterally, has cut himself off from his GSIs, who are his most important allies in proper test development. GSIs are the essential "eyes and ears" of any course. GSIs are in the best position to know on a daily basis how and why their students are struggling and what the proper levels of knowledge are to probe in testing. By not making use of the help of his GSIs in test construction, Professor Jones has potentially unleashed a flood of unfairness, despite his good intentions. Moreover, by excluding staff input, another kind of fairness is also jeopardized, this time regarding GSIs. How fair is it for GSIs to be potentially blindsided by tests that they must subsequently defend but for which they had no input and with which they may even disagree? Everyone in this example is compromised, not the least the GSIs. By keeping his GSIs out of the loop Professor Jones also risks forfeiting his professional responsibilities as a mentor for future prospective teachers. Where is there a better place to begin the mentoring process than to offer GSIs supervised practice in test development, and to provide a principled understanding of the assessment process more generally?

Nothing Professor Jones has done is lethal, of course. On the surface, his policy of unilateral test construction seems perfectly reasonable. His solution for test fairness has worked tolerably well for years. Yet things could be better. Had Professor Jones unpacked the notion of fairness in its various forms and considered issues less narrowly than attending exclusively to a single facet of fairness, perhaps he might have considered using available testing solutions that in a single stroke can address all the issues we have raised here, and as part of the bargain help convert the ordeal of testing into a more constructive experience for everyone. Some of these alternative testing strategies are found in Chapter 7.

## THE TEST: AFTERMATH AND RECRIMINATIONS

Now what about student allegations that even study guides and sample tests designed to prepare students for exams are often useless and unfair? Consider these blistering indictments: "Study guides do not guide, but mislead"; "Practice tests are decoys for what is really going to be on the test." Students reach such unjustifiable conclusions because they often treat practice tests as a kind of shallow diagnostic checklist. This tendency is particularly manifest when students study using samples of multiple-choice test items. For example, when students get these practice items correct during self-testing, they typically move on, giving little thought to why their particular choice is best among the distracters, nor do they always reflect on the ways they studied that made their correct choice more than merely a guess. If they get the item right, what more do they need to know for the test? What they do not take into account sufficiently is the fact that it is not these particular practice items that will make up the actual test, but rather other items with different correct answers, which can only be detected by the same kind of studying that they disregarded in arriving at the correct response on the practice items. In effect, they are fishing for correct answers, not attending to the reasoning that makes a particular answer correct. But, worse yet, to the detriment of good study habits, when their practice choices prove incorrect, students often merely take note of the right answer, not necessarily pausing to determine why it is right, and then move on. They blithely assume that simply *knowing* the correct answer to a particular question satisfies their understanding of the concepts being tested. This reminds us of the deep truth hidden in a comic moment: "Life is not a multiple-choice test." It can be added that this is true because in real-life tests, the same answer may be correct in one circumstance and wrong in another. Determining the difference depends on a far deeper reading of questions asked on the test than students are often willing or able to consider. Are students being treated unfairly as they sometimes claim, and their frustrations justified, or does the problem lie elsewhere in student misunderstandings about what counts as effective test preparation? This analysis leads us not only to the realization that fairness is in the "eye of the beholder" – perceptions that are often driven by self-centered considerations – but also to recognition of the fact that there are no simple answers to the question of whether there is *any* grading policy for which everyone can feel fairly treated, even with those policies expressly designed with equity concerns in mind. We will take up this question again in Chapter 8.

## WHO IS IN CHARGE HERE?

Fundamentally, the mismatches outlined in this chapter come down to a question of who possesses and exercises power. Ultimately, of course, it is students who must harness the power of learning for their own purposes. In reality, however, students often feel powerless and resent it, even though their presumed impotency can occasionally afford them cover by blaming others if things go badly for them. By contrast, instructors exercise considerable authority by creating and taking charge of course policies, a power they may not always exercise wisely when it comes to matters of combating student passivity and encouraging independent thinking.

Meanwhile, GSIs are often caught in a "power vacuum," uncertain of the extent and latitude of their authority, in part because of their relative inexperience as teachers, but also because instructors sometimes delegate authority to them without proper guidance and oversight. Sometimes, this "hands-off" policy is an expediently driven decision based on the assumption that since "GSIs know their students best," it is they who will make the wisest decisions in matters of grading.

Whenever teaching and learning responsibilities are unclear, all the stakeholders, especially GSIs and students, may well wonder who is actually in charge. Substantial power to make policy may reside with the head GSI, but only sometimes, and likely for some issues and not for others. GSIs represent the first line of problem detection, but they may have only limited or uncertain decision-making power regarding the correction of problems.

When GSIs are expected to create policy – sometimes on the spot and without guidance – they are put at a disadvantage. Not always knowing what to do, or where to turn, their decisions are not always practical or pedagogically wise. Moreover, the tentative, arbitrary nature of some of these judgments can give the impression that while GSIs may have been delegated the power, in fact they may have little actual authority. For this reason, students are likely to have little confidence in the finality of decisions. Decisions can easily be overturned by instructors, creating even more confusion. Sensing uncertainty in the matter, students may try to extract unreasonable concessions from GSIs or even lobby for the waving of a ruling. If a GSI should agree to such variances in policy, even thoughtfully and on a case-by-case basis, charges of favoritism can easily follow.

## CONCLUSIONS

All the foregoing suggests the need to create an alliance among all the parties. For us, alliance building means establishing a relationship in which students and staff work together for common purpose. We believe this is best achieved when instructors craft their courses around subject matter problems and issues in their disciplines of scholarly and professional interest to them personally, and whose solutions and the intellectual processes by which solutions are achieved can be shared in partnership with students.

This arrangement elevates students to an apprenticeship role as distinct from being a novice, with all its faintly pejorative connotations. The notion of "power sharing" comes closest to capturing this ideal. Sharing as a process is a critical conduit for the values we seek to encourage, including mutual respect and shared sources of personal satisfaction. Yet such partnerships do not imply equality among all the participants. Education is rarely a pure exercise in democracy. The roles of expert and novice can never be equated. But alliances, unequal in status as their members may be, can nonetheless foster trust and sharing. It is these qualities that are enhanced when instructors struggle to be intellectually honest, not always right or even righteous as they pursue their craft. It is this struggle that moves and excites students. More than anything else, students want to feel they are facing the challenges of learning with and not against their teachers.

# 4

# Prospects for Intrinsic Task Engagement

## INTRODUCTION

Rewards and punishments are the lowest form of education.
    – Chuang-Tzu, philosopher (4th century BCE)

The vision of schooling represented in self-worth terms is that of a battlefield set in motion by a struggle among students for self-acceptance in a context where achievement incentives and rewards are in short supply owing to competitive pressures, with the result that the rules of academic engagement favor deception, sabotage, and lackluster effort. At the same time, instructors and GSIs also struggle to establish a sense of their personal value as teachers, which in turn largely depends on their students' expressions of appreciation and gratitude, often an unlikely occurrence given the kinds of mutual antagonisms that can so easily arise. This potentially tragic combination of discouragement and defeat among all the parties is made all the more harsh and unforgiving by the pervasive presence of a misunderstanding by students and instructors of their respective roles and responsibilities.

But if the threats to intrinsic task engagement are not already dire, things are made potentially even more problematic by the very nature of intrinsic motivation itself. What is it about intrinsic motivation that may, if educators are not careful, limit or even preclude the deliberate cultivation of a love of learning as a central educational goal? This question raises two inter-related concerns. The first concern involves the question of whether or not intrinsic task engagement is merely the creature of successful academic performance, a suspicion that follows from the well-known generalization that human beings tend to like and appreciate those things they do well.

If this is so, then the love of learning may be largely restricted to those individuals who do exceptionally well academically. Does this mean that less successful students will be consigned to a colorless life of boredom and indifference? Is caring for learning merely a phenomenon of success? And what about those students who do perform well, but without an accompanying sense of satisfaction because being successful for them is only a way to avoid failure? Can they ever truly be intrinsically engaged? These are the kinds of questions that confront any instructor who hopes to promote intrinsic motivation as a significant educational goal in its own right.

The second concern raises the paradoxical specter that rewarding an activity for its intrinsic value may disrupt rather than reinforce task engagement. If this is true, it is potentially devastating news. How else can teachers encourage intrinsic task engagement without rewarding it? Let's consider each of these two issues in turn.

## INTRINSIC MOTIVATION AND SUCCESS

First, what about the possibility that task engagement is solely the creature of being successful? There can be little doubt that intrinsic motivation depends in an intimate way on being academically successful. Individuals tend to find value and satisfaction in what they do well. And, conversely, it is equally true that when facing failure, individuals are likely to anticipate little or no personal benefits from their work. This being the case, the options for encouraging student involvement in learning for its own sake may be seriously compromised, since no one can always be successful, especially owing to the pervasive presence of competitive climates.

Adding to this concern is the fact that the psychological processes associated with intrinsic task engagement are actually far more complex than one might initially imagine. First, the causal relationship between success and intrinsic engagement is not simply unidirectional, that is, with success being the instigator of task engagement. Rather, the relationship is bidirectional and circular. More specifically, intrinsic motivation operates in a reciprocal fashion by prompting increases in the quality of one's achievements. How does this arrangement work? Our undergraduate informants have provided convincing personal anecdotes on this point (Covington, 1999). For example, they observe that doing well stimulates students to study more, and the more one learns, the more interesting the material is likely to become; then this increased interest stimulates more study, and consequently better grades. Thus, intrinsic motivation possesses considerable positive leverage.

Second, not all successes will engender intrinsic engagement. As we have argued, the reasons for succeeding are as important as the event of success itself. For example, little of intrinsic value will likely come from success experiences if they simply propel students, like overstrivers, into another round of frantic over-preparation driven by the fear of failure. Even with enormous effort, no one can succeed indefinitely. Yet, over-strivers must succeed, and repeatedly, as their primary means for protecting their sense of worth. This strategy demands unremitting perfection. But their search for perfection, and their requirement for nothing less, undermines intrinsic motivation and is their eventual undoing.

Third, the meaning of success, and its inherent motivational value, also depends not just on the reasons for succeeding but also on the self-perceived causes of success. Success becomes meaningful as the progenitor of self-confidence only if it can be attributed to the efforts of learners themselves, say, through hard work and perseverance. By contrast, if one attributes success to luck, or to an easy assignment, or to the help of others, then it is a hollow victory. In these cases, success adds little to the growth of one's self-confidence. Individuals must be the architects of their own successes. Otherwise, successes can raise the specter of students being unmasked as imposters, seeming to be more able than they really are.

## Solutions

So how do we promote intrinsic task engagement given its complex nature and the various forces ranged against it? We start with the observation that if task engagement depends largely on being successful academically, then we need to overhaul those grading systems that rely on rank-ordered competition to define the quality of student work. As we have argued, there are other noncompetitive definitions of success and personal excellence that promote intrinsic engagement.

At the same time, we cannot neglect the issue of failure, not necessarily to reduce its frequency, but to place it in a more positive perspective as feedback for self-improvement as well as to offset the possibility of failure becoming a threat to one's worth. The key to making these changes lies in answers to the question: "Are there reasons for learning that can be so personally compelling as well as problems so important that a commitment to their solutions can offset the troubling reactions to disappointing grades as well as reframe the significance of academic setbacks?" As we shall see shortly, the available research is quite promising regarding the possibilities for moderating the negative effects of failure and promoting meaningful successes, particularly when personal interests become involved.

Our proposed ingredients for such change consist of three mutually reinforcing elements: (1) maximizing meaningful successes; (2) promoting an appreciation for the positive uses of failure; and (3) injecting personal interest into the learning equation.

## Maximizing Success

In the face of the many complexities addressed already, remedies for the dependency of intrinsic motivation on material success seem to be in short supply, and worse yet, some are likely wrong-headed. Regarding the latter possibility, consider the suggestion that if we simply increase the likelihood of all students becoming successful, then task engagement will flourish! But no responsible teacher would seriously entertain using grading policies lax enough to ensure the certainty of students always succeeding. To do this would jeopardize academic quality control and ensure grade inflation. Also, bringing the achievement of all students to a uniform level will only result in mediocrity, and in the process destroy the spirit of individual initiative so crucial to noteworthy accomplishments. True task engagement depends not on the perpetual certainty of success, but on taking intellectual risks, and on occasion, failing. Although it is true that we seldom tire of success, it is not the easy victory that satisfies us for long. It is the challenges and associated risks that invigorate us. Nor is victory simply a matter of habitually repeating the same successes, even spectacular ones. Routine can quickly dim one's feelings of pride in accomplishment. By contrast, it is dissatisfaction with the status quo – not satisfaction – that has proven to be a prime motivational force.

Our proposed solutions for encouraging intrinsic task engagement focus largely on grading policies, but *not* on the rules of grading per se, that is – not being concerned simply with the number of points needed for a grade of A. Such local decisions must be left to individual instructors in the context of specific courses. Rather our concern here is with the nature of the grading standards themselves. First and foremost, the rules of the learning game need be arranged in ways that maximize the possibility of all students being successful, grade-wise – but successful only when the quality of their work warrants it. As already considered in previous chapters, this involves altering the yardstick by which academic quality is measured; in this case, measured against the prevailing standards set by an instructor, a technique generally known as *criterion referenced grading*

No CURVE!

(Campbell, 2012). Under this system any number of students can achieve a given grade as long as their work meets the proper criteria. This promotes positive reasons for pursuing success. Also, students will be more likely to take credit for their successes because they will perceive them as being caused by their own effort. In effect, students can take ownership of their successes, which encourages self-confidence and promotes task engagement.

### Failure with Appreciation

So far we have concentrated mainly on the psychological makeup of success, that is, one's reasons for succeeding and the causes students attribute to their successes. But what about failure? After all, students do not always succeed in their efforts to learn, a reality that calls to mind the droll observation that "failure is always an option." Is it possible to promote a love of learning and subject matter appreciation, even in a losing cause, grade-wise? The arguments presented so far would suggest this to be unlikely. Yet, a more thoroughgoing analysis indicates otherwise. What conditions might promote caring about learning even in the face of disappointing grades? We put this question to students asking them to recall a time, if any, when despite receiving a disappointing grade, they still felt they had learned a lot that was worthwhile and that they remained excited about the subject matter (Covington, 2002). Our informants consistently cited three reasons for undiminished enthusiasm in the face of disappointing grades.

First, students commented on the pivotal role of teachers and especially the importance of teacher enthusiasm for their subject matter as critical to sustaining student engagement, irrespective of grading outcomes. The available anecdotal evidence compliments this observation by identifying the causal mechanisms involved in the transfer of enthusiasm from teachers to students. Teacher charisma encourages students to create positive, non-ability explanations for their disappointing performances such as inadequate effort, an explanation that increases the likelihood of students trying harder the next time around (Feldman, 1976; Perry, 1981).

Second, students reported maintaining enthusiasm for subject matter material, despite disappointing grades, when what they had learned was germane to their larger life and career goals. They also noted increased personal commitment to learning when working on tasks that produce things of value to others, including, for example, the creation of educational materials such as new bibliographies for the next time a class is offered or the improvement of instructional manuals (Maslach, 2015).

It appears that benefiting others can rival the significance of the grades as a source of personal satisfaction.

Third, students observed that the negative impact of disappointing grades was also offset when instructors deliberately reinforced positive reasons for learning, such as rewarding curiosity. Later in this chapter, we will explore the kinds of intrinsic rewards that can reinforce intrinsic reasons for learning other than the prospects for good grades.

### Engaging Student Interests

When educators consider how best to arrange the conditions of learning so as to maximize intrinsic task engagement, one candidate inevitably comes to mind. It is organizing learning around student interests, whether it is teaching fractions to third graders as a way to calculate the odds in the lottery or assigning book reports on the topic of Mars to aspiring young astrophysicists. Our research and that of other colleagues (e.g., Renninger, Hidi, & Krapp, 1992) verify the psychological value of such strategies, and for several reasons.

First, the degree of subject matter interest has proven to be a powerful predictor for many of the behaviors associated with intrinsic task engagement (Covington & Wiedenhaupt, 1997). As personal interest in a task increases, so too does the frequency of self-reports from students describing themselves as being caught up in the act of learning, of experiencing feelings of wonder and joy at their discoveries, and of having serendipitous experiences – unexpectedly discovering something of value in their work beyond what was initially anticipated.

Second, what becomes of the positive impact on intrinsic engagement of pursuing one's interests in light of the realities of being graded? When student interest is high, the importance of grades as a goad to performance is significantly reduced, since positive reasons for learning – largely intrinsic in nature – emerge to sustain student involvement such as pride in having improved one's skills. And whenever task-interested students acknowledge that they will be graded, they believe that the presence of grades will actually inspire them to do their best work (Covington & Wiedenhaupt, 1997). This upbeat sentiment stands in stark contrast to the reactions of these same students when they have little interest in a task. They now tend to perceive grades only as a way to ensure a minimum of participation. It is such perceptions that lead them to worry about grades as they work, of not feeling smart enough to do well, and to complain that they did not get enough credit given the amount of work required.

Third, in addition to transforming the purpose of grades and their perceived role in the learning process, being interested in the subject matter also transforms the meaning of effort expenditure (Covington, 2002). We have argued that effort expenditure represents a potential threat to those students caught up in a competitive mentality. However, becoming task-absorbed via interesting problems shifts everything. Effort expenditure no longer needs to be a matter of calculated defensiveness – that is, expending just enough effort to get the job done, with excuses available should one fail. Rather, effort patterns begin to comply with more rational calculations. Effort becomes proportional to the difficulty of the task. As the difficulty of problems increase, so too will student effort and ingenuity, and with hard work comes pride in accomplishment.

Fourth, when individuals are following up on an interest, then onlookers, like one's fellow students, report that requests for help such as the asking of questions or the seeking of guidance – behaviors that would normally be interpreted as caused by ignorance, or worse yet, by stupidity – are now seen as part of the legitimate process of being task absorbed (Newman, 1990; Newman & Goldin, 1990). Expending effort is no longer threatening to a sense of worth, even failed effort. Failure in the pursuit of a meaningful goal becomes just part of the process, a sentiment admirably captured by the observation that, "if at first you fail, you are about average." As long as students are challenged by intriguing problems, their calls for assistance and even temporary failures will not necessarily count as a threat to their sense of self.

Fifth, it is clear that studying topics of personal interest enhances intrinsic task engagement in the event of success. Of equal importance, however, the negative impact on intrinsic engagement of receiving disappointing grades is mitigated to a remarkable degree when students are pursuing their interests. Just how remarkable can be gauged by the results of a thought experiment in which we asked undergraduates to estimate the degree to which they would likely value what they might learn from working on a final task in a series of assignments (Covington & Mueller, 2000). Half the students were told to imagine they had received good grades on all the preceding assignments, while the other half were told they had received disappointing grades. Not surprisingly, a string of prior successes was far more likely to prompt students to anticipate enjoying their work on this last assignment than was the case if they had endured a series of prior setbacks. Clearly, success breeds an appreciation for what one is learning. But what was not so obvious – and quite remarkable – was the extent to which personal interest moderated these findings. When the assignments on which students had received a prior string of disappointing grades were of personal interest, then the anticipation of valuing what they might learn next was far greater than when these students had succeeded repeatedly on tasks of little interest! Personal interest can surpass even the prospects for success when it comes to sustaining motivation.

## The Idiosyncratic Nature of Personal Interest

We asked students what it was about the nature of personal interest that buffered the negative effects of disappointing grades. Basically, they indicated that it was the fact that at its core abiding personal interest possess a private, protected state of mind in which the rewards that sustain it are undiminished by even a mediocre record of performance. Take, for example, the child whose keen interest in baseball – he knows the batting averages of hundreds of professional players – remains undiminished even though he is always the last to be chosen in a scratch game of afterschool baseball. The intrinsic rewards that nourish such abiding interests even in the face of discouragement involves having the freedom to pick and choose whatever catches one's attention, taking pride in being the caretaker of arcane or privileged knowledge, and discovering hidden personal talents. Simply put, personal interests carry with them a flood of intrinsic rewards. This is why students in the experiment just described anticipated learning so little of personal value from work of no interest to them, even though they succeeded on the task. By default, the only payoff for them was the grade, which all too often involves feelings of relief for not having failed, not feelings of personal satisfaction.

How can educators best take advantage of the various motivational benefits of interest-based learning? Consider two techniques for this purpose, one quite familiar and the other less so, but promising.

First, the more common strategy is illustrated by our previous example of assigning a book report on Mars to a young astrophysicist. Here personal interest acts in the service of a larger, more inclusive pedagogical objective. Learning about Mars, although certainly a positive goal in its own right, was the instigator of acquiring the skills of literacy, an otherwise potentially boring activity without apparent real-world benefits in the minds of children. Besides the many positive anecdotal reports, several empirically verified benefits also recommend the use of this technique. For one thing, it needs to be modified only slightly to feature the advantages of choice, as when, for example, students can pick any book that interests them. This arrangement combines the motivational benefits of both having choice and of personal interest. Feelings of being in control of events via the mechanism of choice, even to a modest degree, are a powerful contributing factor to task engagement. For example, allowing individuals the choice of writing an essay on any one of Shakespeare's tragedies produces more effort than if individuals were simply assigned one of the plays. For another thing, not only does the availability of choice enhance a sense of personal ownership, but when the topic to be studied is also linked to personal interests, any help or assistance needed is seen by others as part of being task absorbed, not a sign of stupidity (Newman, 1990).

The second, less familiar use of personal interests is for students to turn assignments of little initial interest, even boring or tedious tasks, into more interesting or at least tolerable tasks. The story is told of a food inspector who turned the utterly mind-numbing job of counting pretzels on a conveyor belt into the more interesting task of keeping his eye out for shapes that resembled the profile of Elvis Presley. It worked! By making this change in his job, the inspector's vigilance was sustained for the original task. What about turning boring tasks into interesting ones? Might this general technique work when applied to schooling? But first, is it feasible? The challenge is twofold. First, the given assignment must be sufficiently flexible and open to accommodate the infusion of a wide variety of student interests, including unconventional stores of knowledge, which often result from following one's unique passions. Second, whatever changes result from this infusion of interests, they cannot hijack or distort the pedagogical purposes of the original activity. An actual incident will illustrate this latter concern. Some years ago, while in college, the senior author modified without permission an assignment in a comparative literature class, which called simply for the creation of a biographical listing of major literary references to any historical figure of the student's choice. The only recognizable similarity between this task and its alteration was the selection of a historic figure – in this case, St. Paul. Otherwise, the alteration became a psychological analysis of St. Paul's personality traits that might account for his abrupt, unexpected conversion to Christianity. The purpose of the original assignment was swallowed without a trace, which must have irritated the instructor, if we are to judge from the final grade of F!

Given these constraints, is an enforced marriage of personal interests and conventional subject matter goals really all that possible? Over the years, the answer from seminar members has been an unqualified "yes." In fact, it seems that most everyone has employed this strategy at least once, and successfully. The consensus is that it is worth a try, either for an instructor to offer this option or for students to exercise it, but with permission obtained first.

REWARDING INTRINSIC MOTIVATION TO DEATH

As previously discussed, one obstacle to cultivating intrinsic task engagement as a legitimate educational goal is that caring for learning may simply be the by-product of being successful academically, and hence, caring is potentially held hostage to grades. Our counterarguments, bolstered by the prevailing evidence, indicate the limits of this misleading generalization.

A second obstacle to the proposal that intrinsic task engagement becomes valued in its own right also involves the phenomenon of success. There is concern among some observers that when teachers directly reward student interest in learning, they may unwittingly discourage the very intrinsic values they seek to strengthen (Kohn, 1993). But why shouldn't teachers strengthen task engagement by rewarding it?

Several theories have been proposed to explain this surprising consequence of using rewards. One explanation focuses on the extrinsic nature of most school rewards – extrinsic, because such payoffs as social recognition or monetary prizes are unrelated to the act of learning itself, and thus likely to distract students from enjoying the inherent benefits of learning (Condry & Chambers, 1978). A second view focuses on the subjective meaning of tangible, extrinsic rewards regarding the individual's feelings of self-determination. The argument is that the offering of rewards may create an experience of feeling controlled by others, thereby eroding feelings of autonomy and freedom, which in turn leads to a reduction in creativity and task involvement (Deci, 1975; Ryan & Deci, 2000). Yet, a third theory suggests that receiving rewards if a student is already intrinsically involved may discount the value of that activity when the individual concludes that "if others must pay me to do this, then it must not be worth doing for its own sake!" This theory is referred to as the *over-justification effect* (Lepper, Greene, & Nisbett, 1973).

The underlying assumption common to all three theories is that extrinsic rewards and intrinsic rewards are incompatible, if not antagonistic, with extrinsic rewards typically trumping the value of intrinsic rewards by means of distraction, by discouraging independent thought, or by implying that activities are of little value.

### Reevaluation

We believe that the assertion of incompatibility between these two fundamental sources of rewards – one external, the other internal – is overblown.

Actually, far from being antagonistic, a positive, additive relationship is more often the rule than the exception. Everyday commonsense observations attest to this. For example, experience tells us that hobbyists (whose motives are presumed to be predominantly intrinsic and self-satisfying in nature) often convert the pursuit of a personal interest – say, stamp collecting – into a professional livelihood, combining business and pleasure, with no harm necessarily done to the personal enjoyment of stamp collecting. Additionally, extrinsic rewards frequently bolster personal satisfaction in one's accomplishments. Money, for instance, is the epitome of tangible reinforcements. Yet, giving a young aspiring magician $20 to buy a new magic trick is likely to sustain her interest in the world of legerdemain. Although it is strictly true that money is unrelated to the processes of becoming a skilled magician, qualifying it as an extrinsic inducement, it is nonetheless instrumental in "making a good thing last," which opens a floodgate of intrinsic rewards. Incidentally, this example provides a compelling rebuttal to the over-justification effect, the notion that rewarding an already valued activity can lead to a loss of interest.

The lesson to be learned from this example is that tangible, extrinsic rewards such as social recognition can promote intrinsic task engagement so long as the underlying reasons for engagement are positive. Recall the evidence suggesting that when students are interested in an assignment, they report that the prospects of being graded – the ultimate tangible, public reward – actually inspires them to do their best work (Newman, 1990).

Moreover, the presumed conflict between those two sources of rewards is likely less a matter of incompatibility than a matter of student priorities. The potential conflict of motivations arises mainly because the demands of academic life leave little room for students to pursue either motivational goal fully. Given the pressure of schoolwork in the face of sometimes overwhelming personal and financial burdens, students must often choose between attending to the personal meaning of what they are studying and narrowing the focus of their studies, for efficiency sake, to what they believe will be tested. Students make it abundantly clear the choice they are often forced to make. But they also lament what is lost in the bargain. Students typically prioritize their goals, in this case, as acquisition over appreciation. But that does not necessarily mean these goals are incompatible. They have merely been prioritized. Prioritizing is a far different matter compared to a state of incompatibility. From this perspective, our task as educators is to help students redress these priorities in favor of caring about learning.

### Solutions

The foregoing discussion suggests that the productive life of the mind can be hamstrung by a relative absence of the kinds of intrinsic payoffs that encourage caring about what one is learning. Our evidence suggests that although virtually all students focus on the prospects of getting a good grade, they are also more likely to invest greater time and energy (beyond what is necessary for that good grade) in those assignments for which there are additional tangible yet intrinsically oriented payoffs (Covington, 1999; 2002). These payoffs include giving students the opportunity to share the results of their work with others. These are the means by which individuals gain the respect of their peers and the admiration of their mentors. Also, recall that other similar payoffs have already come to light in our canvassing of undergraduate students regarding positive learning experiences, despite otherwise receiving disappointing grades. These include the personal satisfaction that comes from producing things of value to others and making progress toward one's life goals.

What other kinds of intrinsic rewards can instructors imbed within academic work that will encourage intrinsically rich personal meaning to emerge? Several possibilities have been the subject of our research program. These include self-improvement as a source of rewards as well as the benefits of novelty, surprise, and the offbeat.

### Self-Improvement

Another motivational trigger for intrinsic task engagement is a growing sense of personal improvement and mastery over events. In order to explore these dynamics, we asked undergraduates to recall a time when they were coaxed, bribed, or otherwise coerced into taking up some new activity that in the beginning commanded little enthusiasm, but that in time became a source of great personal satisfaction. Virtually every student had at least one such experience to relate. The circumstances of moving from "chore to joy," as we put it, varied widely, as did the activities themselves, although learning to play a musical instrument was the most frequently mentioned extracurricular event, and learning a foreign language dominated scenarios drawn from school settings.

At five different points in a timeline narrative, students rated the importance of each of several reasons as motivating to continue learning. These reasons included literally being paid in one form or another (e.g., borrowing the family car; increased weekly allowances) as well as feeling a sense of obligation to comply; fearing the withdrawal of privileges if they did not persist; and becoming increasingly skillful or knowledgeable. Increasing one's knowledge and skills was consistently rated as the most important of these motivating factors at each of the five points from the inception of learning until mastery was achieved, and irrespective of the nature of the activity undertaken.

This experiment demonstrates that being aware of one's own progressive improvements not only can sustain learning but, as this example illustrates, can alter the goals and purpose of learning for the better. Witness the transformation of an undesirable chore into a source of pride and joy.

A problem-focused approach is well suited to capture an awareness of improved learning, because significant changes in students for the better are most likely to come from working on authentic problems of substantial consequence. Moreover, a problem-solving focus has the advantage of revealing the many dimensions of improvement that are multilayered and interactive. At one level, improvement means being able to do things more efficiently – better, faster, and with fewer errors – as well as exchanging ignorance for knowledge, that is, learning something now that was not known earlier. At another level, improvement means becoming familiar with the nature of problem solving itself, that is, learning how to orchestrate mental skills and subject matter knowledge into a plan of action – in effect, knowing what steps come next, which according to some observers is a practical definition of wisdom. As to a third level, our observations suggest that the most potent, forward-reaching basis for the continued will to learn comes from personal changes as distinct from improvements – profound, transformational changes in perspective of the kinds reported by our informants in Chapter 1 when they were asked to describe what it was like personally when they became intrinsically engaged. For one informant these changes involved a reordering of life priorities: "Being able to work through these problems may have been the first time I really began to see myself as a chemist." Then there was the personal discovery of the complexities of the creative act: "My feelings were both excitement and trepidation – excitement that I would produce a high quality of work in a medium that interested me; trepidation in the sense that I didn't want to fail." And for another informant there was the sudden realization that learning might be a source of enjoyment: "At first I was shocked. I became very intrigued with the fact of going to classes for its enjoyment rather than anything else!" These changes in perspective come from lessons taught by struggles with significant problems of personal interest.

How might students best detect personal improvements on so many levels simultaneously? Consider the possibility of using a problem or challenge of significance in the form of a capstone task, a concept we introduced in Chapter 1. The general paradigm is simple enough. At the beginning of the term, instructors present a problem or task to their students – perhaps a simplified version of a capstone task, which is subsequently administered a second time toward the end of the term. Evidence for improved problem-solving ability comes from comparing initial performances against the quality of problem solving as work progresses. Many variations in this paradigm are possible. Chief among these is the length of time elapsing between the two administrations of the problem, ranging from a relatively brief duration of only a few days to much longer periods such as the whole school term, as in the case of this example. The advantage of a longer duration is that it allows for repeated reassessments of the quality of student work along the way, particularly at any key junctures or stages in the problem-solving process.

A number of benefits occur when a problem is introduced at the beginning of the term when problem-solving baselines are first established. For one thing, this is an ideal time for instructors to introduce the course – its goals, rationale, and the directions it will take, all with reference to the end game in the form of the capstone task. For another thing, this is an opportunity for students to propose their own personal goals, especially those stated in terms of self-improvement. This is a matter of not only deciding what improvements to track, which itself has undeniable motivational benefits, but also treating dimensions of change as goals to be pursued. Students need to ask themselves what they must do to implement change. Having this in mind from the outset is exactly why experienced group leaders ask participants to indicate in advance what they hope to accomplish, and then subsequently to access the degree to which their expectations were fulfilled. This procedure sets out an agenda for change as well as specific goals to be pursued.

An especially intriguing pedagogical wrinkle is for instructors to conduct an initial problem-solving session by encouraging students to relate all they know (or think they know) about the problem at hand, including their assumptions about the truth or falsity of alleged facts, their best guesses as to solution strategies, and the like. This allows instructors to gauge the entry-level skill proficiency of their students and then tailor their instruction accordingly. Also, of critical importance is the opportunity to unmask erroneous assumptions about the nature of the problem, identify false reasoning in advance, and comment on any other handicaps likely to be encountered on the way to solutions. Recall the disastrous consequences of applying thinking strategies that once were appropriate in high school but now, in college, are outdated (Chapter 3). Instruction on the first day of class in the form of admonishments, warnings, and words of wisdom from an instructor could avoid many frustrations later on. All these benefits are predicated on the assumption that the problem in question is sufficiently familiar that it can be approached even by beginning students. It may be that a simplification of the problem is called for without undue distortion of the full-blown version of the problem.

How best can students track their improvements in such a problem-solving paradigm? Our recommendation is by the use of diaries, journals, and portfolios. The use of portfolios, whose usual purpose is to display a body of work, would be best suited for tracking changes that occur serially over several assignments, as in the case of artistic productions. Diaries and journals seem most suitable for tracking changes in the course of addressing a single problem, from start to finish. For example, as we will see shortly, journals have been used successfully by students to record their progressive understanding of the art of scientific investigation by creating research projects of their own (Chapter 5).

Diaries and journals also provide an excellent opportunity for students to take advantage of the process of self-monitoring, which amounts to reflecting on one's own thought processes during problem solving. It is not always a tidy spectacle, to be sure. Thinking is often a labyrinthine, meandering event, rarely pursued in a straight line toward solutions, but rather inevitably sidetracked by false starts, distracted by countless, sometimes conflicting options, and energized by unexpected insights. Concealed within this ménage are a host of mistakes, confusions, and mental inefficiencies from which lessons can be extracted, proving that failures have their benefits if properly exploited. And then there also are occasional successes – insights that lead one's thinking in more productive directions, or the recognition of the inappropriateness of a strategy in advance of its application. These are the positive inner experiences that students sometimes feel go unnoticed by instructors, a situation that can be corrected by including journals and diaries along with the final term paper, with the project report, or with the results of a student research project. In this connection, we have found it most helpful in the interest of sustaining task engagement when students are encouraged to share their problem-solving triumphs and travails with their peers, including answering the question of why the task mattered to them and what they learned – just another expression of self-improvement.

*Novelty versus Familiarity*

Arranging learning along a dimension of task novelty can also release personally satisfying rewards that are inherent in the challenge of dealing with the unusual and the offbeat. Yet novelty is not always welcome. For some students, novelty is equated with unfamiliarity, and as a consequence can elicit the fear of being placed at risk for failing. We set out to determine whether casting tasks in a novel form would encourage intrinsic involvement without triggering a fear of novelty itself (Covington & Wiedenhaupt, 1997). In an introductory psychology class, we cast a series of assignments in two forms. One version required a traditional essay of the kind quite familiar to students, and the other version required students to take a novel approach to the same task. For example, the traditional essay version on the topic of using rewards and punishments to shape human behavior only required a straightforward definition of terms that were readily accessible by simply consulting the textbook. By contrast, the novel treatment of the same topic required the writer to list the kinds of rewards that can make college a positive experience (i.e., positive reinforcements), the punishments students might be attempting to avoid (i.e., negative reinforcements), and the schedules of self-reinforcement on which they might find themselves while keeping up with their class work.

What, if any, was the perceived value of novelty for promoting positive task engagement while avoiding the potential risks of novelty? A complex answer emerged from this study. Before being assigned randomly to work on one or the other version of the assignments, all students compared each pair of assignments – traditional and novel. Most students perceived the traditional versions as likely to be far less difficult, and certainly less time consuming because students had long ago mastered the mechanics of writing essays based on simply rephrasing information from a textbook. Also, students judged that they would likely get a poorer grade on the novel version of the task. Yet, despite these misgivings, students preferred to work on the novel version by a wide margin!

What was so attractive about novelty that students considered putting themselves at risk for a disappointing grade, and to add injury to insult, with nothing to show for failure other than the waste of time that might be used more profitably elsewhere? First and foremost, students cited the challenge implicit in the novel task, which was described by them variously as a mixture of intrigue, surprise, curiosity, and opportunity – opportunity being the chance to think more deeply about issues. Also prominent in their answers were references to having fun and the freedom to exercise their own creativity.

When the assignments were completed, student interviews indicated that the earlier predictions were borne out regarding the value of novelty, particularly the feeling that one's efforts led to something uniquely their own. Other reactions were consistent with classic descriptions of intrinsic engagement, including students being oblivious to the passage of time as they worked, and choosing to describe their efforts as "determined" and even "excited."

By contrast, the students working under the traditional essay condition were more likely to concede that, despite their initial judgments of the relative simplicity of the task, they felt that they ran out of time to do full justice to the project, were in too much of a hurry to finish, and ultimately did just enough to receive minimum grade credit as well as expressing greater dissatisfaction with the quality of their work. Underlying these general reactions we detected a pervasive feeling of frustration, likely because without the availability of the kinds of intrinsic payoffs that the novelty group found in abundance, the traditional group only saw their task as just another way to earn a grade that in their minds magnified the risks of doing poorly.

Will the positive outcomes documented here regarding novelty always hold true? Clearly not. We can easily imagine tasks that are so removed from a student's preparation and current capabilities that any potential feelings of intrigue and challenge will give way to confusion, self-doubt, and even panic. From an educational perspective, then, the introduction of novelty is a calculated risk, but one that appears worth taking in the interest of encouraging intrinsic task engagement, creativity, and pride in undergraduate education.

Indeed, novelty is one more reason that a problem-focused approach to schooling is appealing. The main source of novelty here is the immersion of students in authentic intellectual processes through which important problems or questions of enduring value are addressed. Not only is the pursuit of such an enterprise novel, by reason of its rarity, but the teaching problems that make up the problem-focused curricula are themselves often cast in provocative, intriguing ways. At the risk of getting ahead of our story, consider selected examples of such teaching problems found in Table 5.1 of Chapter 5.

These problems have been suggested by our seminar members as the backbone of their proposed courses. Each of these problems is clearly novel, or at least intriguing in its ability to surprise, and occasionally bemuse – albeit for serious purpose – as well as being designed to capture a sense of the audacious and the offbeat leavened with high drama.

These emotional reactions are intended to beguile and draw students into becoming active participants in the proposed courses. In addition to these motivational benefits, there is the enormous capacity of a problem-focused curriculum to appropriate novelty in many forms. For example, from just this small sample of course proposals listed in Table 5.1, we can extrapolate the possibilities of novelty taking the form of games to be won or lost, as illustrated by the proposed course in economics (#2). Solutions to problems can also be the result of model building (#5 & #6); and, as a further example, problems can be addressed by students imagining themselves residing in a fantasy world (#7).

This is not to suggest that a problem-focused approach to learning is novel in the sense of being something new. Actually, what John Stevenson (1921) called the "project method" of teaching was already well established in American educational circles long before the turn of the 20th century. Nor is there anything particularly novel about the mental strategies that animate the problem-focused approach. They are already reasonably well understood, as we shall discover in Chapter 6. If there is novelty – or at least refreshment – it resides in the ultimate goal of a process-oriented curriculum: enhancing the ability to think productively.

The expression of novelty need not always be of the "industrial-strength" variety illustrated by some of the examples in Table 5.1. Smaller doses of novelty, so to speak, can also transform an otherwise convention-ally structured course in major ways.

Consider the challenge facing a seminar participant regarding her proposed course in Chinese history. The goal was for her students to understand Chinese history not exclusively from a western perspective, but rather turning the tables so that her students would see history though the eyes (and reasoning) of the Chinese themselves. Stimulating changes in perspective of this magnitude is no easy task. Here the reversal of perspective was aided by presenting students with an alternative global map of the world with China positioned at the *top* of the globe – not looking at it from the side, but looking downward from above, across the vast arc of neighboring landmasses and oceans below it. This novel spatial rearrangement was intended to help explain the origins of China's unique culture over the centuries, and particularly its relations with nearby neighbors, those with whom China would most likely form alliances or become competitors, and even make sense out of the choices for the most effective trading routes. These dynamics might not otherwise be as easily uncovered by a more conventional spatial placement of China on the world map.

## CONCLUSIONS

Obviously, promoting intrinsic task engagement is a complex matter. The prospect of employing personal interest for this purpose pinpoints many of the problems facing teachers. To hear teachers tell it, some students are simply disinterested in learning. But this realization also seems to suggest a solution: simply arousing student interest or curiosity, whether it be through novelty or by way of opportunities for self-improvement. Yet, the problem of student disinterest is more complicated, and so are the potential solutions. The problem is not that some students are simply unmotivated to learn as much as it is that they are often already highly motivated, but for the wrong reasons. And if the solution was solely a matter of arousing student interest, then this also is too facile a proposition. Fundamentally, it is the reasons for learning that have to change for the better, a task that cannot be accomplished by simply raising interest level in the short term. And even here we wonder if in the final analysis, teachers can really command student interest on a sustained basis. Instructors can gain students' attention and even discourage inattention. But arousing interest for the long term? Yes, perhaps. And short of that, at least teachers can arouse curiosity. Yet, all too often curiosity alone is short-lived, with little staying power.

In any event, how can there be much positive arousal if the classroom climate is suffused with fear and self-doubt? Another thing that makes task engagement so hard to sustain is that students often arrive in class with erroneous conceptions about the nature of the subject matter. Novelty may falsely promise an intrigue that cannot be sustained when the true nature of things becomes clear. For example, college physics may lose its fun-filled appeal when rolling balls down incline planes gives way to the abstract principles of gravity and friction and their notation in mathematical terms. What are instructors to do in these cases? And how should they deal with situations in which students are required to take a course in which they have little or no interest and may harbor resentment at having to be there?

Despite the difficulties raised by such questions, suffice it to say that virtually any subject matter topic can be presented in ways that will enhance the chances for intrinsic task engagement, even among initially  disinterested students. This observation is based on our finding that while subject matter interest among students may be spotty and as yet undeveloped, their interest in learning per se remains high and that they deeply value the intrinsic rewards that can result from learning.

As educators, what we must seek to stimulate is the deeper, sustaining aspects of task engagement so that the pursuit of curiosities become congenital – a way of life, despite the pressure of grades. It means the painstaking creation of teaching/learning climates that invite students to invest in already developing interests as well as in nascent curiosities by wrestling with significant subject matter problems. It also means providing a measure of safety from the fears and confusion that can force the pursuit of potential interests underground.

# 5

## Solutions as Goals

Had I been present at the
act of creation, I would have
had some helpful suggestions!
– Anonymous

### INTRODUCTION

We come once again to the central question of this book: Can intrinsic task
engagement and a love of learning coexist – let alone flourish – in the face
of a competitive performance ethic based on external incentives such as
school grades? Assuming that Professor Jones comes to accept our analysis
of his teaching travails, how might he proceed to revitalize himself as a
teacher and reinvent his course for his sake and for that of his students?
Where should he start? It all seems so complicated. Indeed, as we have
presented it, the hidden agenda has taken on all the appearances of the
proverbial "sticky bun" – a gelatinous mass with no apparent center, only
an ever-changing surface of bulges and valleys that constantly threatens to
absorb and hold captive the best intentions of any passersby.

In the course of our investigations, the deeper we probed, the more
complex and convoluted the issues became. Complaints from students that
at first appeared only tangentially related to our main inquiries jostled and
crowded their way onto the scene, and at times seemed to overshadow our
central focus. Yet, all these allegations were symptomatic of deeper underlying processes, typically associated with some aspect of self-worth dynamics. And then, as we expanded our inquiries to include instructors and
GSIs, the circle of frustration and recrimination broadened. For example,

we found that nothing frustrated instructors more than when students reject learning for the sake of grades. Yet, at the same time, students often accused instructors of disregarding the same intrinsic aspects of learning that these same teachers, in their turn, lamented that students have come to disregard. And GSIs were caught in the middle. There is a powerfully destructive circularity at work here, with more victims than villains. Clearly, grading and "grade grubbing" are implicated in this cycle. But the crisis cannot be attributed solely to an overweening grade focus on the part of students or to any other single issue. Many factors besides cutthroat competition over grades contribute to the threat to intrinsic task engagement and to a love of learning. This host of complications includes, among other things, a lack of clarity of learning goals and how to achieve them, the dismissal by students of the potentially constructive role of failure in the process of learning, and mistaken student beliefs regarding the nature of scholarship and intellectual inquiry. Moreover, many of these contributory factors lie outside the reach as well as beyond the traditionally defined responsibilities of instructors to address, let alone to correct.

We are reminded of a tangled skein of interacting, self-defeating factors akin to the legendary Gordian knot. What is cause and what is effect has become blurred. The circularity is complete. But unlike the ancients, we cannot undo the problem by a single stroke of a sword. Rather, by analogy, the knot must be untied painstakingly, and with great patience. We will be guided in this restorative process by our analysis of the problem in terms of the hidden agenda.

Once having laid out all these complexities, it is now our responsibility to offer broad, durable solutions, and not just a laundry list of isolated teaching tips, but rather coordinated solutions that together wheel around common themes. Our approach to course design involves the interplay of two themes: a student-centered perspective combined with a problem-solving focus.

### STUDENT-CENTERED LEARNING VERSUS TEACHER-CENTERED LEARNING

So again, where should we start? Why not start the process of course design by carefully stating one's course goals in subject matter terms? This seems reasonable, especially in light of the premium we have placed on establishing clear expectations for students. Indeed, goal setting *is* an important step, and often the first one stressed by any number of textbooks for effective teaching. The arguments in favor of the primacy of such goal setting are typically buttressed by reference to Benjamin Bloom's (1956) venerable taxonomy of teaching objectives. There is much to recommend this taxonomy. For example, it recognizes a number of cognitive objectives that are couched in terms of the learner – that is, learning goals, not teaching goals, which is exactly the right emphasis. These goals also range comprehensively from lower-level objectives such as understanding subject matter terminology to general mental strategies of inquiry, including the analysis and synthesis of information. This suits our perspective perfectly, especially recalling our emphasis on higher-level thinking skills. Closer still to our tastes, the taxonomy has an extensive listing of motivational objectives that have inspired much of our thinking. These include active participation in the process of learning and showing self-reliance when working independently.

Bloom's taxonomy presents an enduring challenge to anyone who hopes to improve their teaching effectiveness. So why not start with selections from this set of abstract goals and then proceed to unpack these abstractions in terms of the instructional scaffolding necessary to achieve them? This, too, is a vital step. But like goal setting, it too may be premature. As vital as these steps are by front-loading course design with questions about what content to cover, more fundamental questions of *why* students learn – the motivational basis for learning – can easily be pushed to the sidelines and become marginalized.

There is one significant limitation to Bloom's taxonomy as revealed by our motivational analysis. There is another list of goals that in many ways trumps Bloom's subject matter objectives, which has largely gone unnoticed. These are the goals of students – or as we have recast them, the *reasons* for learning.

At best, students' reasons for learning are only incidentally related to the instructor's subject matter goals; at worst, they are in conflict. Our analysis of data collected from several hundred freshmen reveals just how wide the gulf is between these two perspectives, which is part of the hidden agenda. We asked students to list in order of priority their personal goals for the courses in which they were currently enrolled. Not surprisingly, the first priority was to get the highest grade possible. Second came the goal of subject matter mastery – score one in favor of student-teacher agreement. Third came the need for students to prove themselves competent, and fourth, a negatively couched goal: not to make mistakes! Count goals one, three, and four as not only discrepant from but in fundamental opposition to the kinds of academic goals featured in Bloom's taxonomy. Moreover, taken together, these three goals are of a single piece. It is the essence of self-worth theory. It is all here: proving one's competency via achieving high grades with the constant fear of falling short as a person!

This analysis suggests that the primary task for instructors is to craft learning structures that reduce this mismatch of goals between students and the teaching staff by the creation of an alliance in which specific subject matter goals become derivative – not in their importance of course, but only in their priority for consideration. What must come first is planning for an alliance, not just a truce. Following this comes a consideration of the subject matter content to be taught. Not the other way around! From a motivational perspective, the point is that it matters little what subject matter goals instructors may propose if the needs of students are not adequately addressed.

It is no easy proposition for instructors to modify a traditional emphasis on questions of subject matter content in order to include as a co-equal priority questions about *why* students learn, not just *what* they must learn. Why should this reprioritizing be difficult (Barr & Tagg, 1995)? After all, educationally speaking, is it not the case that teachers are primary? A teacher-centered approach has almost always been the norm, and for good reasons. Most obviously, it is teachers who plan and conduct courses, not students! Also, it is teachers who dispense the necessary information, evaluate student work, and give grades; in short, they are presumed to be the experts; they know best. Clearly, instructors do know best about what it means to be experts in their fields, but they are not always equally informed about how students *become* experts! And, why should they? They are not usually hired as experts in pedagogy. Nonetheless, some instructors have accumulated years of teaching experience, and have even survived the teaching wars, perhaps much like Professor Jones has done. And, as a result, like Professor Jones, they may believe they know a lot about teaching. But their knowledge may largely be misplaced – that is, if a teacher wants to do more than simply survive and mark time.

Once again, why should adopting a student-centered perspective prove so difficult? It all has to do with one's prevailing theory of instruction. In the case of Professor Jones, we are asking him to put aside his entrenched view of teaching as the transfer of information to students, unaltered and intact, as well as his preferred choice of delivery being lecturing. Replacing these convictions with what to him seems foreign is uncomfortable. The alternative perspective on learning favors the view that knowledge is constructed by the learner, not merely absorbed, during which time individuals seek to reconcile new information with mental models that they have built through past training and experience (Ambrose, 2010). The instructional demands implied by this view of learning are admittedly great. Jones is absolutely right on this point largely because he must relinquish much of his authority to the novice who now enters center stage as the discoverer of ideas, not just the recipient of them. Also, to achieve this student-centered view, other forms of instruction must be employed besides lecturing, including working with students in problem-focused groups and encouraging students to pose and then answer their own questions. All these activities are free ranging, often unpredictable in their occurrence, and at times seemingly unproductive pathways to know-ledge. This means that Professor Jones risks losing control not only over content and coverage, but also given the fact that he has had little experi-ence with student-initiated learning techniques, it is inevitable that he will initially make missteps and mistakes in their application, leading to embar-rassments and perhaps even to his appearing incompetent.

One final observation regarding the difficulty of maintaining a student-centered focus on course design. It can be attributed to a paradox of sorts. Instructors know so much about their subject matter fields, and have known it for so long, that it may be difficult, if not nearly impossible, to put themselves in the shoes of the neophyte learner with their limited knowledge, their burden of misinformation, and the legacy of self-doubts and confusion. We have proposed the use of metaphors as a way to bridge this expert-novice gap (Covington, 2001). We asked instructors to imagine what it would be like, metaphorically speaking, for them to negotiate an unfamiliar task with little or no prior experience, and with their intellectual reputation at stake with the possibility of failure being real. The experience of designing and delivering one's first college course is a possible equivalent here. Their responses to our request were revealing. Consider the provoca-tive analogy proposed by one instructor of being trapped in a funhouse hall of mirrors. Everyone has been there: bewildered, alone, and not knowing where to turn, perhaps frozen in place for lack of direction! Instructors told us that entertaining such vivid personal images helps stimulate the right questions to ask about the teaching and learning enterprise, not only questions that might not otherwise occur to them but also questions that come from the student's perspective. This is the gift of metaphors. They can put us in the place of others. And, as a gift, metaphors are potentially a far more cost effective and less daunting way to reacquaint oneself with the plight of the naïve learner compared to what Professor Jane Tompkins did to achieve this perspective. She taught a course whose subject matter she knew no more about than did her students! She describes it as "the most amazing course I've ever taught, or rather the most amazing course I've never taught because each class was taught by the students" (Tompkins, 1990, p. 658) Tompkins learned right along with her students and in the process came to appreciate more fully their struggles because they were her struggles too. Metaphors can help shortcut Tompkins's commendable journey.

## Solutions as Goals: A Problem-Solving Approach[1]

The heart of our approach is the notion of solutions as goals. This organizing theme is well suited for neutralizing the hidden agenda. As a consequence of the unburdening of fear and the safety that follows, the way is paved for intrinsic goals to flourish. As we see it, the crux of the matter involves organizing student learning around solving significant discipline-related problems or questions of professional and even of personal interest to instructors. These problems, whose solutions become the ultimate goal of any course, are sometimes referred to as *capstone tasks*. The problem-solving process becomes the polestar around which all our recommendations will circle. Everything falls into place and is harnessed to the notion of solutions as goals, from the first day of class to the last day, and hopefully beyond.

How does a problem-solving model address the hidden agenda? The answer comes by way of three interrelated themes: ensuring coherence and transparency, building alliances, and establishing grading equity.

### Ensuring Coherence and Transparency

It is in the best interests of students, motivationally speaking, to know the intended destination of a course. Yet, rarely are course objectives and the means to these ends laid out in sufficient detail in advance. Course objectives often remain abstractions, with little justification for why what students must learn fits into a larger, coherent picture. Students report becoming disoriented in these circumstances, particularly failure-threatened students (Covington, 2001). They become lost in what to them is a bewildering, often confusing barrage of academic demands in the absence of a coherent overarching rationale. Consider the following lament, "I get scared when the syllabus is spotted only with paper due dates, quizzes, and midterms without knowing what the instructor's expectations are. It makes studying much harder." Less illuminating but far more common are complaints about professors being "random" or "going off on tangents." Professor Jones is notorious for presenting course goals in highly abstract forms without unpacking these goals in terms of the underlying scaffolding of facts, concepts, and mental skills necessary for their attainment. No wonder that so many copies of his course syllabus end up in the wastebasket!

As the first fundamental imperative of learning, it is critical that students not remain strangers in a strange land. What is needed from the beginning is a conceptual road map; in effect, a virtual tour of where they are expected to go, and why the journey can be both satisfying and important (Nilson, 2007). Our experience suggests that the key to creating this big picture is for instructors to begin course instruction at the *end* of things, specifically by introducing a capstone task of significance early in the course, or ideally from the very outset, so that the end game becomes as clear as possible in the beginning. The strategy of providing such an early warning target can be a great clarifier regarding the nature of the journey ahead.

By its very nature the capstone problem establishes the broad outlines of the curriculum by dictating what students must learn, when they must learn it, and in what detail. Thus, subject matter material no longer needs to be perceived by students as simply bits and pieces of disembodied information, cut adrift from higher objectives whose only purpose is to be dutifully memorized and passively stored. Now all subject matter content and teaching activities can take a meaningful place in acquiring the scaffolding of skills needed for solutions.

Above all, the notion of solutions as goals reinforces the student's role as an active participant in the problem-solving drama, and in the process reduces the fear of the unknown and the unpredictable as adversaries. Indeed, unpredictability and the inherent nature of messy, ill-defined problems can become challenges to be savored rather than feared. These organizing aspects of the search for solutions also ushers students into communities of scholarship and research. Students become immersed in the academic culture of the discipline and many will take their first steps toward expert status: They will learn what counts as meaningful and manageable questions to ask, and come to appreciate the history and the legacy of the answers, all of which provides a picture of the larger context within which the problems and issues in a given field are situated.

Even the quixotic, labyrinthine nature of problem solving itself provides a meaningful rationale for why failures or temporary setbacks along the way are an inevitable part of any complex intellectual undertaking. Thus, more positive interpretations for failure are now available. It is not that failure necessarily implies falling short as a person, but rather that failure, to recall the observation of Max Bierbaum, "is more interesting than success!"

## A Fable

Perhaps the positive advantages of working backwards in the initial planning stages of course design can best be appreciated by reporting an amusing incident in which experts suffered the unfortunate effects of starting at the beginning, as course designers are often tempted to do, say, by ordering the textbook before fully considering its appropriateness to one's goals. The experts in question here were mystery writers. In the 1930s, a group of leading mystery writers was challenged to create a joint novel (*The Floating Admiral*; Christie, 1931) in serial fashion. The first writer (chosen by lot) wrote chapter one. The next writer took up the story in chapter two with the requirement that the addition fit the story and plot constraints laid down in the first instance. Successive authors took up the trail whose individual contributions, chapter by chapter, became more improbable as each writer struggled to place all the preceding demands in a coherent framework, which eventually was to include a plausible explanation many authors later for "who did it." The final story was an ingenious improvisation. But for all its cleverness, the ultimate effect was to witness an improbable and far-fetched storyline, without the kind of satisfying tension usually associated with the unraveling of a good mystery story. Effective teaching also involves telling a good story, one filled with tension and drama, insights and resolutions, but not like the haphazard, disjointed, and implausible effort of the kind created by these mystery writers.

A problem-focus approach implies working backwards in one's initial planning of a course in much the same way that mystery writers actually work, starting at the end of things. Mystery writers typically start with the culprit – usually not the butler. Then they painstakingly cover the villain's tracks by misdirection and false leads, layer after layer, until the deception is close to impossible to detect for the hapless reader who must start at the beginning. This is the advantage that instructors should always enjoy – knowing where things will or should end, educationally speaking, and naturally, of course, without introducing all the subterfuge and deception that is the mystery writer's craft. Mystery there should be in learning, but mystery conceived as a fog that slowly lifts as problems come into focus and yield up their secrets. Otherwise, pedagogically, mystery serves no good purpose when it obscures goals and clouds the means to those goals.

Incidentally, some readers may be dismayed by the transparency we advocate. If students are given the exact task in advance on which the quality of much of their work will be judged, isn't that simply teaching to tests? Do not our proposals make things too transparent? Briefly, anticipating our full reply in a later chapter, we will only point out here that there is a vast difference between teaching to a specific test – clearly a bankrupt policy – and rendering transparent the road to solutions for problems that are worth teaching to, that is, prototypical in their demands and structures that will generalize to as yet unknown future problems.

### ALLIANCE BUILDING AND INCLUSION

Now, what of the second aspect of the hidden agenda, and how might a problem-solving focus help ameliorate this obstacle to learning? As already noted, many college students, especially beginners, uncritically accept their role as mere collectors of information – vessels to be emptied at test time. Such a mindset might have served them well in high school, but it no longer works in college, where instructors expect students to take on the role of independent thinkers. At the same time, students expect instructors to motivate them to learn, and can feel betrayed when they are not offered the kind of support and guidance they enjoyed in high school. Undergraduates quickly sense the uneasiness in this relationship with instructors, as reflected in the sardonic observation of one student: "Going to a university is a lot like sitting outside a government laboratory and waiting for a scientist to come out and give you a quiz every few days."

Is it possible to arrange undergraduate teaching in ways that create an alliance between teachers and students similar to the collegiality enjoyed by instructors and their graduate students? If so, then one of the most likely avenues is for instructors to draw undergraduate students into their intellectual world, the passport being the opportunity for them to work on the kinds of issues that intrigue instructors.

Turning over responsibility for solving capstone tasks to students allows them to become active participants in learning. The student's role is transformed from being a mere novice, with all the pejorative implications of that status, to that of apprentices, with the instructor as their mentor. In becoming problem solvers in their own right, students are opened to the same rich sources of plentiful intrinsic rewards of the kinds that drive all scientific and scholarly investigations: successfully testing claims of evidence, discovering connections that might otherwise go unnoticed, and satisfying long-standing curiosities.

It is around these shared payoffs that students can emulate their mentors, and instructors can take pride in their students' achievements. These become the small, shared miracles that instructors treasure and that reciprocally reinforce the teaching/learning alliance. It is a world in which teachers and students make common cause in a struggle for greater understanding of something that attracts them both. No more confusion here about who should be motivating whom. It is the quest for solutions that can motivate everyone.

The process of alliance building proceeds best when instructors talk frankly with their students about the potential mismatch of their respective roles and responsibilities, which can threaten a constructive working relationship. Throughout the coming chapters we will consider several approaches to providing such disclosures, each differing by an instructor's preferred teaching style, but all suitable for a variety of classroom situations and subject matter disciplines. Finally, it should be noted that the matter of alliance building extends beyond the instructor-student axis to embrace the professional relationship between instructors and their GSIs, as well as the critical link between GSIs and their students.

But what are the benefits of such alliances for teachers, more exactly? For one thing, teachers simply become better at teaching! When teachers introduce students to the grandeur of what they love about intellectual inquiry via researchable questions, they automatically become alive to their passion. They teach with more enthusiasm, intensity, and conviction, and students respond in kind. The research on this point is clear. A sense of instructor enthusiasm, and its most obvious outward manifestation, that of expressiveness, is the key to arousing student commitments to learning. Whenever students describe the ideal teacher, expressiveness is always at or near the top of the list. This priority is justified. Students sense what researchers have come belatedly to discover. When instructors teach in an animated fashion – upbeat, open, and with enthusiasm – students tend to attribute their own successes to personal effort rather than to sheer ability or to luck (Perry & Dickens, 1984). Feeling that one is the agent of one's own successes is critical to the quality of the teacher-student relationship because if students believe that success is more a matter of luck or caprice, then teachers can do little to arouse student effort no matter how animated they may become. Indeed, in the latter case, a teacher's casual jokes can easily be misinterpreted by students as taunts or sarcastic putdowns. By contrast, when a problem focus dominates, teaching becomes an autobiographical journey, or as one colleague put it, "A short philosophy of teaching might be, love your subject and convey that love; all else is secondary."

And there is more. Including students in the search for answers to complex, imprecise problems will lead them to understanding better the true nature of being an expert and the real meaning of intellectual inquiry. Here the search for answers is open-ended, and success depends on more than the instructor simply being a "walking encyclopedia," as the naïve view of scholarship would have it. In the beginning, students may want precise, definitive, and tidy answers, but as they join the struggle to understand complexity and things heat up, these views give way to a more sophisticated appreciation of the inquiry process, particularly if instructors lead the charge. In this atmosphere, instructors are allowed to make mistakes, even admit to them, and still remain admired by students because they are allies. It is the teacher's struggle to maintain an intellectual integrity that moves and excites students, not simply being right.

## Ensuring Grading Equity

Earlier, we briefly outlined the case against grading policies that operate on quotas by artificially limiting the number of top grades. Quota systems often cause an underestimation of deserving student work that exacerbates the fear of failing and encourages a cutthroat scramble for a limited number of good grades to the detriment of intrinsic task engagement. And, the more scarce the good grades are, the greater the importance they assume in the minds of students as evidence of superior ability, and hence one's worthiness as a person.

By contrast, in the problem-focused approach we advocate, the problem itself becomes the final arbiter of excellence, not an arbitrary statistic or quota. Here the merit of ideas is judged by how much they have advanced the possibility of achieving solutions. Students are in competition, not with one another, but with the problem itself by their attempts to fathom its mysteries, to clarify the implications of the problem, and to discover and then correct the malfunctions or misunderstandings that initially created the problem. In this context, for example, instructors would ask rhetorically of their students when judging merit, "What is the value of your proposals for making headway toward a solution?" In a problem-solving context, questions like this one constitute the criteria that define excellence measured in absolute terms. Here there is no quota on good ideas. Good ideas are always welcome. Scarcity of good ideas in problem solving is of no benefit to anyone. Artificial quotas are now irrelevant. They are replaced by a struggle of students to meet an instructor's standards in the process of solving problems. This does not mean that everyone will be equally successful, only that no one is excluded from success as a matter of grading policy. We do not suggest that this line of reasoning is without qualification. For example, one reservation follows directly from self-worth theory. Since this way of counting excellence allows for plentiful rewards – anyone can win – will not the abundance of these rewards degrade their value in the minds of students since evidence of one's brilliance depends on scarcity? After all, the test for brilliance is that few can win! And what of those students who tend to thrive under competitive conditions like over-strivers? Will they not be angered that their unique status by reason of a superior GPA will be threatened by the successes of so many others? What is left to distinguish them from everyone else?

Also, there is a second, related concern. Does the possibility of plentiful rewards imply that academic standards are being short-changed by "grade inflation," that is, awarding better grades than is justified by the quality of student work? All these questions will be the subject of considerable discussion in subsequent chapters.

### THE BLUEPRINT

A worthwhile vision is one thing. But translating abstractions into the realities of actual classroom life is a far different matter. In order to achieve this transition, we have developed a practical blueprint for course design from a motivational perspective. As recalled from Chapter 1, this blueprint serves as the curriculum for a graduate seminar consisting of advanced Ph.D. candidates co-taught by the authors whose challenge to seminar members is: "What would an undergraduate course in your discipline look like based on motivational principles intended to enhance a love of learning and true task engagement, above and beyond, subject-matter mastery and achievement goals?" The blueprint consists of a series of steps, or assignments, that unfold throughout the remainder of this book. (These assignments are found in Appendix A). The first step, which is presented in this chapter, challenges course designers to formulate a capstone problem that will become the central focus of their proposed course.

### Step 1: Envisioning Teachable Problems and Goals

This first assignment we give our seminar members consists of several parts. To begin, they are asked to seek group consensus on a single, overarching teaching goal, irrespective of their disciplines, that serves the ultimate purpose of all higher education. Although minor variations in emphasis invariably surface, the main conclusion closely reflects the results of virtually every polling of college faculty regarding their educational priorities. The ultimate purpose of higher education, our seminar participants say, is to equip students to solve problems, to address issues, and to raise questions of seminal importance in a given discipline, and in the process prepare students for the transfer of these thinking skills into the future. This perspective is seconded by psychologist Carl Rogers when he remarked: "Since we don't know what problems the future will have . . . the best way of preparation for the future is to learn to solve complex problems today."

With this goal as a working theme, we then ask participants to sketch out in a barebones form one or more teachable problems, issues, or controversies central to their discipline around which their problem-focused course might be organized.

Seminar participants need not look far to find inspiration. The number and variety of significant teachable problems is endless; to mention only a few themes that transcend disciplines: the solving of an enduring intellectual or historic mystery, addressing a long-standing paradox, confronting a dilemma that has long stifled intellectual progress, investigating the contrary finding that nags at conventional wisdom, or the clarification of a doubtful proposition. Over the years, some 200 seminar participants have taken up the challenge of creating capstone tasks. A sampling of these problems is presented in Table 5.1 along with the departmental affiliation of each contributor.

In anticipation of creating a capstone task, we provide seminar members with a set of seven themes (adopted from the criteria of "essential questions" McTighe & Wiggins, 2013) that participants are encouraged to incorporate in their work, which we believe will reinforce both the motivational and the learning goals we espouse.

## Enduring Issues

First, when possible, the problem focus should be on *big* problems – weighty, significant, even compelling issues which in one guise or another will continue to present challenges into the indefinite future. This makes such issues and problems deserving of a deep, abiding commitment of talent and energy that can capture the imagination of the neophyte as surely as it will an instructor.

## Multiple Solutions

Second, when possible teachable problems should be amenable to multiple solutions and in those cases where only one solution is most defensible or

TABLE 5.1 *A Sample of Teachable Problems*

| | |
|---|---|
| 1. | Students design human habitats that are sustainable and resistant in the face of change (Architecture). |
| 2. | Teams of students create two microeconomic systems, one based on rational rules of decision-making and the other governed by rules with irrational elements in which individuals do not always make decisions in their own best interests. Which system is more likely to win Monopoly games and why? (Economics). |
| 3. | Students will learn the basic principles of fluid mechanics by working on projects such as reducing drag on a ship, designing submarines to compensate for a wide range of underwater pressures, and designing pumps with the proper pressures and power inputs (Fluid Mechanics). |
| 4. | The goal is to help students develop an intuitive understanding of chemical reactions by studying the dynamics of why things explode! (Chemistry). |
| 5. | Students develop a theoretical model that predicts the political results of the growing interface between two major social changes in our time: globalization and democratizing (Political Science). |
| 6. | Students create an actual functioning machine designed to perform some useful purpose based on their understanding of mechanical principles (Mechanical Engineering). |
| 7. | By making use of psychological principles, students will act as advisors to an imagined family in response to a series of developmental crises that befall a fantasy child (Psychology). |
| 8. | Spanish literature majors will trace changes (e.g., distortions) in the translations of pre/colonial Latin American manuscripts, from their origins centuries ago down to the present time (Literature). |
| 9. | Students create a visual representation of the mechanisms by which nerve cells reliably transmit information from one neural partner to the next (Biology). |

feasible, there might be several routes to the solution. Being confronted by multiple options demands the ability to reformulate ill-defined problems in their simplest form to determine the best path ahead, a point that recalls Friedrich Nietzsche's high regard for simplicity: "He is a thinker. That means he knows how to make things simpler than they are." The very nature of the kinds of problems we envision, being largely ill defined and subject to multiple interpretations, makes for endless variations in thought and action. And the deeper one probes, the more intricate and intriguing the process can become. It is at these levels that intrinsic rewards abound, including the thrill of discovery, the beguiling challenge that continues to draw one forward, and the satisfying of curiosity.

## Multiple Sources of Information

Third, teachable problems should also require students to consult – and, if need be, reconcile – multiple sources of information and then make selective use of these sources in the most productive ways. Here the emphasis is on "selective use." In a world increasingly awash in a rising tide of information, most of which is of little or, at best, only marginal value for solving any given problem, students must come to appreciate the vital necessity of stating problems in "solvable" terms – that is, to limit the arc of their inquiries – and at the same time always being alert to the question of what one needs to know but does not know, and of knowing how to find it.

## Solutions by Cooperation

Fourth, when possible, teachable problems should also accommodate some degree of group work. Today, solutions are increasingly the result of a social process in which the expertise of many participants is brought to bear on issues in a coordinated, cooperative fashion. Problem solving often depends on a social process, especially when multiple interpretations are the rule. Recall our earlier point that task engagement is largely a phenomenon of social interactions that themselves are potentially rich in intrinsic payoffs.

Given the growing necessity for cooperation, it is becoming clear also that practice in conflict management, group planning, and the joint resolution of issues must form a critical part of any advanced curriculum. As the potential of proposed teachable problems unfolds, we hope to find them well suited for strengthening such interpersonal skills.

## Representative of Disciplines

Fifth, the teachable problems selected as a central vehicle of instruction should be broadly representative of the kinds of problems addressed by a given discipline, featuring traditionally accepted, discipline-wide methods of research, and requiring the application of contemporary theories. When possible, these problems should have substantial historic roots and a legacy of scientific or scholarly inquiry. Every subject matter field can define its history and current status in terms of the kinds of past problems it has addressed, the nature of solutions proposed, and the intellectual and practical obstacles overcome. This history is an essential part of any discipline-based, problem-focused curriculum.

## Engaging Playfulness

Sixth, when possible, teachable problems should reflect game-like features for all their serious intent. Rules both constrain and inform the limits of game-play, and for some problems there is the prospect of winning and losing to add drama, and a sure-fire way to create task involvement. There is even the possibility of creating game-like adversaries in the form of, say, biological invasions as well as the perversity of human nature itself. One should not be put off by the unfortunate implication of games as mere sources of amusement, recreation, or frivolous diversion. The word "game" has rich surplus meaning far beyond the barest dictionary definition. On the serious side, games can mean any test of skill, courage, and endurance, as in the "game of life." Games can also refer to objects of pursuit, especially business and vocational pursuits, as in the "sales game." Also, we play for high stakes, risk danger, and sometimes gamble recklessly, all for the sake of "winning the prize!" It is the combination of the joyous and creative coexisting with the serious side of play, the analytical, empirical, and the deliberate, that most recommends game-play and roleplaying of the kinds envisioned here as ideal vehicles for encouraging both the will to learn and the capacity to think. Abt (1986) puts it best in suggesting that, "In dreams begin responsibilities ... and in games begin realities." These realities benefit particularly from the fact that serious games provide a union between thought and action. They offer an unparalleled opportunity for an active yet risk-controlled exploration of significant intellectual, personal, and social problems.

## Professionally Challenging

Seventh, and arguably the most important attribute of all from a motivational perspective has less to do with the pedagogical character of a given teaching problem than with the instructor's own interests. Ideally, the chosen problem should be of more than just passing interest to the instructor. Better yet, if possible, it should represent a deep, abiding professional involvement or curiosity. Perhaps it is a part of one's current research program or a question of long standing that until now has been put aside for lack of time or opportunity to pursue. This kind of instructor involvement is infectious. Teachers teach best when they are personally committed to a topic. Students respond in kind to such enthusiasm, particularly when instructors share in their struggles, thoughts, and even their missteps. Such an undertaking provides the means by which students and their mentors can continue to create a process of inquiry that is not easily exhausted. Beside these motivational benefits, this is an ideal way to encourage a student-centered climate by allowing instructors to reacquaint themselves with the world of the neophyte.

### CASE STUDIES

Recall that the blueprint features three case studies in order to provide a continuous narrative reflecting the kinds of ongoing progress that seminar members will make as they work their way through the labyrinth that is course design. These case studies are now more fully elaborated beyond the initial sketches presented in Table 5.1.

### Spanish 190: Early Textuality in Latin America

This advanced undergraduate course introduces students in the major to the art and science of philological sleuthing, which involves documenting the history of changes, alterations, and even deliberate distortions of the meaning and purpose of ancient manuscripts. The capstone task for students will be to track and document progressive changes in an ancient manuscript of their choice from its origins in the Spanish medieval period in Latin America down to the present day. Some of the research questions that support this process, and which students may choose to address either individually or in small groups, are: (1) In what ways do we see old texts still being used and referenced today in renewed ways, perhaps far from the intentions of the original authors? (2) What are some tools and concepts that help us articulate conventions and compare styles of textual criticism? (3) How can one proceed if the origins of the text are largely obscured or even unknown?

The culminating event of this course is the delivery by students of a final, polished version of their analysis of the "travels" of an ancient manuscript. Students must create a visual representation of the trajectory of changes in the text through time using any graphic form of their choice, such as a linear timeline, a branching "tree model," or the use of maps or diagrams. In addition, this graphic must be accompanied by a written narrative speculating about the historical factors responsible for the changes represented in graphic form. The criteria for judging the quality of workmanship will depend in part on the minimum requirement that students include two different versions of the same manuscript in adjacent time periods or epics – and, the more versions they include in their timeline, the better. Also, the greater the time interval between the origins of the manuscript and the latest modern version, the better.

## Neurophysiology 195: How Nerve Cells Communicate

This seminar member proposes that one of the best ways to learn to think like a neurophysiologist is for students to create a model of the mechanisms by which nerve cells reliably transmit information within a neural circuit. This is the central challenge of this proposed upper-division course. More specifically, the essential question becomes: "How does a single nerve cell receive, process, and if need be, modify and transmit electrochemical information downstream to its neural partner?" She suggests that this model be represented in the form of a flowchart that evolves progressively as new information becomes available, allowing students to create more and more sophisticated versions of their model. This progression could be likened, metaphorically, to placing successive transparencies in layers, one on top of another, thereby creating an increasingly complex and detailed image. One advantage of such a procedure, motivationally speaking, is that it provides students with tangible evidence of a progressive improvement in their understanding of a highly complex topic. Ultimately, such improvement would depend on the mastery and application by students of three major subject matter concepts: Action Potential, Synaptic Transmission, and Synaptic Plasticity.

The culminating event of this course comes in two interlocking parts. First, students must submit the final version of their model of neural transmission as well as an accompanying written narrative describing and explaining the flowchart sequence of simultaneous neurological, chemical, and electrical events. The project is graded in terms of the sophistication and elegance of the dynamics portrayed. Sophistication is defined by the number and accuracy of the principles, facts, and concepts incorporated in the model. Elegance is defined by the extent to which these extremely complex, interactive dynamics are presented in as simplified and economical a form as possible without distortion of the content.

The second part of this activity takes the form of a traditional final exam (to be completed in class without benefit of notes). It requires students to evaluate one or more research articles drawn from the literature on neurology from the perspective of judging the appropriateness of the methodological approach taken, judging whether or not the resulting data addresses the question as posed initially, and evaluating the potential significance of the findings for one's own flowchart model. The larger purpose of this test is to assess the growth of scientific reasoning during the term, with special emphasis on the attribute of "ingenuity" in scientific thought. One semester of introductory neuroscience is highly recommended.

Psychology 2: Childhood and Adolescent Development

In this lower-division introduction to human development, students develop a case study of an imaginary fantasy child of their own creation. The child's life-chances are in jeopardy from conception, given a genetic disposition to a potential incapacity, a mental or emotional difficulty, or a handicap of the student's choice. The central challenge of this semester-long project involves students acting as a psychological advisor to the child's parents, caretakers, or guardians in a progressive effort to assist the child to thread his/her way through a series of childhood and early adolescent developmental crises, that is, avoiding or overcoming psychological obstacles and mental traps, while at the same time marshaling positive, compensatory resources (e.g., constructive child-rearing practices). Solutions to each crisis depend on the creative application of information drawn from lectures, discussion sections, and readings as well as student-initiated research conducted individually and in small groups.

The capstone task (in lieu of a traditional final exam) calls on students to develop a list of good child-rearing practices in the form of advice to be given to parents or caregivers. Students will have a choice of format including a public-health pamphlet or even a brief booklet. They also can decide to work alone or in small groups as long as group members take equal responsibility for creating the final product.

## SOME OBSERVATIONS

We pause here to note the progress made since these three case study designers first imagined the possibilities of a capstone task (see Table 5.1). In addition to telegraphing the broad outlines of their capstone tasks, various other aspects of the design process have made their appearance, although only in nascent form. For example, we can detect the emergence of hints regarding the curricular structures of problem solving, including, for instance (in the case of Psychology 2), how various aspects of a problem might be divided into several solvable parts and then sequenced through time. Even strands of actual subject matter content have been put on the table, as in the case of Neurophysiology 195. Moreover, we note a tentative listing of possible criteria for judging the quality of student work in Spanish 190 and Neurophysiology 195. Furthermore, many aspects of the seven problem attributes listed earlier (e.g., "solutions by cooperation") have been incorporated in the proposed courses.

But things are still in flux. As the details of the big picture come slowly into focus, many previous ideas and decisions will be revisited, sometimes strengthened, often revised or even replaced to accommodate continuing insights. All these dynamics come down to the fact that course planning never takes a linear, straight-line course. This evolving process is all part of a dynamic in which we can liken a capstone problem to a "vital center" that, like a magnet, draws or attracts all elements of the design process to itself.

Course planning is affected by many factors, some beyond the control of designers, such as projected class size or budgetary limits, while other factors are inherent to the instructional process itself. Chief among these latter factors are potential limitations of the pedagogical philosophy involved. In this case, there are two concerns regarding the suitability of a problem-focused approach that need discussion. The first concerns a question of the accessibility of students to problems that also hold a professional intrigue for instructors, and the second, whether or not students are likely to achieve a full sense of closure for their work on these problems. Let's consider these concerns in turn.

### Short of Closure

We have been making the case that, when possible, the choice of capstone tasks should be of significant professional interest to an instructor. Obviously, however, problems complex enough to intrigue professionals are unlikely to be fully appreciated, let alone actually solved, by beginning or even by advanced students. Their grasp of a given field is simply too uncertain and incomplete. Moreover, time is a limiting factor. A single school term will almost certainly be too restrictive a time frame for addressing any complex, multifaceted challenge worthy of professional attention. Additionally, students may not have ready access to the necessary technology or the information-gathering resources needed to secure a solution. This problem is especially acute in the biological and physical sciences where breakthrough research today requires highly sophisticated technology.

Fortunately, however, there are ways to represent significant intellectual and scholarly challenges on a sufficiently reduced scale of complexity to make them approachable for even beginning students, and without over-simplifying or misrepresenting the essential nature of the challenges. For example, a historical problem-solving perspective can be adopted that challenges students to address a greatly simplified, and therefore more approachable, forerunner of the same problem that has evolved into its current and far more complex form, but without sacrificing the problem-solving benefits. An example of such "down-sizing" involves the fact that modern commercial jets share the same basic aerodynamic principles with the Wright brothers' early flying machines. Students can deduce these common principles using actual data generated by the Wright brothers, and then perhaps apply these findings by constructing actual flying models of their own. Another example: one of our seminar participants was pondering the problem of how best to present the principles of kinematics and projectile motion in as simple and comprehensible a form as possible for beginning mechanical engineering majors with the added requirement of including the study of friction and air resistance. Hardly simple, until he thought to challenge students to apply these principles very directly by building medieval weaponry such as catapults. Final grades could be based on the accuracy of firing at a target. Perhaps, he mused, this would be the simplest and most reliable grading measure ever devised! Also, we must remember the capacity of games and game-like play to project reality. The proposal to use Monopoly to represent decision-making dynamics in the context of microeconomic systems is a case in point (see Table 5.1, #2).

Also, the problem of limited access to the necessary resources and technology can be addressed by providing simulated versions of complex equipment – simulated in that, for example, students are simply provided with critical information that they could neither discover nor recreate on their own. Providing students with slides of, say, actual neural networks, as in the case of Neurophysiology 195, or providing photographs of neutron scatter plots are only two examples. Although stimulation techniques sidestep the procedural side of inquiry, they do not avoid the reasoning and speculation needed to extract meaning from such data. The mental skills involved in such problem-solving simulations go to the heart of high-level cognitive processing that includes the challenge of making connections among events, determining, for example, how all the scattered neutron data points fit into a unified whole, or planning the optimal order for acquiring information to avoid the haphazard accumulation of data. An intriguing strategy in this latter instance is for an instructor to provide

students with the needed information, and even provide hints for profit-
able avenues of inquiry. But this information is released only in limited
amounts, say, one fact or concept at a time, and then only when called for
by students, thereby requiring them first to create an organizing plan in
which the information they seek will be guided by an overarching view of
the essential nature of the problem.

The social sciences and humanities are often less severely restricted
areas of study in terms of the availability of critical information. The
fantasy child case study (Psychology 2) is an example here. Psychological
theories and widely acknowledged facts and findings that might be
considered in defusing childhood crises are readily available from multiple sources. Having said this, while it is true that solutions are stalled
not only by a lack of information or its availability, as is the case of lost or
destroyed portions of ancient manuscripts (Spanish 190), it is also true
that problem solving can be hamstrung by an overwhelming surfeit of
information. In this case, the burden of identifying pertinent information,
and identifying that which is not pertinent, is the responsibility of
students.

Needless to say, the less experienced the learner, the more effective
such problem simulations or simplified historic recreations can be. And
solutions need not be actual, that is, fully accurate and complete, but only
approximate. For the moment, approximate is likely good enough.
Within the arc of their limited experience and insofar as the information
given to them goes, even the novice can create credible solutions sufficient to form a gateway for a more sophisticated future understanding of
the issues. At this stage in the academic development of students, it is
neither the creation of actual products nor of viable solutions as much as
promoting the processes of intelligent inquiry that should be the main
educational objective. The broader purpose of a problem-solving
approach is to assist students in witnessing the exhilarating process of
making intellectual breakthroughs on their own, even when their efforts
fall short of full closure. The positive motivations that sustain the learning
process at all levels of sophistication has to do with feelings of rightful
pride and satisfaction in what one has accomplished, even though completely satisfying solutions may remain elusive. The long-term instructional goal of motivating the will to learn depends on emphasizing the
sustaining rewards that come from progress, not necessarily from completion. We have already considered some of the sources of these self-
reinforcement mechanisms in Chapter 4.

## Moving Targets

Assuming that achieving even approximate, not actual, solutions is sufficient for promoting cognitive goals, the fact remains that these solutions are still simulations. Will the disappointment of falling short of creating actual, workable solutions discourage students from participating wholeheartedly as apprentice problem solvers? Perhaps so. But this potential danger has advantages. It is a segue for a message to students regarding the fundamental nature of problems. Students must appreciate that problems are "moving targets." They are notoriously restless. In reality, solutions are rarely final or completely satisfactory. This sense of things being incomplete is true for the professional as well as it should be for students.

Sometimes problems metastasize, then become dormant for a time, only to resurface later in a more virulent form that defies earlier solutions. Moreover, many problems are perennial, with only inadequate patchwork solutions holding things together for the moment. In yet other cases, the same problem may appear in various guises from one generation to the next, and consequently must be solved not once, but many times. Furthermore, the effectiveness of solutions also change, sometimes evolving over time with increasing sophistication often caused by technological breakthroughs, through improved theorizing, or by collateral advances in related fields. Then some problems stubbornly resist any progress toward solutions, let alone closure. In these instances, perhaps the only thin compensation lies in the cynical observation that, as one observer put it, "if a problem can't be solved, at least we can admire it!" This sentiment is challenged by Arthur Schlesinger (2008) who revealed the deeper meaning of this quip: "Problems will always torment us. That is why they are important. The good comes from the continuing struggle to try to solve them, not from the vain hope of their solution."

It is this kind of "goodness" that sustains our humanity, and in the context of higher education is often best nurtured when students become cognizant of the commitment of their teachers who invest their professional lives in the faith that the struggle is worth the price, irrespective of the outcome. There is a parallel here between the struggles of students to learn and those of their mentors to inquire, each party dealing with challenges that test the patience, fortitude, and ingenuity of everyone. This, too, is part of the alliance between apprentice and mentor, namely providing a window of opportunity that allows students a glimpse into the professional world of academics and scholarship.

STUDENT-GENERATED RESEARCH

In concluding this chapter, we will consider an additional advantage of a problem-focused approach: *student-generated research*. We have argued that the preferred goals of all higher education involve practice in solving problems of significance, and as part of the bargain exposing students to the scientific, scholarly, and artistic processes by which these solutions are achieved. It is this process of inquiry that carries the transfer value of learning into the future. The single activity that most promotes this spirit of sustained inquiry is student-generated research. Our proposed problem-focused approach provides the ideal vehicle for student research. An important part of defining a problem involves identifying the research questions whose answers and lines of further inquiry lead to solutions. This is why we encouraged our case study participants to couch their capstone problems in terms of researchable questions.

An emphasis on student research is nothing new. Much has already been made of the value of such research as a vehicle for transforming the teaching mission of American colleges and universities, most prominently advocated in the Boyer Report (1998). The various benefits of student research presumed by this committee – mainly that it transforms students into active learners – has generally been supported by subsequent empirical investigations (Kuh, 2008) as well as by our own campus-wide observations and interviews with both instructors and students.

By student-generated research we mean research designed and directed by students to further their understanding of the subject matter issues that animate their coursework. Ideally, students should take center stage not only in conducting research of their own design but also in deciding on the timing of the research process – when and in what order to sequence their inquiries, as well as deciding what questions need be addressed.

The acquisition of research skills has been characterized as a developmental process through which students move in a series of four increasingly demanding steps: exposure (information gathering), immersion (designing research), application (data gathering), and participation (data analysis and interpretation). Such schema can be misleading if it is assumed that students must master these steps in a more or less inflexible order, one at a time, before a given step becomes a sufficiently firm foundation for the next step. To our mind, this is too rigid an arrangement. It is not clear that this research progression actually reflects increasingly complex steps. Nor is it the case that research inquiries always start at the same point in the sequence. This fluidity suggests that students should experience the process of research as a meaningful whole, albeit at levels of difficulty consistent with their experience. But can all these major aspects of the research/inquiry process be sufficiently grasped as individual elements by beginners, yet also be understood as an interlocking process? In fact, they can!

This was well illustrated by the results of an activity undertaken by us in a large enrollment freshman course in psychology. On the first day of class, the instructor asked some 425 students to jot down a question of personal interest that they believed might be answered by insights drawn from the field of psychology. The only requirement was that the question include either the word "how" or "why," or both. The kinds of questions posed were truly breathtaking in their variety. They included more or less conventional restatements of classic issues in the field, such as "Is an individual's behavior controlled by the situation or by the characteristics of the person?" as well as idiosyncratic questions, often of an autobiographical nature, including, "Why do people talk in their sleep?" or "Why does homesickness happen to some individuals and not others?" If nothing else, this outpouring of possibilities underscores the point made earlier about the kinds of expectations students harbor regarding the nature and reach of any discipline. Some of the topics chosen for inquiry, as interesting and profound as they might be, lay outside the traditional province of the science of psychology, a lesson learned belatedly by some of our participants that required their changing to a new or restated question.

Students were then invited to investigate their particular question, a process that could last as long as the entire term. The culminating event of the entire project was for students to design a research study of their own – in effect, creating their own capstone task, one related to their initial question. Although there was no expectation that students need actually carry out their proposed research, they were nonetheless asked to study the history of the question, reformulate it in researchable terms, suggest a rationale and methods for testing hypotheses, and speculate about the implications of any hypothetical outcomes of the research that they might imagine.

These investigations would be largely self-initiated and self-directed, but students were also offered broad guidance that they might chose to follow in the form of a series of activities, all of which were completely voluntary. The purpose of these activities was to expose students in immediately understandable ways to the various steps in the research process described earlier. For example, arrangements were made for students to tour campus library facilities to learn about the latest search engines in order to facilitate the information-gathering step. Also, students were urged to interview one or more faculty members whose research interests coincided with their project. In yet another assignment, students were told to imagine themselves providing a two-minute oral presentation before a group or committee of their choice (e.g., a select committee of the U.S. Congress) whose fact-finding mission coincided with the student's own topic. The committee's question was: "What three things had students discovered about their questions that might interest the Committee?" This exercise was designed to expose students to the "interpretation" portion of the model. Participants were also invited to identify these same steps in a more formal context by identifying them in published research articles.

Students could finish their work at any point in time, perhaps dropping out due to the pressures of other time commitments or simply because they had satisfied their curiosity. In addition, students were warned in advance that there would be interruptions in their work, certainly lasting days or perhaps even weeks. No problem, the instructor emphasized. That's the true nature of inquiry! Students could also expect to lose enthusiasm and momentum from time to time, but also would likely experience rekindled interest. Furthermore, students were put on notice that their reasons for pursuing the project would likely change, that the question itself would almost surely change, that their initial question might become multiple questions, and that the occasional confusion and frustration they would certainly experience are part of the cost of all worthwhile inquiries.

The key to this project centered on students maintaining a journal – actually a research diary. This was intended as a chronological repository of each student's thoughts, insights, descriptions of the steps taken, and their feelings about the process of intellectual inquiry along the way. Students were also asked to rate their progress on a weekly basis regarding their inquiries, as well as to provide estimates of their growth in self-confidence as researchers. These later data were especially significant given our emphasis on feelings of self-improvement as a source of intrinsic rewards. Then at the conclusion of their project, whenever that occurred, students were asked to evaluate their entire experience. As part of this exit interview, students were asked to mention the most unexpected positive things they discovered about the research process and about themselves as researchers – again, questions designed to provide evidence of personal development.

Once students completed a project to their satisfaction, they received a token amount of extra course credit, insufficient to compensate for the totality of time and effort expended by them but not so insignificant as to be ignored.

The overall results of this experiment were remarkable in several respects. First, there was the matter of sheer participation. Of the total course enrollment, approximately 200 initially undertook the assignment, and of that number roughly half actually completed all aspects of the project. These students reported experiencing a significant shift in motivation between the start of the project and the finish. At first, they were mostly interested in pursuing the research project because of the extra credit. Extra credit was the spark that jump-started their involvement. However, once students became involved in their topic of interest, typically the prospect of extra credit was lost to the intrinsic goal of satisfying their initial curiosities. As one student put it, "At first, my primary reason for doing the project was extra credit. But this reason got forgotten when I became deeply involved in the project. I really wanted to do the project and continue with my research." The transformational power of this conversion to an intrinsic commitment was forcefully expressed by another informant: "I got so involved in the project that observing people became second nature to me. This suddenly was not a project anymore, but rather a study that was part of me."

The decision of students to participate in the first instance, and the willingness of many of them to continue, reflected a self-selection process at work such that those students who stayed the course were likely different than those who dropped out or simply chose not to start. Thus, the staying power of this project likely depended to some degree on the personal characteristics of the participants such as their interests, ambitions, and motivations. But we must not dismiss the inherent attractiveness of the task itself aside from self-selection. And there was much that was attractive. As can be readily appreciated, the entire project was engineered to maximize the various sources of intrinsic rewards discussed in Chapter 4 that would hopefully sustain students. Exit interviews indicated that student commitments to continue working over such an extended period, and despite all distractions, could be attributed largely to the fact that they were allowed to work independently – buoyed up by the realization that they were being trusted to do so, and by the fact that their independent, self-guided actions were in the service of investigating a topic of personal interest. We have already noted, and will continue to remark on, the vital importance to task engagement of being in control of one's own learning in the context of issues of great personal significance, and within a broad, supporting circle of encouragement offered by other students and of guidance by an instructor of whom, in this case, they could freely avail themselves. Moreover, the intrinsically sustaining influence of the phenomenon of continuous discovery was also clearly at work here, as one student put it so convincingly, "My enthusiasm grew as I was finding out more and more interesting information."

Let's now consider the academic benefits of pursuing this student generated research project. We were pleased by the depth of understanding and sophistication exhibited by the participants regarding the research/inquiry process. A variety of comments by students confirmed this assessment. For example, in many instances students spontaneously remarked about the serendipitous nature of their inquiries – in effect, having found something of value when looking for something else. Students rarely used the term "serendipity," of course – that would come later, as their scientific vocabulary grew. But recognition of this self-generating process at work by any description was the important step. So too was the realization that research is a bourgeoning, ever-expanding process as reflected by the wonderfully naïve yet prescient question posed by a student, "Is it OK if I now have two questions, not just one?" All students agreed that their original question went through a series of transformations. It was narrowed down, refined, made more specific, or took a new path altogether. Basically, the research question they were pursuing continued to be carved and shaped by the research itself. This process highlights the self-generating aspects of personal interest. It feeds on itself, evolves almost incessantly, and has the possibility of renewing itself with each newfound piece of information.

Finally, students unanimously agreed that a school term is definitely not enough time to pursue a question that truly ignites one's curiosity. Some even said it would take years. In agreeing with this prediction, one student wryly added: "I guess that's how one becomes a professor!" Neither were students completely satisfied with what they found about answers to their questions, and wanted to know more and pursue the numerous side-questions that branched out from their main inquiry. Most important of all, students looked back on all their varied experiences as a total package consisting of many parts, which for them defined the broad dimensions of self-generated research. It was clear that they appreciated how different phases of the research enterprise fit together. They came to appreciate that when they made missteps, they could backtrack and start over. They became comfortable with controversy, and in many instances expressed satisfaction – at times approaching "smugness" – at identifying inconsistencies in the published literature or detecting obvious gaps in available information. They demonstrated all the moves of more advanced students. This meant that these students were now in a position to profit more fully from the study of research methods in more advanced courses, and always in the context of the bigger picture of intellectual inquiry, which for the first time was coming into focus for many of them.

## CONCLUSIONS

In our view, a problem-oriented curriculum serves the single most universally valued teaching goal, irrespective of subject matter discipline: fostering the ability of students to think in creative and productive ways, and to transfer that knowledge and those skills for purposes of solving problems that are initially unfamiliar, novel, or seemingly unrelated to one's past experience and training. The capacity to apply one's skills in unusual circumstances and in unprecedented ways is essential when it comes to facing an unpredictable future. Yet, as we have argued, these are the very skills that often receive the least attention in schools. They are served more in their absence – as noble but elusive goals – than in their observance, particularly because of the widespread belief that once students are provided a starter-dough of facts, they will automatically put them to productive use. As we have argued, the available evidence gives the lie to this assumption. Thinking is potential, not automatic. And, thinking and learning are not the same thing, even though the quality of thought depends closely on what has been learned. Maintaining this symbiotic relationship in proper balance is one of the greatest of all instructional challenges. In Chapter 6, we will explore various ways that the universal processes of learning and thinking can interact in a seamless fashion. We will also consider how best to encourage the transfer of knowledge. The application of one's current thinking to problems remote from one's experience is not simply a by-product of having learned to solve somewhat similar problems. The transfer of knowledge, too, is not automatic, but rather depends on the expectation that certain thinking strategies can be applied universally, as well as on a willingness to plunge into the unknown armed only with a measure of personal confidence, a repertoire of robust, broadly applicable thinking strategies, and an open, searching mind.

The importance of the transfer of training has already been underscored in these pages, but the sheer urgency of the message – approaching the apocryphal – has never been better expressed than by longshoreman Eric Hoffer, when he stated that, "In a time of drastic change, it is the learners who will inherit the future. The learned usually find themselves equipped to live in a different world from the one that no longer exists."

Finally, what is our ultimate purpose in recommending a problem-based approach to teaching and learning? Our purpose is to encourage teachers to view the many difficulties and grievances expressed by students and instructors, which we have chronicled from a new perspective. No small part of such a renewal involves focusing attention squarely on the motivational objectives of education. Whether or not the proposal of *solutions as goals* can be justified depends largely on how well it satisfies the many issues documented in previous chapters. We will continue to argue that it does. We believe that a problem-focused approach is exceptionally economical. It offers a relatively simple, straightforward rationale for addressing the vexing issues we have cataloged, and has the further merit of being effective, a fact that is both empirically and anecdotally supported.

# 6

## Scaffolding Problem-Solving Strategies

My interest is in the future because I am going to spend the rest of my
life there.
                        – Charles Kettering

### INTRODUCTION

In Chapter 5 we followed the initial efforts of seminar members to create a
significant problem, issue, or task worthy of the attention of both instructors and students. The rationale for this activity as the starting point for
course design assumes that the goal of university schooling involves the
seeking of solutions to significant problems during which time students,
starting as apprentices, move toward expert status.

In some respects, the setting of goals, especially when stated in lofty,
abstract terms, is one of the easiest parts of the design process because
there is no shortage of worthy goals. They are literally "a dime a dozen" –
easy to conjure up and difficult to dismiss. The heavy lifting comes in
translating these abstractions into tangible realities, because as long as
goals remain abstractions, they tend to float free of the actual limitations
of time and resources that must eventually shape and restrict all lofty goals.
Goals in the abstract act much like a "wish list" – an important list, to be
sure, but representing hopes and visions, not necessarily realities. Wishes
made without substance often become merely vacuous entries in course
syllabi. Left in this form, they run the risk of fostering the kinds of
disconnects that we have identified in earlier chapters: disconnects between
goals and the instructional means to achieve them or disconnects between
the qualities of mind sought by instructors for their students and what it is
that students are actually tested on.

By first selecting a significant teaching problem or question as the central focus of their proposed courses, instructors can avoid many of the dangers associated with a "laundry list" approach to goal setting. Here the process of goal setting is firmly anchored to the teaching problem at hand because the primary goal is inherent to the problem itself – that is, its resolution. Not only does the problem imply this goal but the nature of the problem itself also broadly dictates the mental processes by which this goal will be reached.

In the first section of this chapter, we will consider the ways that our three case study participants transform abstract goals such as "learning to think like an expert" into a scaffolding of tangible problem-solving strategies that empower these goals. The results of this analysis will bring into sharp focus several additional issues closely related to the process of goal setting. These issues will be considered in the remaining sections of this chapter. Let's telegraph them in advance.

First, goal setting implies the establishing of standards and the need to communicate these expectations to students regarding what counts as "excellence" in thinking. Otherwise, without this information, how will students know when they have met or surpassed these expectations? Standards are the yardstick by which instructors gauge the progress of their students, determine if changes in instruction are needed, act as feedback to students for improving their work, and ultimately form the basis for grading policy.

Second, goal setting is inherently linked to the means by which goals will be achieved, which, among other things, raises questions about content coverage. This issue involves decisions not only about which subject matter material to cover but also in what depth, or conversely, put in terms of minimums, how little must be covered and still satisfy one's course goals. There is never enough time or resources to cover everything, so invariably something has to give. And the reality of insufficient time is exacerbated by the fact that problem solving is inefficient. Problems take time to address, let alone solve, especially the kinds of problems we advocate – complex, ill defined, and often unfamiliar. Thus, whatever principles of problem solving are taught in the brief time available, they must stand as proxies not only for all the material left unattended owing to time pressures but for addressing those future problems whose nature and specific content, being as yet unknown, simply cannot be the topic of any current course. We will argue shortly that the challenge posed by adequate content coverage can only be met satisfactorily by reformulating the issue as a matter of the transfer of knowledge.

Third, the topic of goal setting also brings to mind the question of just why students need to be apprised of course goals in the first place. The answer is patently obvious. Goals are the rallying point around which students are expected to organize their studies and chart the direction of their work. Yet, for all their prominence in the course syllabus, the listing of course goals often remains a mere "boilerplate" for many students, thought of by them as only an obligatory gesture to some utopian ideal, with little or no relevance to their understanding of the underlying course structure. Yet, these are the very goals cherished by instructors as part of the legacy of their research and of their commitment to the academic life. If for no other reason, these goals deserve more consideration and respect. How might students come to appreciate the central importance of goals as intellectual guideposts for negotiating a given course?

And finally, what does goal setting have to do with motivation? We will also address this question throughout this chapter and well beyond.

## MISSION STATEMENTS

If the ultimate goal of higher education is to learn how to become effective problem solvers, then what must students know about problem solving? Answering this question occupied our case study participants for the next several steps in our course design blueprint, following the creation of a capstone task in Chapter 5.

## STEP 2: ENVISIONING DISCIPLINE CHARACTERISTICS

What is the subject matter of problem solving? That depends heavily on the discipline within which a given problem resides, particularly on the purpose or mission of the discipline. Thus, we asked our seminar participants to create a brief description of the essential mission, purpose, or defining characteristics of the subject matter discipline they plan to teach. We intended that their mission statement cast the widest, most inclusive net not only to capture the broad purposes of their discipline but also to set its boundaries – in effect, staking out the entire context in which the relevant subject matter knowledge of their discipline resides. The mission statements of our three case study participants are presented in Table 6.1. The scope of these target descriptions can be recast more narrowly, say, as subdisciplines within the broader discipline, which might constitute an upper-division course within the larger schema of departmental curricula. Note that the mission statement of our psychology participant does attempt to capture a

TABLE 6.1  *Envisioning Discipline Characteristics*

Spanish 190: Early Textuality in Latin America
    To trace progressive changes in the translations of ancient manuscripts from the
    Spanish medieval period down to the present day and document the historic
    factors responsible for these alterations, using analytic tools available to
    philologists.
Neurophysiology 195: How Nerve Cells Communicate
    To understand the mechanisms by which nerve cells reliably transmit information
    within a neural network, and to appreciate the scientific research process on
    which this understanding is based.
Psychology 2: Childhood and Adolescent Development
    To analyze human behavior in terms of sound psychological principles, and to
    understand how these explanations (theories) can be tested for their truth value,
    using rules of evidence and methods of scientific inquiry.

particularly broad view of his field, because he plans to develop an introductory level course whose traditional purpose is to survey an entire discipline.

STEP 3: IDENTIFYING SPECIFIC LEARNING OBJECTIVES

If our question is what a student must learn to become an effective problem solver, then let's proceed to decompose these mission statements into specific teaching objectives (goals). Take, for example, the developmental psychology case study whose mission statement for the larger field of psychology was boiled down, in its essence, "to the ability to analyze human behavior in terms of sound psychological principles, and to understand how these explanations (theories) can be tested for their truth value, using rules of evidence and methods of scientific inquiry." Clearly, for this designer, the essence of his field and the basis for "learning to think like a psychologist" lay in the craft of theory-building, that is, appreciating the role of theories in the process of inquiry, of recognizing the limitations of theorizing, and accepting the obligation to assess the validity or usefulness of theoretical explanations by scientific means. How, specifically, then, might his vision of the purposes of psychology as a discipline be expressed in the form of actual learning goals? This question leads him to create an initial, tentative list consisting of three main learning goals for his course (Table 6.2). This list represents subject matter knowledge expressed as learning goals and their subgoals. As we shall see, this list will soon be revised and expanded as the bigger picture of the course evolves.

TABLE 6.2 *Outline of Learning Objectives for Psychology 2*

---

Learning to create plausible theories
    Theories are based on psychological principles.
    Theories are clearly, convincingly represented.
    Theories clearly address a problem.
    Theories are empirically testable.
    Theories are consistent with available information.
Learning to gather evidence
    Identifies pertinent information.
    Employs multiple sources for generating information.
    Recognizes information necessary to test theories.
    Seeks information to test theories.
Learning the rules of evidence
    Recognizes whether theories fit the facts.
    Seeks to establish reliability of information.

---

## STEP 4: NECESSARY MENTAL SKILLS AND KNOWLEDGE

Now, what mental or cognitive skills, subject matter concepts, and information are needed to achieve the learning objectives listed in Table 6.2? On reviewing the mission statement of the psychologist, answers readily present themselves. For example, students need to know how to create theories, to know what the various ways to gather evidence are, and how to test theories.

The two other case study participants created their own lists of necessary skills, strategies, and information. We then combined all three lists into one, which is presented in Table 6.3. The entries are not entered by discipline, nor are they listed in any particular order. But now order is what is needed. Because our approach is problem focused, it is appropriate that these entries be organized in ways consistent with what is presently understood about the nature of problem solving, irrespective of subject matter or discipline.

## THE NATURE OF PROBLEM SOLVING: A HIERARCHICAL MODEL

A leading authority on the nature of problem solving, Hunt (1994) has remarked: "Problem solving is a bit like beauty, morality, and good art. We are in favor of it, we know it when we see it, but we cannot define it."

TABLE 6.3 *Prerequisite Mental Skills and Knowledge*

- How to take effective notes.
- Function of the lymph node.
- What counts as proof for a position.
- Interpreting graphs.
- Arithmetic operations.
- Organizing information into an argument.
- Characteristics of global economy.
- Conventions for academic citations.
- Knowing when more information is needed.
- Reading text for meaning.
- Moving from abstract goals to concrete implementation.
- Understanding marginal analysis.
- Assessing reliability of sources.
- Recent history of events.
- How to show work on a problem.
- Internet search.
- Refining broad propositions into researchable questions.
- Trend analysis.
- Conducting effective interviews.
- Heritability.
- Choosing the best paradigm.
- Grammar and mechanics of writing.
- Picking out key themes and arguments.
- How to build generalizable claims.
- Recognizing subtle differences in language usage.
- Stating problems in solvable terms.
- Recognizing interconnections.
- Deciding what one must learn.

Certainly, we know good problem solving when we see it, and because so much has been written on the topic, there must be plenty of eyewitnesses around! Yet, at the core of things, despite all the speculation and research, Hunt is essentially right. It is largely the quality of the results of problem solving – good, mediocre, or bad – that is most easily detected. But when it comes to defining the processes themselves, things are not so easy. Fortunately, however, a consensus has emerged in recent years sufficient for our purposes. Simply put, thinking can be defined as the mental operations involved in solving problems. Today many cognitive psychologists conceive of these operations in terms of three different levels of knowledge that are arranged in a top-down, hierarchical structure in pyramidal form (Covington, 1998).

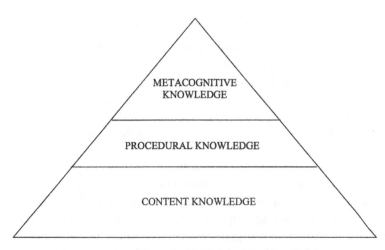

FIGURE 6.1 Hierarchical Model of Problem Solving.
Martin V. Covington, Making the Grade. A Self-Worth Perspective on Motivation and School Reform, copyright Cambridge University Press 2001, reproduced with permission.

Let's consider each of these levels of knowledge and how they interact, as reflected in a simplified version of the model portrayed in Figure 6.1.

## Content Knowledge

The fundamental requirement for all thinking is the availability of information in the form of hundreds, even thousands of facts and other data arranged in charts, graphs, and texts – what is referred to collectively as *declarative knowledge*. Writing conventions and technical terminology are also part of content knowledge, as well as theories and informed conjecture. Content knowledge also includes social systems such as the credit banking system and how it operates, as well as naturally occurring systems such as how weather patterns are formed. In the aggregate, content knowledge represents what is currently known or strongly suspected to be true about any subject matter topic.

The sheer diversity and magnitude of content knowledge is reflected in the broad pyramidal base of our model. The placement of content knowledge at the bottom of the pyramid in no way implies an inferiority of status. Rather, it underscores the foundational role of content knowledge as the basic ingredient of all thinking. But obviously there is more to this pyramid than content knowledge, and the higher one climbs, the more critical becomes an instructional role in promoting productive thinking.

## Procedural Knowledge

*Procedural knowledge* is best thought of, for our purposes, as the means by which we create new information or seek out existing information. The central procedural tool is question asking. Questioning fulfills a variety of problem-solving functions. Questioning seeks information, tests assertions, verifies hypotheses, and satisfies a rhetorical function in which inquiries are not intended to be answered directly, but rather to reframe a problem or excite new directions of thought.

Our case study participants also included a number of procedural tools for inquiry in Table 6.3, ranging from entry-level familiarity with search engines for conducting internet and library searches to those procedures necessary for conducting empirical research such as titrating chemical compounds with a high degree of accuracy. Some procedures are well rehearsed, if not over-learned, as in the example of chemical titration, so that here problem solving follows in an almost invariant "script-like" fashion. Yet, in other instances, procedural knowledge implies the operation of complex strategies of thought. For example, one seminar participant mentioned the need for "selecting relevant literature" – not just any literature, but "relevant" literature. The ability to be selective in this sense presupposes a deep understanding of the problem at hand as well as a secure grasp of a vast amount of content knowledge before procedural operations can be effective. This point makes clear that the three knowledge categories presented in Figure 6.1 are highly interdependent in their operations.

## Metacognitive Knowledge

Both content and procedural knowledge can be portrayed as being potential elements of thought – potential in that they await higher-level orders for their mobilization. They are the tools of thought but not the plans of action that determine which of these tools to use, in what combinations, when, and how often. For this organizing function we turn to the realm of *metacognitive knowledge*. At the pinnacle of the knowledge hierarchy stands an overall executive function whose purpose is to assemble all subsumed knowledge in a systematic approach to a given problem. The old adage, "the whole is greater than the sum of its parts," fits the process of problem solving perfectly. Effective thought is more than the sum total of all subordinate knowledge.

We can subdivide metacognitive knowledge into two distinct but closely related functions: *planning* and *self-monitoring*.

## *Planning*

The best way to think about the metacognitive assembly process is in terms of planning. The metaphor of a military campaign is useful in conveying the complexities involved here. Successful generals position their soldiers (procedural subroutines) in an overall marching order best suited to a given terrain and purpose, whether it be to go on the offensive, to stand firm, or to disengage and withdraw in order to fight another day. These tactical moves and countermoves are controlled by broad plans of action similar to somewhat less violent pursuits such as plotting one's next move at the negotiating table or on the playing field.

But on what strategies are these broad plans based? Whatever their specific nature, such strategies are born out of the experience of experts. Pursuing the military analogy, this means, for example, "protecting one's flanks" as well as "securing one's supply lines." "Protecting the middle" is no less important to chess players than to generals, or for that matter to TV evangelists who must control their main revenue base among the elderly and the gullible.

## *Self-Monitoring*

Once a plan of action is initiated, it is necessary to guide it to a successful conclusion. This involves self-monitoring. Inevitably, plans must be reshaped in response to unforeseen obstacles or to potentially advantageous windfalls of new, unexpected information. Plans must be subjected to continuing reappraisals regarding progress, or the lack of progress, toward the original goal. Indeed, the original goal may have to be abandoned and a more accessible objective pursued. An initially appropriate plan can quickly become inappropriate or even counterproductive as circumstances change. Self-monitoring is the "internal gyroscope" that keeps one's efforts properly focused on a distant, elusive target.

One of the most useful descriptions of self-regulating engagement is the model proposed by Carver and Scheier (1986). They theorize that whenever individuals encounter an obstacle to thinking, they reassess the likelihood of eventual success if they continue on the same course but with renewed energy, or if they should modify or abandon their current approach altogether. Such appraisals depend not only on one's understanding of the nature of the task but also on one's past experience with similar tasks. They also depend on judgments about one's own intellectual strengths, limitations, and preferred styles of thinking. It is only later – sometimes much later – that the wisdom of these earlier, in-progress decisions becomes clear, say, when students receive feedback in the form of a final project grade.

However, such summative appraisals (a final grade) by themselves usually provide little information about the quality of self-monitoring at those countless decision points along the way. Eventually, students must develop their *own* internal "metacognitive checklists" in order to recreate Albert Camus's celebrated definition of an intellectual: "someone whose mind watches itself." Such self-consciousness is a cognitive equivalent of what it means to achieve the status of an expert in a given discipline.

### STEP 5: CATEGORIZING PROBLEM-SOLVING COMPONENTS

In order for seminar members to familiarize themselves with our hierarchical model and its categorical distinctions, we asked them to assign all the entries in Table 6.3 to their proper cognitive levels in the three-tier hierarchical schema. The results of this exercise are shown in Figure 6.2.

Seminar members often express frustration with this task because it was not always clear to them where a given entry belongs, and sometimes entries might even satisfy several functions. Any classification schema invariably invites such ambiguities. Our hierarchical model is no exception. The importance of this model as a classification schema lies not in establishing a uniform agreement of categories in order to simplify the world of problem solving. Simplicity is not the goal. Rather the goal is to make sense of complexity. The point being that the distinctions which define boundaries between the three adjacent knowledge domains are semi-permeable, that the roles of knowledge are interchangeable, and can serve different functions at different times depending on the task. We often use this exercise as a teaching moment to reinforce these realities. We ask pairs of seminar members who assigned the same item in Table 6.3 to different knowledge domains to explain their respective reasoning. Invariably, both individuals are completely justified in their decisions given differences between them in such matters as their respective capstone problems, the structure of their subject matter fields, and the different kinds of solutions sought. This is the best outcome possible. Being capable of such nuanced reasoning represents the highest order of metacognitive analysis.

### A SUMMARY

The hierarchical metaphor of thinking serves the purposes of course design in several ways. First, and foremost, it presents the phenomena of thinking and problem solving as a highly active, self-conscious event, involving the simultaneous interplay of many cognitive elements. This is contrasted to a view of thinking as largely an automatic event, played out primarily at an

Categorizing Problem-Solving Components

| Metacognitive | Procedural | Content |
| --- | --- | --- |
| - What counts as proof for a position. | - How to take effective notes. | - Function of the lymph node. |
| - Organizing information into an argument. | - Interpreting graphs. | - Characteristics of Global Economy. |
| - Knowing when more information is needed. | - Arithmetic operations. | - Conventions for academic citations. |
| - Reading text for meaning. | - How to show work on a problem. | - Understanding marginal analysis. |
| - Moving from abstract goals to concrete implementation. | - Internet search. | - Recent history of events. |
| - Assessing reliability of sources. | - Trend analysis. | - Heritability. |
| - Refining broad propositions into researchable questions. | - Conducting effective interviews. | |
| - Choosing the best paradigm. | - Grammar and mechanics of writing. | |
| - Deciding what one must learn. | - Picking out key themes and arguments. | |
| - How to build generalizable claims. | - Applying marginal analysis. | |
| - Recognizing subtle differences in language usage. | | |
| - Stating problems in solvable terms. | | |
| - Recognizing interconnections. | | |

FIGURE 6.2  Categorizing Problem-Solving Components

unconscious level, and likely devoid of trainable elements. As we will argue momentarily, it is the former view of thinking as a trainable process that best serves our motivational goals contrasted to the belief that thinking reflects a fixed, immutable capacity.

Second, the hierarchical model directs our attention to those vulnerabilities of thought where remedial interventions would be most effective and why. We believe that the ultimate "choke point" for productive thinking is usually not an insufficiency of information – although at times such insufficiencies *can* prove fatal – but rather it is more likely the failure to arrange and assemble information in effective ways as well as the result of inadequate or distracted self-monitoring.

Third, the model brings to light an otherwise mysterious process in a sufficiently simplified form useful for framing higher-order curriculum objectives. This means that curricula can be arranged and justified in ways that reflect our best current understanding of the dynamics of problem solving and thinking. Thus, the application of the model can give the course design process the added force of authority and scientific credibility.

Now (and fourth), what about the issue of motivation? And not just motivation seen as fear-driven forces, which induce students to spend more hours studying but only at the expense of further apprehension and resentment. Our view of motivation is fundamentally different, that is, motives as goals – goals that draw, not drive, but rather beguile students with the self-rewards that come from discovery, inquiry, and the satisfaction of curiosity. Is there any evidence that learning to organize one's thinking in more strategic, metacognitive ways will benefit these positive motives? Are strategically minded individuals willing to think more deeply, and when academic disappointments occur, is the impact of failure moderated and its meaning for them altered in more constructive ways? The accumulating evidence favors these propositions. Students who have been trained to be better planners tend to link the concept of intelligence to the quality of executive, metacognitive functioning (Covington, 1998). For them, intelligence represents the ability to think in strategic ways – analyzing and reframing problems or identifying the sources of difficulty, to be distinguished from intelligence conceived as IQ, which is widely believed to reflect a fixed capacity. Armed with mental rules and plans of action, strategically-oriented students are more willing not only to try harder but to do it in smarter ways. Strategies, then, suggest a more fluid kind of ability – more a resource than a capacity. From a self-worth perspective, the advantage of this view is clear. If strategically-minded students should fail in their problem-solving efforts, legitimate explanations other than incompetence are not only available but plausible. Perhaps the wrong strategy was employed, or an appropriate strategy was used but for an insufficient amount of time. Thus, for these students, failure does need not necessarily imply "failure as a person" owing to incompetence, but rather as a "failure of effort," which can free them to try harder and in smarter ways.

But, of course, there *are* limits to the effectiveness of such inspired persistence. Everyone eventually reaches the limits of time, of energy, and even of one's innate capacities. It is at these points that the true value of believing ability to be a resource, not a fixed commodity, comes to the fore. The response no longer need be a hopeless struggle with *this* particular problem, but rather of *changing* the problem, making it simpler, or more receptive to one's unique skill set.

## THE INTERIOR ARCHITECTURE OF COURSE DESIGN

So far we have concentrated on the cognitive building blocks that comprise the problem-solving edifice. These are the basic "mortar and bricks" of problem-solving, but by themselves they are not enough. Ultimately, effective problem solving depends on organizing one's intellectual resources in the right patterns and sequences to match the nature of the task at hand. The core of this event is nothing less than "knowing how to know." Yet, when viewed only in these terms, this centerpiece of effective thought remains an abstraction. Effective course design requires that such abstractions be transformed into broadly useful problem-solving tools that share common cause with specific subject matter knowledge.

What are some examples of the kinds of universally applicable concepts that can organize and give substance to scientific and scholarly investigations, and that can also ensure robust transfer to future problems? When we appeal to seminar members for nominations regarding such conceptual tools, they propose a variety of possibilities, many of which in one form or another amount to the concept of *system analysis*.

Most phenomena can be envisioned as part of a system comprised of factors that control problems of interest, whether they be investigating neural transmission or deciphering ancient manuscripts. Perhaps the most common example of system analysis is the "troubleshooting" checklist for car repairs. The car won't start; that's the problem. The trouble must be located somewhere in a complex electrical/mechanical system. The plan of analysis involves systematically checking off possible causes of the malfunction – one by one, and in a descending order of likelihood, starting with the most likely culprit.

This example can be extrapolated to any complex phenomenon whose nature or behavior is subject to multiple influences. For instance, the causes of tropical storms can be located within a system of variables, as can the movement of planets and the behavior of children. These complex systems can often be portrayed in visual terms. Consider the inner world of childhood. We can imagine a series of interlocking systems that act singly and collectively to control, influence, or cause a child's behavior. The first system can be portrayed visually as a small ring that constitutes the child herself with all her innate biological and physical properties as well as genetically triggered dispositions. Next comes a second larger concentric ring enfolding the first ring, which represents all the parental and other family influences that can impinge directly on the child and also interact simultaneously with the first-order factors that populate the initial ring. Any number of successively larger encircling rings can be envisioned, which represent the causal impact of additional systems including the larger social-cultural arena.

Virtually all the teaching problems offered by our seminar participants over the years qualify in one way or another as a system, defined by Merriam Webster (2011) as "a set or arrangement of things so related or connected as to form a unity or organic whole." This definition certainly applies to all three of the capstone tasks featured in our case studies. Solutions depend on viewing issues as part of a larger whole. For instance, the task of describing how nerve cells communicate reliably can only be fully satisfied by contextualizing the process within an interacting system of biological, chemical, and electrical subsystems. Similarly, students are unlikely to offer sound advice to parents and caretakers regarding the successive crises facing their "fantasy children" unless they recognize that the causes of these crises are operating thorough an endless cycling (system) of past and present dynamics that control the future. Finally, a philologist would be disadvantaged in creating a convincing storyline describing the history of changes in an ancient text without keeping track of all the forces – geographic, political, and religious – that are likely to have influenced the process of change over time.

Ultimately, if students are to become truly effective problem solvers, they must identify the causal factors that make up the inner workings of a given system. A system approach encourages students to decompose these factors – to see what makes them "tick," so to speak; to determine what creates this problem in the first place, and to ask and answer additional questions regarding what dynamics are operating here. And, if the dynamics are found to be dysfunctional, say, as in the case of the "fantasy children," to determine how these factors might be realigned or altered for the better. In this connection, system analysis is not only useful for describing how nature works according to causal models; it can also serve as a powerful heuristic or "homing" device for guiding experts to trouble spots in much the same way that the car mechanic uses a "troubleshooting" decision tree to locate the cause(s) of the engine breakdown. And, more often than not, even minor dislocations within a vast, complicated system can cause many times its own weight in mischief. This is the case when one enzyme out of thousands in a biological system does not properly metabolize or when a single sparkplug fails to fire reliably in a car engine.

One widely applicable system model drawn largely from the behavioral and social sciences is the causal principle suggesting that: (1) the consequences of future events, for good or ill, are largely dependent on the wisdom of present decisions; and (2) present problems are in part the product of past decisions or even indecision.

The notion that present choices are constrained, or even precluded, by past decisions has great intellectual and pedagogical reach. Certainly, this is true in the behavioral and social sciences, but it also operates beyond these domains as well. It is applicable when industrial design students identify a chain of disastrous choices made by panicked plant operators at Chernobyl that led to a core meltdown of a Russian nuclear reactor in 1986. At what various points, an instructor might inquire, could the reactor have been shut down safely, and why was it not? What improvements in staff training might have provided the necessary margin of safety? Could the human/machine interface be redesigned to increase this margin? By contrast, a more constructive response to potential disaster by the American Apollo 17 astronauts led them to a safe landing. Why were their choices in a decision tree more effective? The application of a forward-reaching inquiry in the health sciences is equally compelling. How can adolescents be convinced that current efforts by them to gain acceptance among their peers by smoking may have disastrous future health consequences? And, the notion that the past holds the key to understanding every human tragedy is alive and well whenever English literature students explore the biographical timeline found in *King Lear*. This past/present/future axis is particularly pertinent whenever a problem structure is chronological in nature.

### STEP 6: CONSTRUCTING A CAUSAL SYSTEM

Following a group discussion of the importance of causal systems, seminar members were challenged to propose a system of their own creation, around which students might organize their problem solving efforts.

Once prospective causal systems were identified, we then challenged seminar members to create a visual metaphor for their proposed system. The benefits of metaphors are considerable here. Metaphors dramatize complex events in simple, immediately understandable ways without significant distortion. Simplicity is a virtue in teaching as long as we heed Albert Einstein's warning "not to make things simpler than they are." Simplicity can be a relatively rare commodity in academic circles where the emphasis is often necessarily on crucial but arcane details. Yet, simplicity is critical for the novice who likely has little or no understanding of the fundamentals of a discipline, or worse yet, possibly harbors misconceptions regarding the nature of the discipline itself as well as underestimating the dynamic nature of the scholarly and scientific enterprise. Additionally, by insisting that seminar participants express their metaphors in a less familiar visual mode than in a more common verbal form, elements of the unexpected, the offbeat, and even the playful will thereby more likely be aroused and unleash a spontaneity that leads to thinking about ideas in new ways.

How have our case study participants responded to the challenge of representing their capstone tasks in the form of causal metaphors?


## Psychology 2

We have already telegraphed the twofold principle around which our psychology instructor plans to organize the kinds of problem solving demanded in his course, namely that "present problems are the creature of past decisions and future events are a consequence of present decisions."

How can this example of a causal system be represented metaphorically in the simplest terms yet without undue distortion? And how might it aid in revealing the underlying nature of his capstone task in ways immediately accessible to his students? His crude drawing of dominos provided an answer to the first question. Yes, "the domino effect" as a metaphor! Everyone knows how this works. Dominos are placed upright, one behind another, forming a long line. By pushing over the first domino in line, the next domino follows suit, falling forward and upsetting each successive domino, one after another, until none are left standing.

Our case study neurophysiologist recognized that a time-ordered structure might also apply to the phenomenon of neural transmission which led her to consider a railroad metaphor, in which boxcars (neural impulses) coupled together move past successive choice points or terminals. Among other implications, the image of switching yards will remind her students of the fact that neural impulses often uncouple from one another, and sometimes converge; in effect, switching tracks which produces complex networks.

Once their metaphors were chosen, we asked each seminar participant to explain to the group how their metaphor might provide students with insights into the dynamic nature of their proposed capstone task. Our psychology participant made a number of observations. First and foremost, he argued that, like the domino effect, time-ordered crises on a human scale are also a cause-and-effect phenomenon. Moreover, the domino effect provides a close parallel to the same dynamics found in a past/present/future system analysis. For example, at *present*, a particular domino – say, one toward the back of the line – is about to experience the consequences of a *past* event (tipping of the first domino), which creates *future* consequences, one after another, down the line. Furthermore, in the case of human crises, the consequences of past causes can continue to pile up, making things progressively worse, a dynamic that can be just as unstoppable as what occurs in the domino effect. And, like the domino effect, a single, seemingly inconsequential event in human terms can lead to enormous, even catastrophic effects totally disproportionate to the original cause. And, without stretching the point too far, even the notion of "hindsight," which psychologist are fond of invoking, is capable of metaphorical appreciation: After the fact, the original causes of a troubling event become so completely obvious, by tracing the process backward from the end to the beginning, that we sometimes wonder how anyone could have missed it.

Our psychology instructor also suggested that it would be useful to consider ways that the domino effect falls short in its parallelism to his capstone task. Basically, psychological dynamics *differ* from the physical dynamics of the domino phenomenon. Human problems are more complicated, and in different ways. For example, there are many causes at play in a time-ordered series of human crises, not just one, like that of tipping over the first domino. Moreover, the cause of the domino effect is straightforward, linear, and repetitive. But in human terms, causes are far less predicable. For one thing, not all causal influences have the same impact. Some influences are a constant presence from one crisis to another, never diminishing in their importance, such as a chronic medical condition. Other factors may impact one crisis and not another. For another thing, some factors may be indirect, that is, they may exert an influence only when another factor is present; otherwise they remain benign.

The larger point here, our psychology instructor says, is when facing the complexities of any problem, his students will always be reminded, metaphorically, that the best solutions are those built on a thorough understanding of the nature of the problem, and what caused it in the first place. Otherwise, one may end up confirming the most ominous of Murphy's Laws: "If you think the problem is bad now, just wait until you solve it!"

This exercise also serves another purpose. As a course proceeds, there becomes a corresponding need to organize emerging knowledge in increasingly more sophisticated and thoroughgoing ways. This progression is well illustrated in the case of our psychology participant by the fact that the initial representation of his capstone problem was cast in the form of a list of learning goals (Table 6.2). Clearly a good start. But in order to focus student attention on the underlying problem-solving processes involved, he might next rearrange the organization of the initial list of goals in a more dynamic fashion (see Figure 6.3) as reflected by their being linked, one to another, and that these relationships in turn are controlled by a causal system of factors. Among other more subtle interpretations, this reorganization also suggests the fact that depending on the particular problem, learning goals are not always co-equal in their contribution to solutions which invites a discussion of the topic of sub-goals.

This need for continuous conceptual updating was also recognized by our neurophysiologist when she proposed that the process of creating increasingly sophisticated conceptions of the dynamics of neural transmission be conveyed to students by adding together successive layers of information, one on top of another, thereby creating an increasingly complex, complete, and detailed image.

We suggest that, when appropriate, course designers plan to share their conceptual models with their students, in visual form or not, with special emphasis on their evolution both for the sake of continuing transparency as well as for a sense of why the course is organized the way it is. Not only is achieving solutions the goal, but the journey to that goal need make rational sense as well. Recall that it is organizing structures that are largely missing for the novice, making it difficult to find one's own way around the conceptual landscape of a subject-matter field.

## Spanish 190

This designer's visual metaphor depicts an apparently hapless manuscript careening through time and space in a "gauntlet-like" fashion at the mercy of translators who imposed their own successive agendas – rewriting,

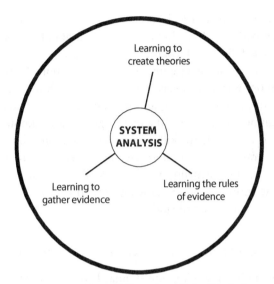

FIGURE 6.3 Revised Learning Goals: Psychology 2

erasing, and overwriting as they went. The importance of this image is that it is easily converted into a two-dimensional grid with the horizontal axis representing a time frame consistent with the length of the travels of the manuscript of choice. The vertical axis would display potential factors within a system of causal influences that may be in play at any point in time, such as periodic political upheavals, economic disasters, or cycles in religious thought. The instructor may choose to highlight some or all of these factors in class discussions, as they might apply to any manuscripts her students might choose. Also, she will almost certainly direct her students to leave room in their grids for more entries, which she expects students will need as a result of their investigations.

Thanks to this organizing grid, a greater number, variety, and complexity of analyses of textual variations over time are likely to occur than might otherwise be the case. It is those empty columns and rows in the grid that beckon to be filled! For example, students can scan the behavior of two or more factors simultaneously in a search for possible interactions among them over time. Causal interpretations of dynamics at these levels of complexity depend on a metacognitive sophistication of the highest order, which one seminar member described as "the ability to see connections and a sensitivity to historic patterns." Consider just one sample pattern: following the widespread migration of indigenous peoples, substantial changes in translations nearly always occur. Of course, students need to be cautioned that patterns alone do not prove a causal link. More convincing evidence is needed. Both metacognition and procedural knowledge work in tandem here. For instance, one might ask if translations following migrations evoke more images of exile, hardship, or banishment than do other translations not preceded by migrations. Knowing what kinds of data will bolster an argument is to reason at a metacognitive level; knowing where to find the data is a procedural skill. Claims are based on informed speculation; things are rarely certain or absolute, but merely more or less plausible. Knowing that claims depend on the reliability of one's sources also involves metacognitive insight; knowing how to assess reliability is likely to be counted as a procedural skill.

## GOAL SETTING AND STANDARDS OF EXCELLENCE

Without some policy regarding the standards of excellence by which students will be assessed, goal statements alone are basically meaningless. Otherwise, how would students know if they had actually satisfied these goals? Moreover, if students are given little or no guidance for how they may achieve or even surpass these standards, then goal statements will become irrelevant. It is easy enough to generate a list of learning goals – perhaps too easy. But it is a far different thing to determine when students have satisfied, exceeded, or fallen short of these goals. Obviously, such decisions depend on establishing the criteria by which such judgments are made. For example, when a student's work falls short according to a given set of criteria, how much of a "shortfall" still deserves an A? Or is it now an A-, or even a B+?

For many students, especially failure-threatened individuals, such a question is an ignition point for much of the fear and resentment that can set student against student and students against the teaching staff. For these students, standards of excellence, by whatever name, implies being graded, and grades have the power to compromise one's sense of worth, let alone influence one's occupational future.

Our seminar participants will do well to take heed of the issues of standards of excellence and grading right from the beginning of their work because there are a variety of overlapping considerations that need to be taken into account along the way. We have already begun taking the steps toward considering the nature of standards of excellence guided principally by our problem-focused approach. For example, we have argued that it is a matter of how well students meet the requirements for the solution to a problem that forms the basis for establishing standards of excellence, not the relative performance of students compared to one another. Then there is our insistence on the need to ensure the transparency of course rationale so students can be apprised in advance of what is expected of them.

So far, so good – but only so far. The realities of grading will remain a constant presence as the design process proceeds, and to the extent that instructors become advocates for the students they serve, they too will vicariously experience the same frustrations over grading as their students. And these frustrations always seem to erupt at the most awkward times. For example, toward the end of one of our seminar meetings, a particularly frustrated participant blurred out, "We have spent weeks thinking of ways to make learning more inviting for our students, more 'user-friendly' and exciting, yet now we ruin it all by having to give grades!" Grading policy need not represent the kind of betrayal rightly feared by this person as long as courses are designed from the outset with the challenge of student evaluation always kept in mind and not merely treated as an afterthought.

But what can be done now, in the early phases of design work, that will best position our seminar members to deal with the task of transforming the role of grading and evaluation in more positive ways? To begin, as always, we must keep the student perspective in mind. Feeling fairly treated is the key that enables students to take advantage of evaluative feedback as guidance for ways to improve. As will be recalled, fairness in grading means several things. First, students expect that the rules by which one can get a good grade are made as clear as possible. Second, students believe that one's work as well as that of others should be evaluated, not one against another, but each judged on its own individual merits against absolute standards.

Let's first take up the matter of the clarity of rules for grading. Our classroom research suggests that the single most welcome formula among students regarding grading policy can be stated as follows: "The better the grades students want, the more they must do, and the better they must do it." There are two pieces to this formula: what students must do, and how well. We can briefly consider each element now in hopes of heightening our "early warning" sensitivities to the issue of standard setting as well as providing a broad context within which to consider grading policy as we go.

## What Students Must Do

What are some useful procedures by which our case study participants can anticipate decisions about what they want their students to do? One strategy is to make a running list of those things that students must do to pass the course, stated in tangible, performance terms whenever possible. In this way, instructors can transform the abstract qualities of "specific learning objectives" into clear, understandable actions. Clarity is always welcome. An excellent example of this approach is presented by veteran college teacher, Robert Fried (2001), who provided students in his children's literature course with three sets of objectives: one dealing with the knowledge of children's literature, another concerned with related intellectual skills, and the third dealing with the attitude and values domain. The objectives within each domain were put in the form of a statement, which in all cases begins with the stem: "I will have successfully completed ED 1405 once..." For the knowledge domain, a sample of objectives includes: "... once I know what the state frameworks in literacy are" or "... once I know how and why traditional nursery rhymes and fairytales have had such durability down through the ages, and why they might be in danger of losing their appeal." For the skill domain, a sample of objectives includes: "... once I have the skills to create a children's book on my own, perhaps with the help of a young person" or "... once I have the skills to teach children how to enjoy reading on their own and with each other." Finally, the attitude domain is represented by several additional objectives, including the statements: "... once I have an attitude that appreciates the power of childhood and adolescent literature to help students become independent and self-motivated readers and learners." The sample of items presented here is drawn from the final form of Fried's course performance statement that he provides to his students on the first day of class.

Using Fried's model, our case study participant in neurophysiology created a sample of specific learning objectives. All of these objectives in Table 6.4 are linked directly or indirectly to a capstone problem. Each objective is in the service of solutions. This makes tangible the overall cognitive scaffoldings, which can become more readily understood by students. Second, each of these learning objectives implies exact counterpoints in the assessment domain. Students can be forewarned regarding the connection between what is taught, and presumably learned, and what objectives will be put on the table for testing. Third, the nature of the standards implies that these objectives satisfy a key ingredient of student-perceived fairness. There is no assumption here that only a few students can achieve these objectives. Indeed, the implicit assumption conveyed by the wording itself is that these objectives are accessible to all students. Anyone can succeed if they fulfill the absolute standards of excellence that stand behind these objectives. It would be the height of

TABLE 6.4 *Specific Learning Objectives: Neurophysiology 195*

- Critique scientific journal articles in cellular and molecular neuroscience.
- Write a proposal for original scientific research.
- Prepare and present a PowerPoint presentation on the above proposal.
- Provide supportive critiques for the proposals of classmates.

hypocrisy to convey the impression that course objectives are accessible to all, then, by "baiting and switching" in the end, employ a relative grading scheme in which only an arbitrary percentage of students could succeed, irrespective of the quality of the performances of the remaining individuals.

### How Well Students Must Do

Obviously, mere compliance with learning objectives is the crudest of standards. Moreover, merely telling students what is expected of them will not necessarily make it so. Without a clear declaration of standards, substandard work will be the inevitable result. So what now can be said early on about the kinds of measures to employ in assessing whether or not students have satisfied an instructor's standards of excellence?

Let's start by considering different kinds of excellence. Should judgments about what constitutes excellence focus on the near term, that is, on accumulated classroom performances in the form of a grade point average (GPA)? Or should one take a longer view of future excellence? Current GPA is a strong predictor of how well students will perform, grade-wise, during the next school term or the next year. But as a predictor of future events such as supervisors' ratings of on-the-job performance, the value of one's GPA is only marginal at best (Covington, 2001). In part this is because of the operation over the long haul of an often hidden yet influential factor in the achievement equation: student motivation. Our analysis of the overstriver is the premier example here. The near-term success of overstrivers in amassing a noteworthy GPA is driven largely by efforts to avoid failing, a motivation that may work tolerably well on the way to the top, but is likely to be counterproductive once these individuals have attained positions of status or power. By contrast, it is a combination of a willingness to master new skills and to cooperate well with others that best predict future job success, yearly income, and self-ratings of personal confidence (Spence & Helmrich, 1983).

None of these observations are meant to suggest that one approach for assessing excellence – either on a near-term or long-term basis – is more appropriate than the other. They are not incompatible. Likely, in practice, these two approaches share in creating an instructor's overall vision of excellence. Actually, the point here is to ask whether there are any benchmarks of excellence that reflect short term achievement and simultaneously track a trajectory toward future excellence, and – of greatest importance – also have implications for the growth toward excellence. We believe there are. Our choice is to reward success at skilled problem solving in the near-term, which fosters both self-confidence and further successes, while at the same time recognizing that the prospects for future excellence are also being secured because current successes at problem solving depend on a well-developed metacognitive capacity that is critical for dealing with as yet unknown future problems.

A second aspect of sustainable excellence is demonstrated competency – not necessarily brilliance, but competency – that is the indispensable minimum for excellence to emerge. The qualities of mind necessary to transform competency into excellence – the "tipping point," so to speak – are motivational in nature. How can they be encouraged as an integral part of the classroom reward system? Once again, Fried (2001) offers an excellent working strategy. He creates thumbnail sketches of what in his course differentiates students in the A range from students in the B and C ranges. For Fried, students in the A range "are self-starters who take the initiative. They do not wait for the professor to tell them what to do"; "approach the subject with an independent and conscientious view-point"; "read articles and commentaries with a critical eye – looking for author's biases that may color the meaning." For Fried, students who fall in the C range "tend to do the minimum to get by"; "tend to wait to be told what to do, or not to do much of anything unless it is clearly required"; or "write in a manner that does not display much originality or reflection on experience."

Fried's strategy offers students a unique invitation to view themselves as true learners – thinking about measuring themselves against the standards that define excellence in the life of the mind rather than trying to determine just what they will be tested on, or judging how little they need to do and still get a passing grade. This perspective places the quest for excellence, no matter how specifically defined, in absolute terms. Everyone can cooperate and endure for the sake of the larger group, and constantly seek new intellectual horizons. These are qualities open to all and become yet another potential source of equity. They are scarce enough. They should not be made even more precious by undervaluing them as a matter of misguided grading policy.

## THE ISSUE OF CONTENT COVERAGE

College courses often attempt to cover far more than can possibly be delivered in the time available. The scope of goals and the list of topics can sometimes appear equivalent to a 10-tome encyclopedia! As already noted, the issue of content coverage becomes particularly acute among survey courses whose typical goal is to provide students with an overview of an entire discipline, yet a less vexing problem for advanced, upper-division classes that tend to address narrower, more specialized topics. Nonetheless, content coverage is always an issue since no course, no matter how limited its scope, can be expected to cover everything of importance, at least not equally well. Often even some of the most significant material can be given little more than a "once-over-lightly" treatment.

The emphasis on coverage per se is sustained in part by the often-cited analogy to a blanket – that is, "blanketing" as much material as possible. We believe this is a misplaced way to frame the issue of coverage, mainly because not every topic deserves equal treatment as implied, analogically, by the uniformity in the weave of blankets. Coverage as a priority in itself offers little guidance for making sound pedagogical decisions regarding degrees of topical emphasis. Rather, it is the demands of problem-solving tasks that should determine what needs to be learned, when, and to what depth.

We believe that the challenge of providing adequate coverage is best satisfied by reframing coverage as a matter of the transfer of knowledge in which the center of instructional gravity should be weighted in favor of training metacognitive strategies, particularly those skills associated with planning and self-monitoring. The universal reach of good planning is the most effective means for confronting often unfamiliar, ill-defined problems whose solution we propose as the centerpiece of instruction. This argument emphasizes instruction for both *depth* and *breadth* of processing. But this is not the kind of breadth of processing that is typically associated with the practice of skimming over material in a superficial way merely for the sake of exposure. For us, the goal of "breadth of coverage" carries an alternative meaning. Here breadth refers to the transfer of metacognitive knowledge across the "length and breadth" of the problem-solving landscape. It is metacognitive knowledge with its essentially limitless capacity for application across disciplines that deserve protracted emphasis. This is precisely *because* not every future contingency can be covered in the classroom, let alone even anticipated.

Having said this, there remains a potential irony regarding our advocacy for coverage within a problem-focused approach to college teaching. Compared to imparting content knowledge, teaching for thinking and especially its transfer to problems not yet encountered is an enormously inefficient proposition. Solving problems takes time, lots of it – time to reflect, to speculate, and then often to redefine a problem and begin again. And group problem solving is the most cumbersome of all. There is time out to negotiate with others for their cooperation; time out to overcome misunderstandings and stalemates; and even time to create controversy deliberately in order to challenge overly simplistic group-generated solutions. Patience is a decided virtue when it comes to problem solving. But patience steals away time that could otherwise be spent on ensuring exposure to other material. Thus, it appears that we are still confronted with a cruel trade-off between promoting depth of processing and maximizing breadth of content coverage. Actually, however, in the end, this dilemma is more apparent than real. It is the mutually reinforcing interplay between general and specific factual knowledge that saves the day. By improving the ability of students to think strategically, they will also increase their capacity to learn more and to retain more of what they learn.

## THE TRANSFER OF KNOWLEDGE

If the issue of content coverage is best treated as a matter of the transfer of knowledge, then the ability to transfer knowledge becomes of even greater importance than formerly appreciated. And if problem solving is the "name of the game," then the application of one's present knowledge to unexpected or unfamiliar future issues is where the stakes of the game are raised to their limits. Few teaching objectives have been given greater billing, generation after generation, or by more college instructors, than preparing students for the future. Yet lurking within this noble goal, there resides a potential dilemma whose resolution will bring us to a fuller appreciation of the intimate relationship between general problem-solving strategies and local domain-specific content knowledge, as well as allow us to draw some important implications for instructional design.

### The Dilemma

The merits of a generalist position are beyond question. Although not a guarantee of a solution, general problem-solving strategies for planning and monitoring of one's plans should at least help in solving problems, both now and in the future. However, not all attempts to demonstrate the value of universal strategies have been successful. Such failures have led Newell and Simon (1972) to conclude that learning broad problem-solving principles amounts to a general/weak approach – general in that broad strategies are obviously applicable to all problems, but weak because their usefulness for solving a specific problem may be only marginal.

At the same time, the accumulation of domain-specific content, say, in mathematics, physics or chemistry, is undeniably important for solving problems in these fields. However, once acquired, subject matter knowledge in one domain appears to have surprisingly little positive impact on performance in other domains. For example, learning to play chess does not ensure that students will be better able to solve logic problems. For this reason, Newell and Simon characterize the accumulation of specific content knowledge as a strong/specific approach when it comes to transfer – strong because subject matter knowledge is a powerful factor in solving problems within a given domain, but specific owing to the fact that the value of this knowledge for solving problems outside the domain is limited.

Here it seems we have the makings of a profound dilemma. If the evidence for the transfer of broad thinking strategies is spotty, and specific knowledge is also of limited generality, can we really prepare students for a future of unknown possibilities where the specific content as well as the very nature of the problems themselves will likely be quite different if not unrecognizable today?

## The Dilemma Resolved

The answer is more hopeful than might appear at first, and depends on recognizing that general and specific knowledge prepare students to solve problems in different but complimentary ways. The key to this insight followed from the results of a classic experiment conducted by Chase and Simon (1973). These researchers demonstrated that master chess players were no better at memorizing the layout of chess pieces on the board than novice players if the patterns were random. By contrast, the capacity of grand masters to remember the various moves of their opponents in real games from the past was prodigious. For example, it was estimated by Chase and Simon that these expert players could call to mind some 50,000 chess configurations that occurred in past game play with opponents. Something profound and specific about chess play is at work here. This phenomenal ability at recall is the result of thinking about chess in terms of meaningful patterns of play, not random patterns. This clearly confirms the "strong/specific" proposition. But what about the "general/weak" proposition? Must general strategies always remain weak in terms of their transfer value? The answer is no, not at all. Instead of asking these grand masters to solve chess problems, Clement (1982) gave these experts unfamiliar, novel problems for which their present knowledge was insufficient. In this situation, the grand masters as well as experts in other fields reverted to broad thinking strategies in an effort to discover the underlying structure of the problems. This often involved creating simple visual representations and everyday analogies of the problems in an attempt to detect the workings of the more complicated case. Also, experts try to identify the specific problem as belonging to a larger class of problems (Adelson, 1981). For instance, before studying the specifics of a particular legal case, experienced attorneys locate the particular decision in the larger context of who judged the case, the type of court that tried the case, and the kinds of parties represented. These kinds of findings have led researchers to describe neophytes who possess general thinking strategies as "intelligent novices" (Brown & Campione, 1990). These individuals may not yet possess all the specific subject matter knowledge needed for exploring a new field, but they know how to get it.

General problem-solving strategies come into their own in the face of unknown contingencies. They are far from being "weak" or of only marginal value. They have great relevance depending on the nature of the problem. Moreover, general thinking strategies and specific content knowledge are not at odds. General strategies are most valuable in the beginning when tasks are overly complicated or unfamiliar. But as the problem solver gradually develops a body of information and experience, a rich subject matter base evolves, which is specific to that particular task, making solutions more routine. Eventually, with enough experience, even highly complex tasks like chess play may take on the superficial appearances of rote functioning. This deceptive case can incorrectly convey to the novice that expertise isn't developed but is innate.

Yet the application of general strategies to unfamiliar situations is by no means automatic. Students have difficulties applying what they know to new topics. These failures are caused by several interlocking deficits working in tandem. First, some critical amount of specific knowledge is needed to which general principles can be applied. Transfer cannot occur in a vacuum. For example, students may understand the broad heuristics for mathematics problem solving in the abstract, but they may not understand mathematics well enough to make use of their understanding in specific situations (Schoenfeld, 1985). This is why creating familiar, everyday analogies for an unfamiliar problem can be so effective (Gick & Holyoak, 1983). The uncommon becomes situated in a familiar context, which permits one's past experience to be brought to bear. But then one's prior knowledge must be available from memory, an obvious point that focuses our attention on the second potential shortfall for transfer, that is, the failure to access the specific knowledge necessary for transfer to occur.

Consider a dramatic example of this failure, and a stark demonstration of the basic frailty of human transfer mechanisms (Bransford, Nitsch, & Franks, 1977). The investigators in this study found that college students have great difficulty solving simple "insight" problems of the kind described here unless they are provided with hints, even though they have the necessary information for a solution already stored in memory. "Uriah Fuller, the famous Israeli superpsychic, can tell you the score of any baseball game before the game starts. What is his secret?" Before being given this and other similar "problems," one group of students was provided information that eventually would clearly be the key to their solutions, statements such as "Before it starts the score of any game is 0 to 0." When some of the students from this group were expressly prompted to use clues previously provided them, their record of problem solving was excellent. However, other students who had the same clues in memory, but were not prompted explicitly to use them, performed poorly – in fact, no better than yet another group of students who had never possessed the clues in the first place.

The ability to access stored information in such circumstances depends on the way that information was originally organized in memory. The most effective organizational schema are those that are rich in connections among all the elements of stored content knowledge, that is, fully integrated into a larger network of meaning. This is why treating facts as merely a series of disconnected, isolated entries into memory creates what Alfred North Whitehead (1929) referred to as "inert knowledge" – information that in principle is applicable to a wide range of situations, but which in reality is available to individuals in only a restricted or isolated set of contexts. Unfortunately, much traditional instructional practice encourages the acquisition of information by students that remains inert.

Third and finally, individuals need some mechanism to guide their search of memory for what is relevant to the problem at hand. We have placed such mechanisms in the domain of metacognitive knowledge, another area of demonstrated deficiencies. For example, it is difficult for students to reformulate problems in ways that make it clear what additional information is critical to a solution. Thus, although students may possess the critical information, they may not know what to search for in memory.

### Instructional Implications

The instructional implications of these findings for promoting the transfer of knowledge are several. First, it must be appreciated that there is a close interplay between specific and general knowledge. They are not rivals, but rather partners. Learning experiences should be structured in ways that general and specific knowledge are mutually reinforcing, which means that these domains grow apace, in a symbiotic fashion. However, since it will likely be difficult to determine with any accuracy just how much accumulated subject matter knowledge is sufficient for general strategies to be effectively invoked, the wisest course for instructors is to create an expectation among their students that all knowledge has uses beyond the limited context in which it is being learned, and to provide demonstrations to this effect right from the beginning in an effort to break the tyranny of "inert knowledge." Students must be made aware of the processes by which transfer is likely to occur so that some degree of self-reflection is achieved as they work. In this regard, one of our co-authors found it useful to present the concept of transfer of knowledge, analogously, in terms of a mental tool kit with its individual cognitive skills and procedures awaiting their executive application in different ways depending on circumstances. Carpenters use hammers differently depending on whether the job requires removing a nail or setting it! The analogy to a Swiss Army knife with all its various functional tools also comes to mind.

These observations remind us of another piece of the transfer puzzle. Context and circumstance is everything when it comes to transfer – in effect, whether the task is to set the nail or to remove it. Recognition of the vital importance of context is guided by what cognitive scientists refer to as *conditional knowledge*. Conditional knowledge means "knowing about knowing," that is, possessing knowledge about the constraints and conditions of the use of knowledge – why, for example, it is useful to search for ideas in systematic ways rather than randomly or to reformulate old problems in new ways. Without such an appreciation, an individual may in fact possess the necessary procedural skills for, say, effective question asking, yet may not apply them unless directed specifically to do so. Such failures to act independently are referred to as *production deficiencies*, and are thought to occur largely in the absence of knowing at a strategic level why questioning can be particularly beneficial in a given situation.

Creating the expectation that both content and procedural knowledge can act like tools with broad utility is one step toward improving the prospects for transfer. Another step concerns maximizing access to content and procedural knowledge from memory. As mentioned earlier, access depends closely on the quality of the mental representation of knowledge held by students. If that structure is incomplete, loosely organized, or lacking a robust network of interconnections among the stored material, as is the case with the novice, then there will be relatively fewer "triggers" for retrieving the necessary information when needed. Such structural deficiencies are one reason we have argued the need for students always to make meaningful what they must remember. In this way, new information can be more fully integrated into an existing store of knowledge. Knowledge structures can be represented through *cognitive mapping*, a procedure that involves students creating a graphic representation of their personal cognitive organization of a concept. In Chapter 7, we will explore various ways that cognitive mapping techniques can be used not only to assess the metacognitive aspects of what students have learned but also to consider its utility as an instructional device.

In the meantime, we can point to several effective ways to encourage being mindful about transfer. One teaching approach is to couch instruction in terms of practical applications whenever possible. This strategy is highly effective for the transfer of procedural knowledge taught in one content area to another. Consider the question posed to college freshmen by Bransford, Nitsch, and Franks (1977): "Try to remember what you learned about the concept of logarithms. Can you think of any way that logarithms might make problem solving simpler than it would be if they did not exist?" These students not only recalled something about logarithms but also were able to explain their value in mathematics.

Another powerful strategy for inducing accessibility to information involves making problem-solving tasks personally meaningful. For instance, Bransford et al. (1977) presented two groups of college students with information about human attention. One group learned about research techniques for the study of attention and attention deficits. Another group was charged with the task of thinking about lapses in attention and the need to control attention in high-stakes academic situations such as preparing for a test or listening to a lecture. Several days after the experiment ended, all the students estimated how much they had perseverated on the topic of attention in the meantime, and under what conditions. The first group rarely reported thinking about the concept once they left the experiment, whereas those students who were prompted to think about attention in everyday, personal, or practical terms reported perseverating on this theme a great deal, and especially when it came to actually studying or listening to lectures. These findings suggest that it may be possible to keep ideas alive by paying more attention to the types of social situations that people naturally find themselves.

## Near and Far Transfer

Another aspect of transfer should also be borne in mind by instructors. It concerns the distinction between what is referred to in the research literature as *near* and *far* transfer (Covington, 2001) and the different causes of the failure of transfer under these two conditions. Near transfer refers to those cases where the new problems targeted for transfer share a close structural affinity with those problems that the individual has already been trained to solve. The simplest example involves applying the same arithmetic formula for determining the area of a rectangle to any new rectangles that come along. The sizes and shapes may vary, but the underlying affinity is transparent. A rectangle is a rectangle! Far transfer refers to those instances in which the principles needed for solving a new problem may share little in common with those problems previously mastered – or what is more interesting, even when they do share a considerable cognitive overlap, this fact is obscured by superficial, surface differences. An example of far transfer involves the same arithmetic formula for determining the area of a rectangle, but this time applied to a trapezoid, whose shape presents a quite different visual configuration. The application of the same old formula to the new situation depends on realizing that a trapezoid is really a rectangle when the areas under the angled portions at each end of the trapezoid can together be combined into a square.

It is a truism that the process of transferring one's knowledge in the case of either near or far transfer is only potential, never guaranteed. People are slow to see the connections between what they have learned previously and the challenges they now face. But this observation is only partially true. And herein lies the danger. Sometimes people think they see a connection, but one that is not there!

For this reason, the failure to solve problems successfully, particularly in the case of near transfer, is not the inability to see similarities among problems when they exist, but an automatic rush to judgment of problem equivalency when similarities do not exist. In these instances, people end up trying to solve the wrong problem. An example of the failure to recognize differences calls to mind the college student who attempts unsuccessfully to apply rote formulas learned in a high school physics course to physics problems in a first-year college class. Although these problems may share superficial similarities, the means for their solution are almost certainly quite different. These traps can only be avoided by being able to detect differences as well as similarities in underlying structure among problems, another aspect of metacognitive sophistication.

## THE NATURE OF FUTURE PROBLEMS

In planning for how to forearm students for future demands, some thought should be given to the subject matter concepts around which instruction should be organized. Take the nature/nurture concept that might organize the Psychology 2 course. Whatever future directions the current revolution in human genetics and bioengineering take, many of the resulting ethical, economic, and political issues will likely profit from being framed as discussions in which the concept of nature/nurture will play a significant part. But beyond the enduring relevance of various broad content themes, there is still the matter of the as yet unknown kinds of problems whose solutions can benefit from such subject matter preparation. There is no limit to the candidates here. Problems are only as far away as the morning headlines. But which headlines? Giving due respect to the dangers inherent in predicting which problems will populate the future, we will risk mentioning three issues that most observers believe will increasingly characterize the future. These three issues offer intriguing possibilities as a basis for creating capstone tasks.

### Low-Profile Risks

The future is becoming more problematic in part because the greatest dangers may not always be the obvious ones. Take the field of public health. The consequences of some health risks, such as using heroin and skateboarding, are immediate, potentially fatal, and capable of graphic portrayal. But other risks, such as poor diet or chronic cigarette smoking, are more subtle. The dangers here involve low probabilities of occurrence over extended periods. Relatively few smokers will die of lung cancer, and in any event, the harmful effects of smoking are often long delayed. Thinking about such low probability, time-delayed risks should be part of the college curriculum – not simply for the sake of, say, the health of individuals but also because students need to appreciate that the shape of the future depends on the wisdom of present decisions. Such understanding is exceedingly difficult to convey because of the compressed view of future time held by many people and often because of a deficiency in probabilistic reasoning.

## Problems without Precedent

More and more problems in the future will be without precedent in human history. One problem-solving obstacle already without precedent, and getting exponentially worse by the day, is information overload. Even today the information glut is so severe that experts working in highly arcane, narrowly defined specialties cannot keep up with all that is potentially important. The situation is staggering. Worldwide, 10,000 books are published each day, and the number is rising. And this does not count the daily blizzard of e-mail memos, abstracts, and reports, the vast majority of which is only marginally relevant to any particular problem. People must be prepared to handle large volumes of information, clearly not to remember it all, but able to make decisions about what is relevant and what to ignore. Practicing such sensibilities would seem particularly crucial during the problem formulation stage of problem solving.

## Interconnected Problems

Future problems will become increasingly interconnected and need to be solved collectively, not in isolation, and not one problem at a time. The future of present decisions will depend increasingly on how well we handle deeply interconnected issues. This argues for a system approach to problem solving, which suggests that, as Michael Polanyi put it, "we can not comprehend the whole without seeing its parts, but we can not see the parts without comprehending the whole." Attention must be paid simultaneously both to our evolving guesses about the nature of the broad outlines of the big picture and to each of the individual puzzle pieces that must eventually fit together to form the whole. The kinds of teaching problems we envision are admirable vehicles for promoting an appreciation of this whole-part relationship, which involves the capacity to view any particular problem as part of a larger system, whether it be biological, psychological, or economic, or what is most likely some combination of all these.

## COMMUNICATING GOALS

So far we have explored several interrelated pedagogical issues including the challenge posed by content coverage and the need to set standards of excellence against which student progress toward learning goals can be assessed. Now let's briefly consider the question of how learning goals are best communicated to students. Taking up this topic now may seem premature. Yet, as a concern, it is never too early to be considered. By putting issues of communication on the table now, we are challenged to articulate what exactly is worth communicating.

The typical means for communicating one's course goals is simply to list them in a syllabus. This is a start, but only that. More is needed than a perfunctory presentation of these objectives. Students not only agree that goal statements are appropriate; they also believe it is reasonable that attention be drawn to them. However, beyond this concession, students are often only paying lip service. Goals can be quickly forgotten, or perhaps worse yet, simply dismissed or ignored, thought to be part of the obligatory "boilerplate" of any class. But whatever the causes of these lapses, it is typical that goals presented at the beginning of a course, even when they are repeatedly reinforced, can rarely be recalled with any certainty at the end of the term. This means that many classes are essentially rudderless events, except to the extent that they are organized around due dates for assignments and test schedules. It is these details that are easily recalled, but often little else. A particularly revealing example of this "tunnel vision" was witnessed by one of the authors. A student had arrived late for class in the midst of the lecture. Unbeknownst to him, his class had been cancelled that day, and a lecturer from another class was substituted whose subject matter was markedly different. As he sat looking somewhat confused, he undoubtedly was rationalizing his unfamiliarity with both the lecturer and the topic by assuming that the lecturer was a guest speaker. He only realized his mistake later when the next exam date announced by the lecturer did not correspond with the date in *his* course syllabus. Mustering as much dignity as possible, he beat a hasty retreat from the hall!

If this example were not so troubling, it would be amusing. As it is, it vividly illustrates a potential disaster in the making. If academic sense-making by students relies largely on the outwardly appearing course characteristics, then the underlying fabric and true purpose of the course will elude them. Why should this be a problem?

First, a sense of purpose is critical for task engagement. The purposes implied by course goals suggest direction, intent, and, eventually, destination – attributes that are all important to proper motivation. Once students have the assurance of clarity of purpose, they can more freely turn to matters of personal curiosity that may be aroused by the curriculum. When students understand the larger purposes of their studies, how they can fulfill these purposes, and come to realize that they are trusted enough to be given this opportunity to learn, they will exceed our expectations.

Second, neophyte learners often approach courses in an atomistic way. For example, they view their courses as a series of discrete tasks to be completed by certain dates. Ask students what the percentage of their grade is accounted for by a given assignment, and they are nearly certain to know. But ask them which goals or themes of the course relate to that assignment, and you will likely get blank stares. Ask them how various units or sections of a course are interrelated or why the course ends with the topics it does, and then those blank stares will often turn to looks of incredulity! Basically, many students fail to see the implications of these questions for their learning. As a consequence, this atomistic view of course structure promotes a superficial stance toward learning, which often amounts to students construing their task as one of memorizing terms, definitions, and concepts in isolation and ignoring the relationship among them. In addition to being tedious and disengaging, learning without meaning leaves students with only a limited understanding that makes analysis, and the application of their knowledge, difficult.

Third, we have argued in earlier chapters that much of what students consider to be unfair about courses comes not from any malevolence on the part of instructors, but rather because students simply do not understand how things work. They tend to remember the simple rules that govern course policy, such as whether or not tests can be made up or what constitutes an excused absence. But what many students apparently do not even attempt to understand, let alone remember, is how course requirements serve course goals. This point was illustrated by an experiment conducted by our staff. In the last few days before the end of a large social science course, students were reminded that every class assignment had been designed to help them realize the main goals of the course. They were then asked to work backwards in their thinking and deduce from these assignments what skills, knowledge, and attitudes the teaching staff believed make up the capacity "to think like a behavioral scientist." The resulting responses indicated that in general students were simply not up to the task of making connections between major course goals that had been repeatedly emphasized throughout the term and the means to achieve them, even when explicitly directed to search for connections. Judging from our observations, it seems that students often are operating in a kind of cognitive "twilight zone," floating around, doing what they are told, usually on time and with generally satisfactory results, but with little understanding of why they do what they do.

How can instructors assure themselves that students appreciate the pedagogical logic of course structures? The best advice comes once again from Professor Jane Tompkins (1990): "Talk to your class about the class ... Do this at the beginning of the course to get yourself and the students used to it. Make it no big deal, just a normal part of day-to-day business, and keep it up." (pg. 659) We have seen such conversations conducted successfully in small seminars as well as in classes whose enrollment exceeds 500 students.

Consider the strategy developed by one of the authors for ensuring a deep understanding by students of the intimate connections among course structures, their rationale, and their goals. On the first day of class, after articulating the goals of the course, he asks his students what topics they think need to be covered in order to realize these goals. Following a listing of these topics, he adds any topics that have not yet been offered, but which are actually part of his course, and he eliminates those topics that will not be included (with a brief explanation as to why). The result is a list of topics identical to those he plans to cover. He then asks his students to arrange these topics in a "logical" sequence consistent with effective teaching practices as students define them, and also to indicate how much emphasis should be placed on each topic. In essence, and not always recognizing it, these students are sketching out an initial rough design of the course they are about to take! Typically, what becomes immediately apparent when various teaching sequences are debated by students is the existence of significant similarities as well as differences in approaches. This aspect of the activity is intended to demonstrate that courses do not simply design themselves, nor is there only one obvious way for a course to be put together. It all depends on what instructors value and how they conceive the purposes of the course. After his students have explained their design rationale, our colleague shares his vision of the course. With this background, his students more readily grasp the reasons for his pedagogical choices, better see the implied linkages between the various parts of the course, and appreciate how the course builds or develops. Interestingly, our colleague reports that because his students have already thought through many of these issues, they are much more likely to challenge him regarding his reasoning. Indeed, they have often prompted him to make more comprehensive explanations of his rationale. And, on occasion, he even has made changes to the design of the course in light of these arguments.

Finally, this activity can be extended by asking students: If my teaching goal is such and such, and we are studying so and so, how might I best teach this class, and then assuming that we have addressed the topic in this way, how might I test your knowledge? Our colleague reports that asking this question at various points throughout a course prepares students for upcoming exams by sharpening their predictions about the most likely test questions. For us, this two-part question holds far more significance than a test preparation exercise. It is basically the formula, posed here as a series of questions, by which all effective course design proceeds. This statement ties all the essential elements of the teaching/learning act together into one unified, transparent entity: goals, instruction, and evaluation. Indeed, this notion of continuity and connection is the overriding theme that we will continue to stress for the sake of both content mastery and motivational considerations.

## CONCLUSIONS

So far our treatment of course goals and their underlying intellectual scaffolding has focused largely on what Benjamin Bloom (1956) has referred to as "cognitive" goals, that is, those intellectual aspects of know-ledge associated with productive thought and problem solving. But Bloom also recognized another goal domain that he dubbed the "affective" arena, which included, in his words, "the manner in which we deal with things emotionally, such as feelings, values, appreciations, enthusiasms, motiv-ations, and attitudes." To this list we would add intrinsic task engagement, which for us is the ultimate legacy of all learning and the central focus of this book. These affective goals inhabit an intangible, highly idiosyncratic domain that is largely intrinsic to the individual. But as we have argued in Chapter 4, these goals, too, can be reinforced and nurtured by many of the same extrinsic, tangible factors and conditions that promote cognitive goals. Common to the promotion of both objectives is a sense of intellec-tual honesty on the parts of both students and instructors, and an atmos-phere of fairness and trust.

But what about this affective goal domain? What about the wishes of instructors to convey their passion for a chosen field? This is a goal, too, and planning here is just as critical as with any purely content goal. But what kind of planning? How does one put into words and actions a sense for one's deep commitment to the academy and an appreciation for the intellectual integrity, dedication, and sacrifice that the examined life requires? These sentiments can be listed as goals, of course. But ultimately lists cannot contain them; listing runs the risk of trivializing them. One delightful example of the struggle to infuse one's teaching with passion is reported by Walvoord and Anderson (1998) when a college instructor who taught classes in a swine management department expressed discontent with a list of strictly content-driven performance objectives being drawn up by her colleagues (i.e., outline a plan for swine management). What she wanted ultimately was for her students to "appreciate the pig. I can't measure that, and I don't know how to test it, but it's important to me and my students, and I won't give it up!" Walvoord and Anderson go on to report that several of her colleagues offered suggestions not all of which were totally serious, given that the topic was appreciating pigs!

Our observation is that intangible goals such as "appreciation" are best conveyed indirectly, by example, through modeling by instructors as they too struggle publicly with the same academic problems that they have assigned their students. Students may not come to love pigs, but they can appreciate the intellectual integrity and dedication of purpose they sense in their instructors. In previous chapters, we took up the question of how best to encourage these intangibles. Suffice it to say that, for the moment, these answers reside, not primarily in an instructor's presentational style or persona, but rather in the hundreds of "behind-the-scenes" planning decisions that go to make up a safe, fair-minded, and intellectually honest learning experience. In Chapter 7, we will rejoin our case study participants as they pursue these objectives, and in particular as they begin to sort out the instructional and assessment implications of our problem-solving focus.

# 7

## Partnering Instruction and Assessment

### INTRODUCTION

Citizens of the 21st century will not be judged by their ability to bubble in answers on test forms.

– Robert Calfee

We now turn to the twin topics of instruction and assessment – twin as in "joined at the hip," yet still retaining their distinctive, individual functions. We will put these two pedagogical elements in play together as key satellites circling the centerpiece of all courses: goals. Goals are the entry point of course design; everything flows from goals. Instruction is harnessed to goals as the means by which skills are taught and knowledge imparted that represent the cognitive equivalents of goals. As for assessment, its first role is to probe the extent to which instruction is successful in achieving course goals, and should student performances fall short, the second role of assessment is to act as an early warning to indicate that some revision in teaching approach may be needed. Finally, the third role of assessment is the means by which students receive feedback regarding the adequacy of their progress toward course goals. Assessment lies at the core of all good teaching and successful learning.

Well – that's the theory, anyway. But the reality is often quite different. Goal attainment can come to grief when assessment concerns override everything else – even goals themselves, since it is *grade* attainment, not necessarily *goal* attainment on which many students fixate. As our research has shown, students are rarely guided in their studies by course goals, which for many of them remain mere abstractions. It is grades that count. This much can be deduced from self-worth theory, which argues that for many students their sense of worth is held captive by grades.

This reality confronts instructors with a special problem. Everything we know about the process of learning indicates that it is a wholly natural, essentially automatic human survival response, whereas probing what students have learned – or in reality, what they have *not* learned – raises the threatening specter of falling short as a person. Such fear is the basic mechanism that drives anger, self-doubts, and in particular test anxiety, a topic we will shortly take up once again. Yet, assessment is indispensable to efficient learning, let alone effective learning. If students are mistaken in their understanding of subject matter material or have missed the point of a lecture, they need to know. Learning flounders without feedback. At the same time, instructors need feedback regarding student progress in order to adjust their teaching so it may become more effective.

If instruction and assessment are two sides of the same coin, then assessment is the worrisome side. In this chapter, we will rethink our methods of assessment in an attempt to lift the burden of fear that can otherwise cripple, if not destroy, this indispensable partnership. Among other things, this means that testing needs to be made more fair and transparent in the eyes of students, yet still retain the validity of its function, that is, to provide an accurate evaluation of the standing and progress of students. But before attempting to reconcile the role of assessment with self-worth concerns, we will begin by addressing two questions vital to the mission of instruction: first, what is worth teaching, and second, how we can best organize instruction around a problem-focused approach.

## THE CONTENT OF CHANGE:
### THE EXPERT/NOVICE DISTINCTION

What kinds of changes in students do we hope to promote? Our short answer is to assist students to grow apace from initially being novice problem solvers to becoming experts and shedding their dependency on authority so that they may become independent, self-assured learners and take intrinsic pleasure in their discoveries. But to what guidelines should we appeal in order that these objectives might be achieved? In effect, of what should a problem-solving curriculum consist? Basically, our favored strategy is to assist students to internalize the ways that expert problem solvers differ from novices. An important aspect of these differences requires an analysis of what makes problem solving so difficult, a lamentable fact underscored by the truism that "for every problem there is a neat, plain solution – and it is always wrong!" This is only one of the many observations that make up "Murphy's Laws," which comprises a user's manual of what not to do when dealing with an unpredictable world of maddening perversity, nasty surprises, and unintended consequences. What, then, are the likely missteps or mental traps in problem solving to be avoided, and the common confusions that keep Murphy's Laws from being repealed? The answers to these questions need to become part of the curriculum.

One strategy is to appeal to the extensive research on the differences in the ways that experts differ from novices in their approaches to problem solving. What do we know about these differences, and how might this information aid in the development of problem-oriented courses? To begin, it is obvious that expert thinkers solve problems quicker, with apparently greater ease, and offer better, more sophisticated solutions than does the novice. But why should this be? First of all, it appears that we cannot define expert status simply by the number of years an individual has been in practice. Although it is true that people typically get better at problem solving with experience, there is a point beyond which sheer experience adds little to one's level of expertise, an observation under-scored by the fact that there remains considerable variations in the quality of thought among long-time professionals in every field. So it is not simply experience alone that makes the expert. What else is at work? Following are some of the generalizations that can be gleaned from the literature that addresses this question.

## Processing Information

To start with the obvious, experts simply possess more relevant facts and information than does the novice. Clearly, as just noted, mere exposure to a field counts for a lot. Yet information alone – even lots of it – is insuffi-cient in itself. The key to sufficiency is the availability of information in working memory. Information is held in memory differently by experts (Larkin et al., 1980). For experts, memory is indexed and stored according to categories that are best represented as files. For the novice, these files are as yet ill-formed or even nonexistent, leading to a potentially chaotic jumble of bits and pieces of information floating free of anchor points.

## Self-Monitoring

Experts are guided in their thinking by a complex system of self-conscious monitoring of their progress toward solutions. As already noted in Chapter 6, this monitoring function is part of a broader constellation of cognitive assembly skills that we have referred to collectively as metacognitions (Carver & Scheier, 1986). Once a plan of action is initiated, it must be guided to a successful conclusion. As we have said earlier, self-monitoring is the internal gyroscope that keeps one's deliberations and decisions focused on a distant target. It is in the realm of cognitive self-regulation that some of the most profound differences reside between the expert and the novice.

## Not Knowing

One critical aspect of self-monitoring is the ability to recognize when there is insufficient information to solve a problem. But how do people know that they do not know something? How does such a void get identified? Not easily, of course, and the problem is compounded by the fact that problem solvers, especially the novice, tend to cling to the safety of what they already know rather than complicate their task by probing their ignorance. Beginning students are particularly vulnerable to this tendency when it comes to preparing for exams. They tend to rehearse what they do know, or think they know, rather than testing the limits of their knowledge. This tendency to over-rehearse what one already knows can lead to overly optimistic estimates about how well prepared they are and how much they actually know. In these cases, when students receive lower grades than expected, they are likely to blame the instructor or the test, or both, not their own inadequate grasp of the material. A related aspect of such limitations is the tendency of beginners to overestimate how well they can recall material after a delay in studying or how well they can perform in the anxiety-arousing context of actual testing, a condition that is quite different from rehearsing material in the study hall.

The effectiveness of self-monitoring is also compromised by the tendency of beginners to be more concerned with achieving solutions quickly, which means they frequently fail initially to formulate the problem in workable terms, despite the well-known dictum: "A problem well defined is half solved." The advantage of a thoughtful approach to problems is lost when the novice pushes ahead, often relying blindly on strategies that have worked before in superficially similar circumstances but do not work now (see Chapter 3). When previously successful strategies no longer suffice, a kind of mental paralysis can set in. The novice simply does not know what to do next. If mental work is uncomfortable, as in the case of someone feeling unprepared or confused, then the tendency is to exit the situation as soon as possible. Early exiting can also be explained by the cult of efficiency that pervades our society. Americans are known for their ability to get the job done, quickly and on time. Efficiency and its partner, speed, can easily become the highest priority. Finally, impatience is also likely driven by a misguided set of beliefs about the nature of knowledge itself. As has already been pointed out, students often view knowledge as fixed and unchangeable, with the result that problem solving may be thought to consist of little more than the application of straightforward, formulaic strategies. Whatever the causes, premature leave-taking is well documented. For instance, when students are allowed to control the amount of feedback provided them, they often exit instruction before mastering the material (Butler & Winne, 1995; Steinberg, 1989).

## The Forward-Reaching Legacy of Fear

Finally, at last, we can report something that the novice typically possesses in abundance. But, unfortunately, it is too much of a bad thing: the fear of being found out as incompetent. We have spent the better part of several chapters considering the self-worth dynamics associated with both learners and teachers. Little more need be said about these issues here except to remark that all the self-regulatory deficiencies just mentioned are most likely to be found among those students we have identified as failure-threatened. What causes these deficits is an absence of what Corno (1993) calls motivational and emotional control strategies. These strategies are helpful in managing negative emotions such as guilt and remorse, especially in those situations in which students judge their efforts to be hopelessly ineffectual or their progress too slow, and thus are likely to set lesser goals or to opt out completely.

### INSTRUCTIONAL PARADIGMS

A second question asks what principles should organize improvements in problem-solving proficiency. We suggest it is the infrastructure of the capstone problems themselves that define a given field of inquiry that should guide the organization of problem-solving instruction. Problem-solving paradigms differ widely, depending on the discipline. Some fields such as the humanities, and the social and political sciences, often deal with problems best described in *spiral* terms, where instruction involves reexamining issues on a repeated basis so that students are led to find deeper and successively more profound meaning on each reconsideration of, say, the Bill of Rights or of Shakespeare's Hamlet. In other fields of inquiry, instruction is best thought of as preparing students to become better able to solve increasingly more complex problems in a kind of *hierarchical* progression, with success at each progressive level of difficulty depending on the thoroughgoing mastery of all prior levels. This paradigm is largely true for the fields of mathematics, statistics, and the physical sciences. Instructional paradigms should make common cause with the distinctive problem-solving structures of a given discipline. We can explore four distinct paradigms that are compatible with our problem-centered focus.

### Spiral and Hierarchical Structures

As just mentioned, instructors can convey a problem-solving perspective by means of a spiral lesson plan – spiral in that the same or similar problems are reintroduced over the course of time. With each reexamination, the problem is solved anew, but with increasing sophistication, depending on the knowledge that has accumulated between problem-solving opportunities. Among our three case studies, this organizational strategy is well exemplified by the Spanish literature course in which the instructor plans to assign students the task of tracking progressive changes in an ancient manuscript from its origins in the Spanish medieval period down to the present day. In order to guide her students through this task of philological sleuthing, she plans to illustrate this scholarly process by introducing via a lecture/discussion format four classic case studies, one at a time, in a serial fashion. The first sample study represents the simplest "barebones" case, intended to provide students with an overall snapshot of the entire philological process. Within the context of a spiral-like structure, each subsequent case study introduces more complexities and difficulties of the kinds typically faced by professional philologists, many of which will soon confront students in their own work, such as the availability of only fragments of damaged manuscripts, the omission of pages from manuscripts, and the illegibility of texts. Along the way, strategies for dealing with these shortfalls will be presented. Also, training in unraveling ambiguities in data will be presented along with the introduction of more complex search engines for information gathering.

Hierarchical structures share much in common with a spiral approach. Both involve the acquisition of problem-solving tools in the face of increasing complexity. Material presented at each step in hierarchical structures is considered foundational "building blocks" for understanding subsequent steps. The main difference between the two instructional paradigms is that spiral procedures tend to focus on discovering increasing complexities within the same or similar problems, whereas a hierarchical approach not only deals with increasing complexity but also typically considers an increasingly wider arc of problems.

The motivational advantages of both approaches are several. First, in the case of the spiral paradigm, by returning repeatedly to the same problem students automatically gain an appreciation of their own conceptual growth, and recognize that although day-to-day improvements are rarely obvious, they do accumulate and lead eventually to entirely new forms of thought and perspective. The same sense of improvement can occur with a hierarchical paradigm, not within the context of the same problem, but in the capacity to solve more complex problems. In Chapter 4 we documented the motivational advantages that come from experiencing a sense of growing conceptual sophistication and skill improvement, and how this source of motivation can be directly introduced into the curriculum.

Second, these gains in competency are tied directly to one's own problem-solving efforts that strengthen the perceived linkage between effort and outcome. Gaining a sense of personal control over one's learning is critical for a positive interpretation of effort expenditure. As we know, trying hard can be a potential threat to one's sense of worth, especially if one tries hard and fails anyway. But if one's efforts produce improved competence, then effort becomes valued in its own right, and less likely to be overcome by the fear of failing (Covington, 2001).

## Chronological Structures

If instructors view the problem under investigation as occurring in phases, or amenable to being broken down conceptually into stages or time periods, then the course will likely be arranged in sequential or chronological terms. Here instruction will typically follow the flow of time from the first or early events to later or last events in an effort to discover how factors or events at a prior time contribute to and shape subsequent events. Our case study exemplar here is the proposed developmental psychology case study. As we recall, the central challenge of this project involves students acting as psychological consultants in an effort to help their fantasy child thread their way through a series of childhood and early adolescent crises (Chapter 5).

In this particular example, any one of the childhood crises taken alone may be no more difficult to solve than any other. But what makes the problem-solving demands greater here as one proceeds is that the solutions chosen for a prior problem may restrict one's freedom of action when it comes to solving successive future problems. Recall this same challenging dynamic at work in the case of *The Floating Admiral* (Chapter 5). What makes this case study example so powerful is that it not only provides a way to introduce students to the demands of increasingly complex mental challenges but also reinforces the widely applicable observation by Peter Drucker, that "Long-term planning does not deal with future decisions, but with the future of present decisions."

## Means-Ends Structures

One of the least appreciated, yet among the most important, problem paradigms involves developing a plan of action to achieve a goal or an end state that can be reasonably well specified from the outset, or at least an ideal goal envisioned in advance. By contrast, for most problems, typically the end state is unknown and its solution requires a plan of action. But in this category of problems, the plan *is* the solution! This is the kind of problem that union/management representatives face as they negotiate a new labor contract. Each side brings an initial strategy, or plan, to the table, designed to achieve an ideal outcome – a plan that consists of an opening position as well as bargaining points and, if required, fallback positions. And although each side has an ideal outcome in mind from the beginning, they are well aware that reaching a final agreement will involve mutual concessions, accommodations, and, ultimately, perhaps even cooperation.

This problem-solving paradigm is referred to as a *means-ends analysis* (Simon, 1973; 1980), because the plan of action must have the potential to reduce progressively the differences between an initially undesirable or neutral state of affairs and a final, desirable, or at least acceptable, end-state; in effect, the end is specified, but the means to that end are not. This problem type is appropriate to any situation in which the constraints or conditions of the end-product can be reasonably specified in advance, especially tangible products of the kinds that, for example, challenge the imagination of engineering students who are given the task of designing a one-passenger solar-powered vehicle weighing no more than 200 pounds that can sustain speeds of 20 miles per hour for a minimum of two hours. Students in film studies courses face the same "means-ends" demands when a cinema instructor challenges them to portray various emotional attributes – say, suspicion, dread, or a sense of wonder – in visual terms using various cinematic tools including lighting, music, staging, and film editing. And it will not escape the notice of readers that the designing of college courses is also essentially an exercise in means-ends-analysis. The hoped-for results at the end of a school term can be imagined, but not necessarily the journey to achieve them.

Our three case study participants are envisioning courses of sufficient complexity that they will likely find that no one paradigm can represent their intentions completely. Perhaps it is our neurophysiologist (Neurophysiology 195) who anticipates the most complex mixture of these paradigms. She anticipates (not surprisingly) that a *chronological* structure would likely be the dominant instructional paradigm, since the downstream partnering of nerve cells is, by its very nature, a time-ordered process (on a scale of milliseconds). Within the first several class meetings, she anticipates introducing a highly simplified time-ordered presentation of the entire nerve transmission process, from one nerve cell to the next. This is intended to provide an entry-level view of the entire conceptual/neural landscape that will be the focus of her course. During each class meeting, she plans to add various concepts that will allow students to create an increasingly sophisticated version of their own neural model.

The key subject matter constructs are "Action Potential" (the unitary electro/chemical signal used to relay information), "Synaptic Transmission" (the molecular process by which a nerve impulse is sent by one cell and received by another), and "Synaptic Plasticity" (how nerve cells modify the strength of their transmissions). It is anticipated that these constructs will be revisited many times, with each encounter leading to a deeper layer of complexity, thus introducing a *spiral* component to the overall instructional paradigm.

Finally, students will learn that neuroscience can also be arranged as a *hierarchical* discipline. Here too there are levels. In order for neuroscientists to achieve an understanding of neural communications as a complex system of time-ordered interlocking factors – chemical, electrical, and physical – they must understand the whole process at a circuit level, a process that in turn depends on a deeper foundational level in which nerve cells operate as a complex interplay of molecules.

This thematic progression from simple to complex inspired our instructor to envision a potential capstone project in which in the last few weeks of the semester, students individually or in groups would attempt to link their nerve transmission models together in various configurations (e.g., in series or in parallel) to recreate higher-order nervous system functioning such as the inhibition or the strengthening of impulses that is a neurological equivalent of the psychological phenomena of learning and forgetting.

## STEP 8: CREATING A TEACHING ASSIGNMENT

As a next step, seminar participants were asked to create a sample "building block" assignment that would foster the skills and understanding necessary for their students to successfully address their capstone projects. This assignment could take a variety of forms, ranging from simple homework activities to more demanding or protracted assignments. The creation of this assignment was aided by consulting a two-dimensional *instructional spreadsheet* (Figure 7.1). The horizontal dimension represents the time frame along which all teaching/learning experiences will be ordered. Participants were further directed to place their sample assignment somewhere along the horizontal time line, indicating its place in the overall instructional scaffolding. The second dimension consisting of vertically ordered entries reflects some of the considerations around which all assignments should be crafted. The topmost entry involves an analysis of the degree to which a particular assignment is likely, in the words of Walvoord and Anderson (2010), "to elicit the kinds of learning and understandings reflected in one's course goals." This amounts to the concept of *instructional validity*. The second entry concerns listing any key subject matter material necessary to complete the assignments. The third entry concerns instruction for any prerequisite cognitive skills and strategies. The fourth requirement calls for a listing of steps or activities (including readings) necessary to prepare students for the assignment.

Now let's consider the sample assignments created by each of our three case study participants and evaluate how they stack up against the spreadsheet requirements. We will focus our attention on the first entry featuring the issue of instructional validity, which is key to all other considerations.

### Neurophysiology 195: How Nerve Cells Communicate

Our neurophysiologist has created a prototype assignment which she plans to present several times throughout the semester. The purpose is to teach students to critique research articles in the field of neurophysiology that pertain to the capstone task. Repeating this assignment also provides practice for the upcoming final exam to assess the growth in her students' capacity for scientific reasoning. The final exam will consist of the same seven-part series of questions that will require an analysis of several research articles that are unknown to students in advance.

Two-Dimensional Instructional Space

| | Assignment #1<br>Week # ___ to # ___ | Assignment #2<br>Week # ___ to # ___ | Assignment #3<br>Week # ___ to # ___ | Assignment #4<br>Week # ___ to # ___ | Assignment #5<br>Week # ___ to # ___ | Assignment #6<br>Week # ___ to # ___ |
|---|---|---|---|---|---|---|
| Connection to Course Goals | | | | | | |
| Subject-matter Concepts Needed | | | | | | |
| Cognitive Skills Needed | | | | | | |
| Steps/Activities Needed to Prepare Students | | | | | | |
| | | | | | | |

FIGURE 7.1 Two-Dimensional Instructional Space

"Choose one of the following research articles, all of which pertain to this week's topic of 'Action Potential.' Read the article carefully, and summarize in your own words responses to the following questions:

(1) What information was lacking in the field that this study aimed to address? In other words, what are the primary research questions that this study attempts to answer?
(2) What are the research methods used?
(3) What are the primary findings?
(4) What conclusions are drawn from the findings by the researchers?
(5) Imagine you are the principle investigator of this study. What additional research questions are triggered by this study that you might deem important enough as a next research step?
(6) How do the findings change or add to the development of your nerve transition model?
(7) BONUS QUESTION: What additional experiments or modifications of the present study might better address the researcher's questions. Also, are there any shortcomings or flaws in the study that would cast doubt on the credibility of the findings?"

### Analysis

Does this assignment "elicit the kinds of learning reflected in one's course goals?" The answer lies in the instructor's mission statement (Chapter 6): "To understand the mechanisms by which nerve cells reliably transmit information within a neural network, and to appreciate the scientific research process on which this understanding is based." Clearly, this practice assignment holds up well in eliciting the kinds of skills and conceptual learning needed to achieve her course goals, particularly those related to becoming a knowledgeable consumer of scientific research. This assignment gets high ratings for instructional validity.

### Psychology 2: Childhood and Adolescent Development

Next, consider the fantasy child case study in which students offer guidance to the caretakers of a fantasy child when facing a series of crises (Chapter 5).

The proposed teaching assignment involves the second of six crises, and comes in three interlocking parts. First, students are called on to create an event that the fantasy child, who is now ten years old, will recall vividly as having happened several years earlier. The memory should be highly dramatic, either positive emotionally or traumatic, but – and, this is the central point of the exercise – the memory is false. The event in question never really happened!

Second, students are then directed to create a *plausible* theory to explain how this false memory might come about and was later recalled as real. Explanations should include two or more of the following psychological principles related to the dynamics of memory: misinformation effect; source amnesia; repression; mood congruence; motivated forgetting; flashbulb memory; and long-term memory.

Students are informed that their fantasy children reacted with indignation, if not anger, when the reality of their memory was challenged. Additionally, students are alerted to the fact that the parents/caretakers are afraid that firmly held, unjustifiable thoughts are sometimes considered symptoms of mental instability. They are confused and worried about what to do.

As to the third and final task, students will be asked to offer advice to the caretakers. Should they be concerned? Is the child lying? How should they handle the situation? Students are given an opportunity to list any questions whose answers are not included in the description of the problem that might help guide their advice. For example, a student might ask if the child had a history of telling innocent falsehoods as part of childhood games. As evidence, answers to such questions have clear relevance to the truth value of various theories, including the possibility of mental illness.

### *Analysis*

What are this instructor's learning objectives? The list of objectives (Chapter 6, Table 6.2) follows from his mission statement, which is "the ability to analyze human behavior in terms of sound psychological principles, and to understand how these explanations (theories) can be tested for their truth value, using rules of evidence and the methods of scientific inquiry" (Chapter 6, Table 6.1).

Although no single practice assignment can hope to touch all the bases in such a densely packed statement, nonetheless, we believe this assignment works particularly well for goal inclusion. The concept of theory building, which takes center stage in the mission statement, is well served by requiring students to create an explanation (theory) for the false memory using well-established psychological principles, particularly since it introduces the attribute of plausibility as an essential ingredient of any good theory. Moreover, the crux of the challenge of providing advice to caretakers turns on students judging the relative "truth value" of two competing explanations for the false memory. To the extent that the theory created by students' accounts for an otherwise bizarre behavior, it may reassure parents that this behavior is not the result of mental instability. Yet, the contrary interpretation of mental instability might prevail depending on various pieces of evidence that are unavailable unless students ask for them. Here the "rules of evidence" as part of the instructor's mission statement are featured, which include the need for students to ask questions in order to test theories. Finally, students are given ample opportunity to build their arguments for advising parents around a past/present/future perspective that has been identified previously as the meta-cognitive organizing strategy best suited to this capstone task.

Taken as a whole, the problem-solving activities featured in this assignment match up well with the proposed learning goals, thereby satisfying the requirements for instructional validity.

### Spanish 190: Early Textuality in Latin America

#### Analysis

Our philologist has chosen to create an assignment in which students develop a scoring rationale for grading their own work on the capstone task. It is not this student-centered emphasis that necessarily makes this proposed assignment unusual. After all, such student participation in designing their course is nothing new (Covington, 1992), and has proven quite effective, motivationally speaking, as demonstrated by our example (Chapter 6) in which one of the coauthors worked in collaboration with his students to create a course outline. Nor should the fact that students are helping create the very rules by which their work will be considered inappropriate. Rather, the intrigue derives from the fact that this is not a "building block" assignment on which the capstone task will be built, but rather the other way around. It is not the means to an end – quite literally, it *is* the end, embodying those conditions that will satisfy the requirements for effective learning championed by Black and William (2009), that is, providing students with the rules by which their work will be judged, thus allowing them to assess their own progress and to determine how they can improve. From this perspective, this assignment is the epitome of instructional validity!

#### SPREADSHEET BENEFITS

Several benefits are triggered by this spreadsheet exercise that apply to problem-focused teaching, irrespective of discipline or subject matter field.

First, limiting the spreadsheet exercise to the creation of just one teaching assignment proved particularly advantageous. Many of our seminar participants remark that all the empty columns on either side of their solitary entry was a stark reminder that the successful completion of any given assignment rests on the adequacy of all prior assignments in preparing the way, and in turn triggered speculation about the adequacy of their sample assignment as a productive building block for all future steps.

Second, the beginning and the end points of the course are made tangible by this exercise – the end point, by our reckoning, being the solving of a significant problem or the creation of a product of interest. Interestingly, this assignment qualifies as a sophisticated example of a means-ends analysis paradigm. Instructors must develop a teaching plan capable of eventually reducing the differences between novices and experts defined by an end state that can be reasonably well defined in advance. This involves course designers in thinking backwards from the end point as well as imagining themselves traveling in the complementary but opposite direction, that is, moving students from the beginning to the end of all things. It is along this bidirectional continuum that instructional decisions must link to and support course goals.

Instructors are not the only beneficiaries of a carefully crafted organizational structure. It benefits students as well, owing to the clarity of the instructor's teaching rationale and the clear linkage between direction and destination. Structure promotes self-assurance, the possibility of personal control over events, and the vision of a successful outcome. This is precisely why students should be made privy to the rationale and underlying structure of their courses right from the outset, and perhaps actually participating in the creation of the course goals as illustrated by our philologist.

Third, as the spreadsheet grid is being filled in, an instructor can look across the various rows of the grid and within columns, and quickly grasp the range of learning/study activities proposed, and the character and difficulty of the cognitive skills and subject matter material to be engaged. This confection of entries can be analyzed for several beneficial reasons. Collectively, the adequacy of these entries can be judged against departmental curricular requirements for coverage and for placement in the overall sequence of courses. Instructors can also better gauge the extent of the intellectual and time demands on students that are required by this total package, raising questions such as whether too much is being required of students given the limited instructional time and resources available. And is the likely tempo and rhythm of activities optimal to sustain student engagement? Better to make any kinds of adjustments called for by these inquires at the planning stage than after a course is under way.

## TEACHING PRODUCTIVE THINKING

We have relied heavily on the hierarchical model of thinking as a means to identify the skills of problem solving as well as to organize these cognitive assemblies into a useful top-down order. This same model can serve as a template for cataloging various instructional strategies for promoting content and procedural knowledge. It can also address the question of how instructors can combine the teaching of local, domain-specific knowledge with metacognitive sophistication in ways that favor intrinsic-task engagement and increases the chances for the transfer of one's learning to the future. The key to these benefits depends on providing assignments that are embedded in a larger problem-solving context, always linked to the tasks ahead, and, taking their purposeful place in the service of solutions, not left adrift or atomized for the doubtful reasons already critiqued.

### Ensuring Content and Procedural Knowledge

Subject matter content is the operating language of all productive thinking. From a problem-solving perspective, facts should be conceived as things to think *with*, not only things to think *about*. In effect, facts should be taught as problem-solving tools. Facts allow individuals to conduct many critical operations such as judging the scale and limits of a problem by reason of its factual constraints; facts can determine the feasibility as well as the desirability of proposed solutions; facts can arouse skepticism or relieve one's mind on some point, or even inspire awe as when we learn that there are as many galaxies in the universe as people on our planet!

Basically, facts should be introduced sparingly, only as needed, and then, most importantly, always associated with problem-solving activities. But before facts can be pressed into service, they must be acquired. How best can large volumes of facts be acquired in ways that allow for their ready availability from working memory? One instructional procedure well suited to answer this question is *mastery learning* (Burns, 1978; Kulik, Kulik, & Cohen, 1979).

### Mastery Learning

The term *mastery* implies "certification," that is, a skill, a concept, or a procedure acquired to a sufficient level of competency to get the job done. The wider meaning of mastery also includes a learning paradigm and an associated educational philosophy that at its most literal assumes that most students can eventually assimilate the basic lessons of schooling if (1) the learning objectives are couched in clear, unambiguous terms, and (2) students are given sufficient opportunities to learn through repeated study and testing, timely feedback, and adequate guidance (Born & Zlutnick, 1972).

The widest application of this formula is associated with "drill and practice" for learning relatively simple concepts and operations including acquisition of statistical notations and conventions and acquiring procedural skills, especially when precision is at a premium – say, being able to reliably reproduce the same results of a DNA analysis flawlessly. The mastery paradigm has proven unparalleled in its effectiveness for ensuring the acquisition of factual material and procedural fidelity (Born, Gledhill, & Davis, 1972; Kulik et al., 1979). Virtually all the research indicates that the acquisition of content and procedural knowledge is greater under a mastery paradigm than under conventional learning procedures where students typically move on to new material whether or not they have mastered earlier assignments. Not surprisingly, the superiority of the mastery paradigm is due to the extra practice and study afforded students who have yet to master the material (Covington, 1985a). Naturally, we would expect students who have additional study/test opportunities to retain more simply because they learned more to begin with.

However, the very effectiveness of the mastery learning paradigm sounds a cautionary note because if learning occurs in a rote-like fashion, it is not necessarily secure, and can remain largely useless. What appears to have been mastered may actually be unstable and fleeting in memory. This point was convincingly demonstrated in a mastery-paradigm study (Covington, 1985a) in which a group of students were required to score 95% of the answers correct on a multiple-choice test consisting of two kinds of items, one requiring rote recall of vocabulary definitions and the other requiring conceptual thought (i.e., the application of these same definitions to real-life situations). Students who failed on the first test try were allowed to take additional parallel forms of the test after further study. This study/test procedure was repeated until everyone achieved the 95% criterion. In effect, by the end of the acquisition phase of this study, everyone had mastered the material to the same level.

But what about retention of the material? Several months later, all the students were given an unannounced retention test over the previously learned material. The retention scores of those students who had satisfied the learning criterion on the first test try – dubbed the "fast learners" – were compared to the retention scores of those students who had taken several tests with extra study in order to achieve the same criterion – the "slow learners." On average, the slow learners recalled correctly just as many vocabulary definitions as did the fast learners. However, the slow learners were decidedly poorer at recognizing the correct conceptual applications, despite the fact that they had originally demonstrated a level of mastery on these items equal to that of the fast learners. So, adequate performances are no guarantee that learning has occurred, or at least not the same kind of learning. Here is what happened. The slow learners did what they do best, that is, they simply memorized the conceptual responses without necessarily understanding the deeper meaning of what they were learning, a laborious process that took them extra study. By merely over-learning the correct responses in a rote fashion, they appeared to have reached mastery. However, when learning is treated as a rote exercise, recall is less resistant to forgetting than when information is internalized and stored in meaningful ways, something that the fast learners appeared better able to do naturally.

This finding – a laboratory parable of sorts – adds an important cognitive addendum to our motivational assertion that everything about the quality of learning, that is, its generalizability and even it durability, depends on the reasons for learning. In short, motives trump everything – well, almost everything. As just noted, the study strategies one uses to learn are also a vital consideration, particularly with regard to the availability of knowledge in working memory as well as the flexibility and ingenuity with which knowledge is applied to good purpose over the long haul. If learning and performance are not always the same thing, then it also must be true that students can actually learn things well but cannot always demonstrate this fact on demand. Both these realities can potentially invalidate test results as accurate measures of achievement. More on this point shortly when we, once again, take up the topic of test anxiety.

## Enhancing Metacognitions

At the pinnacle of the problem-solving hierarchy stands metacognitive knowledge with its indispensable executive function. It controls the assembly of all cognitive processes at the strategic level – when to ask questions, which questions, and detecting the significance of answers.

How can instructors demonstrate the enormous intellectual power of metacognitive reasoning as well as provide meaningful practice opportunities for students to assemble their own thinking in systematic ways? Our classroom observations have convinced us that the single most effective answer is for instructors to create a climate of "cognitive apprenticeship" that allows students to model the thinking of real-life practitioners. This occurs when students witness their teaching mentors solving the kinds of problems *they* are expected to solve – and, in the ideal case, literally watching as the instructor or a GSI talk their way through a problem: musing about what makes it a problem, turning the problem inside and out, and viewing its fullness from various angles. We do not have in mind those instances in which such a thoughtful, reasoned intellectual struggle is replaced by a brief flash of insight followed by a flourish of chalk, resulting in the appearance – if by magic, of a formula on the blackboard, and ending with a dismissive smile of intellectual superiority. This may be going through the motions, but it is not the dance!

As an educational consultant in a large-enrollment introductory physics course, the senior author sat spellbound as the lecturer addressed the topic: "What to do, when you don't have a clue" or "but, there are three unknowns and only enough information to solve for two." Annoyed by this temporary inconvenience, the lecturer set out to solve for the third unknown. In that brief hour, one could gain a deep, intuitive sense and appreciation for the true nature of problem solving, of the importance of improvisational thought, the occasional benefits of circuitous reasoning, and the awesome power of logic – all orchestrated in sequential patterns of directed thought. It was a virtuoso performance. As the lecturer moved toward a solution, he even treated his students to an occasional misstep – deliberately, we all guessed – in which the journey was temporarily derailed, but to good effect. It was a delicious moment savored by every non-expert in the audience of 300 students – watching an admired professional stumble but eventually recover. At several points, he even solicited help from his audience. The rising pride for assisting an admired authority in his field was not lost on students in this interchange.

Providing an overview for students of the entire problem-solving process, from beginning to end, with all its warts and blemishes exposed, also allows instructors to give the lie to misleading beliefs about the intellectual enterprise. Take, for example, the widespread assumption among students that expert thinking is a quick and relatively effortless matter. To counter the notion of effortless thought, one English literature instructor treated his class to a series of PowerPoint projections, each showing the same page in one of his recently published scholarly articles. The first slide presented the final published text on the page in question, resplendent in all its formal typesetting and its pristine margins. Very impressive. Next, working backwards, he displayed the prior penultimate version of this same page covered with numerous editorial markings and corrections. And then came a still earlier version of the same page that had been critiqued by an outside reviewer with several nasty-looking question marks scrawled in the margins along with scribbled comments. Then came the next slide. By now the instructor's own computer typescript containing many typos had replaced the typesetter's formal work. This version was adorned with messy handwritten notes by the author reminding himself of some necessary changes. Somewhere along the way, as one slide replaced another, it became clear to the audience that they were descending deeper and deeper into the very processes of thought by which their instructor was crafting his final ideas out of initially vague but intriguing possibilities. Close to the end of the demonstration – or rather at the very birthing of ideas – the previously intact page gave way to notes scribbled in pencil on scraps of paper. The back of an envelope also appeared with brown stains at one edge – obviously coffee spilled during a late-night session! A painstaking, and at times painful, process was being revealed. No student left that lecture hall without a deeper appreciation of what it takes to create intellectual and scholarly products worthy of the marketplace of ideas. It takes a lot of work, and for this reason the process is anything but efficient!

In summary, what each of these demonstrations conveyed is an invitation for students to enter into a community of practitioners. Most professional occupations, including medicine and law, are taught largely through a process of apprenticeship. For example, consider the fast-track formula for the making of a surgeon: "Watch one (operation); do one; teach one!" (Do not try this at home.) Graduate students in the sciences and in the humanities hone their research and scholarly skills largely by apprenticing to senior researchers who themselves are working on authentic problems that require the resolution of ill-defined issues or the clarification of controversy. These students eventually become authentic practitioners themselves, which is to say, expert thinkers. It is our view that to the extent this same process of apprenticeship can be replicated among undergraduates, the chances improve that these young adults will also eventually become expert thinkers.

The seemingly effortless, virtuoso performance of our physics professor depends on a vast repertoire of cognitive resources arranged in a hierarchical structure of knowledge controlled by an overall executive function whose purpose is to create plans of action that determine how, when, and in what order procedural and content knowledge is purposely assembled. Above all, plans of action are the key to effective problem solving, perhaps second only to wisdom, which, when reduced to *its* essence, is but a synonym for planfulness; in other words, wisdom is "knowing what to do next." In a student-centered learning environment, students evolve as proxy planners through experience, not all at once, of course, but in time, which depends on guided practice provided by instructors as well as peers. And, we now know from experiments of the kind described in Chapter 5, exposure to the scientific and scholarly world of independent thought and exploration can profitably begin in truly authentic ways at least as early as the beginning college years, if not earlier.

## THE INSTRUCTIONAL/ASSESSMENT CYCLE

Being made aware of what one has not learned can be as natural a process as is learning itself. But the reality is often far different. Such disclosures rarely occur in a positive or even a neutral context. This much is clear from a self-worth perspective. Evaluation is feared when the possibility of failure becomes the measure by which one is judged as a person rather than when evaluation is treated as a source of information for how to improve. We have argued that the linkage between performance and worth is in large part due to competition – a process in which the chances for success are often overshadowed by the greater likelihood of failure, since competition typically produces few winners. And ironically, in a competitive environment, even improved performance can count for little, because as one improves, so do others, which does nothing to change one's relative standing in the group. Losers remain losers despite improving. Competition puts virtually everyone perpetually behind the curve. And, as we have noted earlier, even the winners can pay the price of continuing self-doubt while experiencing guilt at having denied success to others.

Even with all this, competition with its relentless odds against succeeding is not the only villain. Fear also comes from simply not knowing where one stands and what counts as excellence. The basic requirement for offsetting this source of anxiety lies in the kinds of feedback provided to students that, according to the analysis of Black and William (2009), consists of three elements: (1) students need to know the measures by which they will be judged; (2) they need to know where they stand on these measures; and (3) students need to know how they can improve.

## PRIMARY TRAIT ANALYSIS

Let's take up the first two of these requirements offered by Black and Williams: providing students with the criteria by which their work will be judged and where they stand. The most frequently used system for creating such criteria is referred to as *Primary Trait Analysis* (Lloyd-Jones, 1977). This technique can be applied to evaluate virtually any activities or assignments including term papers, quizzes, and class participation as well as oral presentations.

### STEP 9: CONDUCTING A PRIMARY TRAIT ANALYSIS

Earlier in this chapter, each of our three case study designers created a sample teaching assignment intended to strengthen the skills or traits thought to advance their course goals. As a next step, they will establish a set of benchmarks or criteria (sometimes called *rubrics*) for scoring the quality of student work on these assignments. Now consider how these three different examples might unfold.

### NEUROPHYSIOLOGY 195: HOW NERVE CELLS COMMUNICATE

As you may recall, the sample assignment created by our neurophysiologist consisted of a series of seven questions requiring an analysis of research articles for practice in preparation for the final exam. Consider Question 7, which concerns the primary trait of "ingenuity of scientific thinking," which is one of the main course goals. The question calls on students either to modify an existing research study or to offer a better alternative design to address the researcher's inquiry.

How might our instructor extract information from student responses that reliably reflects the ingenuity of their thinking? To begin, she ranks a sample of student responses from the least ingenious suggestions to the most ingenious. Suggestions that merely improve a research project will receive the fewest grade credits, while ideas for entirely restructuring a project will receive the most credits on the premise that reframing proposals is the greater mark of ingenuity. Examples of simple modifications might include proposing marginal improvements to an already adequate research design such as simply increasing the sample size, while higher-ranked suggestions would involve major overhauls or novel approaches. These might include creating a simpler, more streamlined procedure, rendering the research more cost effective, minimizing time demands on subjects, or increasing the ease of data collection. Naturally, any recasting of the original research design, no matter how ingenious, that loses sight of the initial research question would receive no credit.

Although our instructor plans to highlight ingenuity of thought as a primary attribute, she might decide to combine the credits given for this dimension with the accumulating credits given for answering all of the remaining questions. In her judgment, this grand total may reflect a deeper overall understanding of the scientific process than might otherwise be detected by considering individual answers alone, on the theory that, as the saying goes, "The whole is more than the sum of the parts."

### PSYCHOLOGY 2: CHILDHOOD AND ADOLESCENT DEVELOPMENT

Earlier, we analyzed the "false memory" teaching assignment for its goal-driven qualities and pronounced it well designed in terms of instructional validity. Recall that, as part of the assignment, students were asked to offer advice to parents regarding how they might best respond to the fantasy child's insistence that a memory reflected actual events, when in fact these events were known never to have occurred. How might our psychology instructor go about crafting a rationale for assessing the quality of student advice?

In this example, the task of creating a scoring schema is a group enterprise consisting of the instructor and the GSIs assigned to his course. This arrangement permits grading by the same personnel who created the scoring schema.

To begin, the instructor suggests two basic criteria or rubrics for judging the quality of student advice. First, he believes that in order to receive grade credits, students must recognize the basic dilemma that drives the fear expressed by the parents and on which the advice should ultimately focus, that is, deciding which of two theories is most persuasive or plausible for explaining the causes of the fantasy child's false memory – either a theory of mental instability or the result of an admittedly unnerving, yet not uncommon, natural occurrence that can be accounted for by appealing to well-known psychological principles. One way to decide between the theories is for students to seek information not available to them unless they had asked for it. For example, they might ask if actual events were mixed in with the falsehoods. Answers to such questions are clearly relevant to the plausibility of both theories. For this reason, the GSIs tentatively agreed that grade credit will be given for any questions students asked that could be reasonably construed as bearing on the larger issue of which theory was the most plausible explanation for the false memory. The number of such questions asked would become a proxy for whether or not students satisfied the learning goal of "seeking information necessary to test theories" (Table 6.2, Chapter 6).

Second, the instructor also argues that the quality of the reasoning behind the advice to parents will also depend on students placing this false memory episode in a larger systematic context reflecting the dictum that the "past controls the present, and the present controls the future." For example, well-prepared students are likely to ask themselves what is it about past events that may give weight to a theory of mental instability or favors a more benign explanation. Questions implying a perspective of reaching back into the past might include asking whether or not there were previous false memory episodes. Thinking that implies a future-orientation might include considering the possible consequences for the child's well-being if this episode was wrongly labeled by parents as the result of mental instability.

After receiving these broad directives from the instructor, the GSIs begin creating a scoring rationale for the learning objectives listed in Chapter 6 (Table 6.2). For starters, we just witnessed their reasoning when it came to judging how well students had learned to gather evidence to test theories – in this case, by asking pertinent questions. Next, the GSIs establish grading criteria for the remaining learning objectives, such as making plausible use of psychological principles. Once the group has a tentative overall scoring rationale in mind, each GSI scores a set of the same student essays. Any substantial differences in scoring among the raters triggers discussions about the causes for the disagreements that may lead to revisions in the scoring criteria, such as expanding a scoring category so that previously undetected nuances in student thinking can be accommodated. However, even with such safeguards, raters inevitably differ somewhat in their scoring of individual essays, because there is always some ambiguity in interpreting any given set of scoring rules. Yet the magnitude of such differences can be limited by the procedures being illustrated in this example.

Taking a further step, the GSIs then proceed to read another small sample of essays using their emerging scoring rationale. Any substantial differences in scoring are again discussed, and more adjustments are made to further sharpen the scoring guidelines. This cyclical process can be repeated until acceptable levels of inter-rater agreement (i.e., test reliability) are reached. Eventually, an overall scoring rationale emerges, which, by mutual agreement, adequately reflects various levels of mastery of the learning objectives (i.e., test validity) and also is sufficiently justifiable and transparent in its logic to withstand the scrutiny of students and instill a sense of fairness.

## SPANISH 190: EARLY TEXTUALITY IN LATIN AMERICA

Recall that Spanish literature majors were challenged to trace changes (e.g., distortions) in the translations of precolonial Latin manuscripts from their origins centuries ago down to the present. As we know, the instructor and her students had already set out to develop a scoring rationale for grading work on this capstone task. They started by identifying the central traits or attributes they believe characterize thinking like a professional philologist. They chose to focus on three attributes: *Ambition, Accuracy,* and *Completeness.* Let's consider what they meant by Ambition, which, it was decided after some discussion, referred to the extent to which students choose to take on the widest, most comprehensive sweep of historical analysis. For our instructor, this required students to go beyond merely satisfying her minimal requirements, first by entertaining more than two different versions of the manuscript of their choice and, second, by choosing versions that maximized the time interval between versions. The more time that elapsed, the more complex and inclusive descriptions of changes would be required, for which students would be eligible for more grade credits. Third, the older the origins of the manuscript, the better – venerability being a factor in receiving extra grade credits because of the more challenging obstacles to interpretation (e.g., availability of only fragmentary material).

The notion of minimums has special significance for us because it is central to the rationale for our proposed approach to grading policy in general (Chapter 6). To recall, this involves a two-stage formula: The better the grades to which students aspire, (1) "the *more* they must do and (2) the *better* they must do it." For example, more specifically, when students only satisfy minimums and little more, either in terms of the amount of work undertaken or of the quality of the work demanded, they might earn, say, only a baseline letter grade of C, which is satisfactory but scarcely memorable. As applied to this particular situation, the *more* that students do becomes a marker for the primary trait of Ambition. The simplest measure of this attribute merely involves counting the number of versions of a manuscript investigated by students beyond the two required, with the possibility of assigning extra grade credits proportional to the extent students choose versions beyond the minimum. A more nuanced assessment might also take into account not merely the number of versions entertained by students but also give some recognition given to the accessibility of each version and the physical condition of the material that relates to the age of the original document. The same "counting" procedure can also be applied to the time interval criterion by assigning credits to the number of years or decades between versions chosen for analysis. Clearly, mere "counting" is the simplest and likely the most reliable of criteria.

But there is a trade-off here. The more ambitious a project becomes in terms of scope and complexity, the more difficult it will be to achieve complete coverage of events and to avoid leaving significant gaps in one's analyses of change. In effect, students may be savaged by the requirements of the other two primary traits, Completeness and Accuracy, which brings us to the second phase of our two-stage formula for judging excellence – that is, doing things better. Obviously, providing more is not necessarily synonymous with doing better. In fact, in this case, the relationship between more and better is likely to be inverse, with the possibilities for achieving accuracy becoming less likely the more ambitious the task. However, at least, this trade-off would provide an opportunity for giving extra grade credits on those infrequent but noteworthy occasions where Ambition, Completeness, and Accuracy all work in tandem for positive effect.

By unpacking this capstone task in terms of its cognitive demands, it was further recognized that the key to doing *better* was that students, like professionals, must hold two interactive perspectives in mind simultaneously – diachronic (the trajectory of a text through time) and synchronic (a "snapshot" of a text at a particular moment). In order to achieve an effective balance, various metacognitive skills must be exercised. Most critical here is the ability to detect changing patterns over time, say, in cultural norms or in styles of rhetoric as well as recognizing political agendas reflected in a text when they are used for purposes of propaganda. Once trends are detected, then properly interpreting them becomes critical. Achieving this level of problem-solving sophistication is the gateway to becoming an expert philologist. It was for this reason that a group consensus formed around a proposal that recognition of changing patterns over time with an accompanying analysis of their significance would receive proportionally greater grade weighting than other problem-solving tactics.

So far, all three case study participants have adopted an analytic approach to Primary Trait Analysis – analytic, because each dimension or trait can be considered separately, independent of any others. An alternative strategy is the *wholistic* approach, which considers the quality of work as a whole. Here only one score is assigned to a student's work on an entire task. This approach is especially helpful when the dimensions one wants to assess cannot be easily analyzed and scored as separate elements.

This does not mean that wholistic scoring proceeds without some basis for judgment. For example, our philologist might still judge student performances in terms of the kinds of criteria discussed here. But rather than simply awarding credit explicitly to each dimension and adding all the credits together, she would consider the entirety of student work in terms of what it reveals collectively about the students' overall grasp of the capstone project. In Chapter 8, we will discover that a wholistic approach also aids in creating a rationale for assigning final course grades.

## A CRITIQUE AND ANALYSIS

As an evaluation technique, Primary Trait Analysis may appear to some as overly meticulous, even mechanical. As one exasperated faculty colleague put it, "I don't believe in rubrics!" Unfortunately, we never learned what he did believe in when it came to evaluating complex intellectual products and in such a manner that students could extract the information that satisfies Black and Williams's requirements for feedback. Nonetheless, despite our colleague's frustration, whether one calls them rubrics, rules, or scoring strategies, in the final analysis the quality of intellectual work is *always* assessed by some kind of decision rules. To the extent that these rules can be made public as well as subject to the general agreement of experts – hence becoming both valid and reliable – their availability satisfies the essence of the first two ingredients of Black and Williams's recipe: that students know the measures by which they will be judged; and they know where they stand on these measures.

Yet, we share the exasperation of our colleague in one important respect. No set of scoring rubrics, no matter how detailed or comprehensive, can ever capture the entire meaning of what it means to generate "elegant" or "creative" solutions in any discipline. Elegance and creativity are concepts always in evolution. Some attributes of creative thinking have been proposed – novelty of thought among them – and are capable of being scaled (Covington, 2014). But in the end, they too fail to do full justice to the province of creative expression. To attempt to define creativity exclusively in terms of formal, behavioral criteria in hopes that its attributes can be reliably and objectively measured endangers the very qualities we hope to honor. Yet at the same time, we must avoid evaluating quality as essentially an undisciplined, blanket application of the assertion that "I know it when I see it!"

Naturally, teachers seek to arrange educational experiences to encourage those attributes that ultimately define "excellence." Happily, creativity and other valued qualities such as intellectual curiosity are likely to emerge spontaneously – however we care to define them, whenever one's reasons for learning are positive and the fear of failure is minimized. Primary Trait Analysis encourages such a learning climate because it involves establishing absolute, merit-based standards.

Several additional benefits derive from the application of the assessment strategies inherent in Primary Trait Analysis. They relate broadly to the motivational value of clarity and connectedness within the instructional process. First, and most obviously, the system involves the development of reasonably clear, transparent assessment that allows students to forge a closer fit between their studies and the goals they are expected to pursue, making it less likely that they will waste time chasing irrelevancies that, given their often unpracticed eye, may otherwise dominate their thinking.

Second, by making criteria explicit, students can begin the task of internalizing the standards of excellence in thought and action that define any field of inquiry. Like the chess masters described in Chapter 6, it is generally the case that all neophyte problem solvers will gradually accumulate a body of knowledge around a set of rules, conventions, and expectations that will replace undisciplined thought and eventually allow students to approach the realm of intuitive functioning. There is likely no better way to set the novice solidly on the path toward expert status than to begin the struggle early on to define excellence of thought in any field, nor any better antidote to the passive mind-set that hobbles many students. Moreover, the quicker educators sweep away the insufficient intellectual compass of the novice, the sooner they will be rid of the vexing accusation by students of unfairness in testing on which we commented in earlier chapters. As long as students fail to grasp the overall logic of the measures by which their progress is marked or fail to achieve a coherent overview of their discipline, they will naturally take exception to what they may mistakenly assume are "tricky" tests, or what they assail as apparently "make-work" assignments – and, worse yet, perhaps conclude that such "unfairness" is intentional.

## ASSESSING PRODUCTIVE THINKING

Now, what can be said about reframing assessment from a problem-focused perspective? The best starting point is to recall our proposed hierarchical problem-solving model (Chapter 6). Why not locate assessment strategies within its structure in ways that coordinate both teaching and testing? For example, if facts are best thought of as problem-solving tools, then it is the student's understanding of this tool-like function that should be the main focus of assessment, not merely providing evidence that students have dutifully memorized facts and figures. And if it is the quality of higher-order cognitive assembly that ultimately determines the effectiveness of problem solving, then it is this metacognitive function that should be the ultimate focus of assessment.

And what are the motivational advantages of a problem-focused approach to assessment? If test anxiety reflects the fear of failing, then self-worth theory discloses the single most threatening aspect of traditional testing that often goes unappreciated. The goal of most traditional testing is essentially negative: to reveal what students don't know rather than what they do know, an observation we have on the authority of none other than the most celebrated of all school failures – Winston Churchill (1923, p. 156):

> These examinations were a great trial to me. The subjects which were the dearest to the examiners were almost invariably those I fancied least ... I should have liked to be asked to say what I know. They always tried to ask what I did not know. When I would have willingly displayed my knowledge, they sought to expose my ignorance. This sort of treatment had only one result: I did not do well in examinations.

Obviously, trying to reveal one's ignorance was not only seen by Churchill as an ignoble pursuit; it also smacked of deception. There is little comfort here for students racked by test anxiety. The assessment procedures we favor turn the tables on Churchill's presumed tormentors regarding the calculus of testing by inviting students to tell teachers what they *do* know, and we would add – of equal importance, giving students ample opportunity to craft their knowledge into coherent responses to significant questions given to them in advance of testing. Before proceeding further with this line of argument, it is critical that we point out that soliciting what students know as our preferred assessment strategy is not intended as the exclusive means for probing their knowledge base. It is as important that students become aware of what they don't know and still have to learn or unlearn, as it is to assess their already secure knowledge. Our point is that special care need be taken so that "ignorance exposed" – in Churchill's words – doesn't imply worthlessness, an ever-present danger according to self-worth theory. What is at stake here is how testing affects student expectations about their own future successes and failures when it comes to learning. These expectations depend to a great extent on how students construe the seemingly perpetual yet natural state of ignorance that characterizes the novice.

In many respects, revealing one's ignorance versus recognizing one's knowledge comes down to the proverbial question of "whether the glass is half empty or half full," and to the motivational implications of this distinction. Psychologically, a vision of becoming "fuller" is a positive, success-oriented motivator, whereas remaining "empty" is potentially debilitating. In this connection, we know that expectations of future successes can be influenced positively by altering a person's mood state. Practically speaking, this means directing students to attend to the positive rather than to the negative aspects of a stressful event, an intriguing premise tested by Sarason and Potter (1983) who encouraged a group of Coast Guard Academy recruits to record only positive experiences (e.g., learning new things) in a daily diary during boot camp. Compared to control cadets, who either recorded negative events or kept no diaries at all, the "positive-event" group experienced greater personal satisfaction, felt less tension during this stressful period, and were less likely to resign from the Academy at the end of boot camp. The results of this study suggest a twofold strategy for encouraging effective learning: on the one hand, focusing attention on one's successes and on the positive consequences of goal attainment, while on the other hand, correcting errors with as little psychological cost as possible. We have already made this latter point by reference to a classic learning paradigm for cost-free recovery from making errors and mistakes in the form of mastery learning. The rationale here is simple: There is no grade penalty for errors except the additional study time needed to correct them. And as to the more general point, we know from evidence introduced in Chapter 4 that self-acknowledged skill improvement – moving from ignorance to understanding – is one of the most powerful of all positive motivators.

What we know about the psychological and educational benefits of shifting the emphasis of assessment from identifying one's ignorance to that of tapping into one's knowledge base comes largely from laboratory studies that have explored this shift using the technique of *customized testing*.

## Customized Testing

Customized testing involves presenting students with a testing procedure designed to fit the particular knowledge base of the examinees (Weiss, 1983). Test items of known difficulty are administered sequentially to students, typically by computer. When examinees fail a given item, a less difficult item is presented next, until, through this procedure, a set of correctly answered questions emerge that provide an estimate of the upper bounds of the individual's knowledge. Psychologically, this amounts to a zone of self-perceived competency where one's knowledge is secure. Starting from this arena of safety, students can renew their studies to further expand the boundaries of their knowledge base. Although ignorance, in the form of inevitable errors and mistakes, lurks just beyond the outer edges of these boundaries, it is less of a personal threat given the presence of a platform of confirmed knowledge.

The most interesting variation on this procedure is customized self-administered testing (Rocklin & O'Donnell, 1986). Here the individual, not a computer, chooses the next item from several levels of difficulty. Such self-testing produces higher achievement scores than occur for students who are administered the same kinds of items in a standard test format. The positive mechanism operating here is likely revealed by related research studies in which students performed better when they had a choice of several practice tests than when they had no choice (Kuhl & Blankenship, 1979). Having some control over the manner of one's testing appears to have a highly salutary effect. As to the issue of test anxiety, it appears that anxiety influences only the choice of difficulty level of the first items selected by subjects for testing. Far easier items are initially selected by anxious examinees compared to non-anxious control subjects. Other than this difference, anxiety levels predicted neither the rate of progress of students toward more difficult items nor the average difficulty of all the items chosen. In effect, self-administered testing appears to ease the otherwise disruptive effects of anxiety on performance. Although customized testing as a research tool does not easily translate into practical procedures for ensuring more accurate estimates of students' knowledge, its general characteristics echo the advantages of providing students with choice as well as some degree of personal control. These characteristics are prominently featured in two other approaches to assessment that also allow students to customize their own testing in order to reveal their current and emerging knowledge bases. The lesser-known technique is *concept mapping*, while the other, *proactive testing*, is already in widespread use.

### CONCEPT MAPPING

Planning for problem solving presupposes a firm grasp of the knowledge structure of a discipline, that is, how the accumulated content and procedural knowledge in a field is arranged or represented conceptually, including what counts as appropriate or even feasible methods of inquiry as well as appreciating the boundaries of what is currently knowable. It is the fluid nature of these organizational possibilities that makes the study of any field so daunting for the beginner. For the expert, subject knowledge is organized in tightly knit patterns, easily accessible to working memory and controlled in their application by strategic higher-order decision processes. For the novice, subject matter knowledge is scattered, often without anchor, and not easily retrievable. The evidence suggests that as the result of training and experience, these structures not only deepen in terms of increased cross-linkages among concepts but at the same time also become more complex and differentiated (Wallace & Mintzes, 1990).

Cognitive mapping represents a promising way to document these kinds of conceptual changes in students. Basically, this involves asking students to create their own graphic representation of the concepts in a field. These could come in the form of flowcharts, networks indicating linkage among concepts, and tree diagrams. A number of scoring schema have been developed to assess the quality of such representations. Basically, these measures tap different aspects of the complexity of the knowledge base, which, for example, might involve counting the number of scientific-ally acceptable propositions embedded in a map. Considerable attention has been given to validating the proposition that the kinds of complexities reflected in these scoring schema relate to actual problem-solving ability in a given discipline (McClure, Sonak, & Suen, 1999). For instance, in one study, schoolteachers enrolled in a college science methods course who constructed the most complex maps regarding the dynamics of life in tidal zones in the oceans produced significantly more scientifically acceptable hypotheses about marine life than did fellow teachers who created simpler maps (Wallace & Mintzes, 1990).

More complex, differentiated knowledge representations do not appear to arise simply because of the tendency of more advanced students to employ more appropriate terminology. Rather, the capacity to create proper inferences depends on the richness of the network of cross-linkages among the concepts. Investigators have explored the reliability of map scoring as well as the ease of scoring. Generally, it is reported that the time needed to train graduate student raters combined with the time for scoring per map compares favorably to those time commitments typically associated with scoring traditional essay tests.

As a technique, cognitive mapping is quite flexible for building the kind of reciprocity that blurs the distinction between teaching and testing. For example, instructors may require students to justify elements of a concept map developed during a lecture, or students may be required to incorporate a list of terms supplied by the instructor into a map of their own or to flesh out a map started by the instructor. Moreover, the topic of the map may be as broad or as narrow in coverage as is suitable to the particular teaching unit, ranging from a broadly focused map (such as using the central concept of "energy" in a physics course) to a more constrained, narrower focus on the topic of, say, "electromagnetic energy."

Goldsmith and Johnson (1989) have described the ideal educational assessment vehicle as being objective in nature, reliable in scoring, yet capable of revealing the fluid representation of knowledge that is ceaselessly changing due to experience and instruction. However, seeking stability of measurement – that is, ensuring test reliability – may appear at odds with the simultaneous need to capture cognitive changes due to learning, which is an inherently unstable proposition. Cognitive mapping seems to strike a balance between the need for measuring the ongoing dynamics of conceptual change and doing so in reliable ways. And if we take seriously the proposition that the quickest way to change how students learn and study is to change the assessment methods, then cognitive mapping represents a powerful ally in any instructor's efforts to focus attention on higher-order thinking goals. Preparing for examinations that feature cognitive mapping requires a different, more active, synthetic learning approach than simply memorizing information, which too often amounts to repetitious chanting in rehearsal of flashcards without larger meaning.

Cognitive mapping also has considerable versatility in responding to various other issues. Take, for example, the potential negative impact of misinformation about a discipline on the subsequent learning of beginning students. Conducting a mapping exercise in the first few days of the new term can reveal such shortcomings in student knowledge. These data can form the basis of discussions with students regarding larger course goals that will almost always depend on effective mental representation of subject matter knowledge. Moreover, cognitive mapping can act as an "early warning" tripwire in the feed-forward process by which instructors can revise their instructional strategies to better accommodate difficulties being experienced by students.

PROACTIVE TESTING

Can testing be sufficiently customized by students to reflect their own unique knowledge base without invalidating the ability of a test to measure true conceptual change, and still serve the goals of instruction? The quintessential technique that answers this question in the affirmative is already in widespread use at the college level. The basics are simple. Students are provided in advance of an exam with a list of potential test questions, usually to be answered in essay form, from which the instructor subsequently picks a subset that will comprise the exam, but without students knowing in advance which questions will be chosen. The test itself is typically "closed book" that requires students to rely solely on any preparations they have made for any or all of the questions.

Here transparency occurs in its truest form, and with it come a number of advantages both for students and staff. For one thing, students know beforehand the totality of what may be required of them. This means that the boundaries of their responsibilities are clear, which allows them to exercise considerable personal control over the scope and complexity of their pre-prepared answers and to estimate with some certainty the total amount of time needed to prepare. Moreover, students no longer need engage in the degrading "cat and mouse" guessing game with GSIs over what will be on an exam (see Chapter 3), that otherwise would likely have resulted in students preparing themselves in a haphazard, patch-quilt fashion. Now test preparation can directly engage the full attention of students secure in the knowledge of the demands placed on them. Furthermore, GSIs no longer need to operate under the restrictions inadvertently created by Professor Jones when he chose, presumably for the sake of "fairness," to develop his tests by himself without input from staff members that left his GSIs adrift and in the dark (Chapter 3).

Everything is clearly laid out in advance so that test preparation can become an exercise in strategic means-ends analysis. In effect, students work backwards, first envisioning the dimensions and attributes that will define a good answer to a given question, and then planning how to craft answers that will satisfy these requirements. Knowing the test demands in advance also alters the relationship of staff to students from one of being potential adversaries caused by student uncertainty and anxiety to one of the mentoring of students by GSIs.

Finally, test questions presented in advance can assume a strategic, pedagogical importance, far beyond their immediate role in assessment. More specifically, the questions can also serve as various points of inquiry around which the course itself revolves. For example, consider the following set of essay questions presented in Table 7.1, which collectively encompass all the major themes and overall structure of an American literature course. A subsample of these questions will make up the final exam.

TABLE 7.1 *Proactive Test Questions for an American Literature Course*

| | |
|---|---|
| 1. | How is the Puritan legacy accounted for in the history of American literature? |
| 2. | What is the significance of the constructs of race and geography in the writing of American literary history? |
| 3. | What thematic paradigms are most useful in thinking about the unity of American literature? |
| 4. | Why are some American writers included in one textbook treatment of American literature and not in others? What do these omissions mean? Why are some writers considered major in one text and not in another? |
| 5. | What questions should a future American literary history address? |

No danger here of the course goals remaining mere abstractions. When posed as questions, goals become the epitome of transparency. And because they are introduced in advance – actually in the first week of class in this case – everything that follows for the remainder of the term, and from every source – lectures, outside readings, and assigned text – will become grist for the mill that will drive the continuous refinement of students' answers to these questions.

Now, finally, what about Churchill's objection that tests only revealed what he didn't know? Does testing of the kinds advocated here address his complaints? And if so, do they change things for the better, both motivationally for the learner as well as providing an instructor with a more accurate picture of what has been learned? Any answer needs to recognize that conventional testing already provides considerable evidence of what students know, by default; if they give the right answer, then presumably they know at least some of the right stuff. And if their answers are incorrect, they presumably don't know enough. Both what one knows and doesn't know is being assessed simultaneously. What's wrong with this?

But this is not the entirety of Churchill's complaint about testing for ignorance. The unspoken portion of his argument is that when students are free to tell what they do know, then *they*, and not the instructor, control the agenda. This allows a more accurate picture to emerge regarding students' unique patterns of knowledge and the creative expression of that knowledge. Moreover, feelings of control – even modest amounts of control – reduce the apprehensions that would otherwise suppress the fuller expression of knowledge acquired. Moreover, with the power of control, students are less likely to perceive themselves as victims of trickery. What could be "more fair" from the perspective of students?

It seems reasonable, then, to deduce that Churchill's culprit may be less a matter of assessing ignorance per se than it is the methods by which it is assessed – not by stealth and guile, according to Churchill, but through the freedom to control the means by which ignorance is detected.

## TEACHING TO THE TEST

In concluding this chapter, it may be necessary to make ourselves clear on a vital point regarding the role and purpose of assessment. Our proposal to reframe the mission of assessment around a problem-solving focus, tempered by motivational considerations, may sound to some like we are prepared to give away the store when it comes to testing students. Are we becoming too transparent in our proposals for assessment, making things too easy for students? After all, hasn't the dominant rationale of testing always been to determine what students don't know? If we turn the tables and let students tell us what they do know and coach them on how best to tell us, don't we invalidate the results of such testing? No, actually the procedures outlined here are more likely to provide better estimates of student learning, largely unsullied by anxiety and apprehension that often attends the testing for evidence of ignorance. It may well be true that transparent, student-centered assessment is less valid than standardized testing for predicting the upper limits of one's capacity to manipulate highly abstract material under severe time pressures. This information is coveted by graduate and professional school admissions officers. But predicting successful graduate training by these measures – in reality, very imperfectly as it turns out – is far from our concerns for the moment. Rather, what is at stake here is establishing a true estimate of what is being learned by individual students as the result of specific instruction in a particular subject matter context. This focus goes to what the ultimate purpose of assessment is – that is, the diagnostic means to maximizing the intellectual promise of individual students. No small part of this function of assessment is a matter of "certification," establishing what students have learned and to what standards. The validity of such tests depends on transparency, on some element of student control, and, perhaps above all, on the perception of "fairness" by students.

It may be useful to make a distinction between "teaching to the test" – in the pejorative sense that this phrase is typically used – and "teaching to course goals," which we advocate. For us, the question of whether or not to teach to goals depends on what kind of goals instructors have in mind. If tests reflect goals that are robust enough to challenge students' views of the world, or powerful enough to stimulate personal and intellectual growth, then tests should be subject to direct instruction. What ultimately counts here, however, is not direct instruction per se, but whether students can make use of their intellectual growth in ways that influence their future for the better. This is a matter of the transfer of learning.

Yes, in an important sense, we do want to give away the store if that means passing on our current storehouse of knowledge, theories, and technologies to a new generation, and in the process assisting them in making the best uses of this legacy. This is all part of a problem-focused philosophy. Note that nothing we advocate regarding transparency involves the degrading of academic standards. Rather, transparency aids in the proper maintenance of standards because it is the teaching of standards and the criteria by which excellence is measured that is at the heart of a problem-focused philosophy. What we would give away, then, are not answer keys to tests, but rather giving away methods for creating future answers. It is ways of thinking, not specific, prerehearsed answers, that should fill the educational storehouse.

This vision of goal-based testing is quite different from those notions of "teaching to tests" usually associated with the bankrupt procedure of pressuring teachers into training students on how to do well on specific standardized tests. Such a regimen forces teachers to concentrate instruction on content, which often features atomized, disconnected bits and pieces of information, lying outside of any problem solving context. Little wonder that many of our high school students demand this kind of teaching/testing symmetry when they reach college. They have grown used to a misbegotten transparency. What they *should* be tested on, they insist, is what they were specifically provided in the class or read in an assigned text – no more, no less. It is difficult for them to conclude anything other than that treachery is at work when they enter college and find that "business is not as usual." Fortunately – at least for the moment – colleges and universities are under no political mandate to "teach to tests," but rather, hopefully, to teach to higher goals.

The kind of narrow preoccupation with superficial instructional coverage that is driven by the performance demands of such politics increases the probability that educators may simply be providing students with a bag of test-taking "tricks." Such instruction may enable students to perform well on standardized tests yet leave them deficient in basic understanding. Moreover, quite apart from the fact that such testing mocks the goals of true learning, their ultimate purpose is counterproductive as well. Unlike the goal-based assessments we favor, much standardized testing functions in reality largely as "gatekeeping" devices that serve to select out those students who can profit most from further learning, rather than to provide diagnostic help for nurturing all students.

## CONCLUSIONS

In closing, we offer a segue to Chapter 8. To assess students' ignorance at the expense of measuring their acquired knowledge will inevitably result in students equating ignorance with stupidity. This confusion harbors a great tragedy. Ignorance is a common, pervasive, yet correctable state of the human condition. By contrast, labeling oneself as stupid amounts to a self-defeating belief focusing on one's inadequacies, real or imagined, that are often thought to be beyond repair. This mind-set makes the banishing of ignorance virtually impossible. Moreover, this tragedy is not only perpetuated by the nature of many traditional assessment strategies; it is exacerbated by the practice of grade rationing. No other classroom practice contributes more to the devastating conviction held by at least one exasperated student of our acquaintance who remarked that "Colleges and universities are the only institutions in our society that take a lot of bright, young people and make them feel stupid!" We take up this accusation in Chapter 8.

# 8

## From Goals to Final Grades

PARENT: What did you get out of the class?
STUDENT: I got an A.

The angry voices first heard in Chapter 1 have echoed down through these pages. Instructors are frustrated by the apparent indifference of many students toward the gifts of learning, while students blame their fears and misgivings on grading policies they perceive as unfair. At the center of things stands an overweening grade focus among many students that threatens to extinguish the power of learning for its own sake. We have been exploring this standoff via the question: Is there life beyond grades? Our observations suggest that the answer is a cautious "yes," but only sometimes, and then all too often only barely. Some students accommodate well to what amounts to a conflict between grades and caring about learning. Others are troubled by the conflict and seek to create personal meaning in the false relief that comes from avoiding failure. Still other students single-mindedly pursue grades, but vow to follow their own interests once the gauntlet of the college years is over. This seems an unlikely proposition.

We have identified the basic causes of this potential stalemate between instructors and students as the result of a hidden agenda. First, the reasons for learning and teaching are often based on fear and mutual mistrust. Second, there is a misalignment of the respective beliefs of students and instructors regarding their roles and responsibilities. And third, students perceive a number of inequities thought by them to be an essential unfairness regarding some grading policies. It is not that students necessarily object to being evaluated. Rather, it is the competitive yardstick by which they are often judged that is the basis of contention. We have argued that these felt injustices are a primary ignition point for much of the anger, frustration, and resentment that sets students against one another, and students against instructors. Why should this be? According to self-worth theory, grades are catapulted center stage by their excess meaning as measures of one's worth. Basically, grades have the power to shape, even destroy, one's sense of worth as a person. Moreover, grades become "gatekeepers" for one's personal and occupational future. Course grades often determine which major, if any, students can declare, whether they will continue to be eligible for scholarships or continued financial aid, and whether they will be viable candidates for graduate or professional study. Moreover, grades enjoy great credibility among potential employers as well as being a broadband signal for parents to gauge the extent to which their children are taking advantage of the educational opportunities provided them. From this perspective, grades become both sought after by students and feared, a dynamic in which ironies abound. For example, effort can become a threat to maintaining a sense of worth, namely that studying hard and failing anyway implies low ability, hence worthlessness. Thus, ironically, grades can work against the very values – persistence and dedication that instructors hope to encourage in their students. Instructors too are caught up in this vortex. They are no less vulnerable than students are. Their sense of worth is also on the line.

In the face of these unsettling realities, our task from the beginning has been to consider ways that instructors and students together can alter the meaning of grades so they become the handmaiden to academic success as well as signaling the value of one's labors. We have made considerable progress toward these ends, with many of the issues associated with the giving and the earning of grades already addressed. For example, we have explored the virtues, motivationally speaking, of instructors being transparent about course goals, and especially the importance of providing a clear representation of the kinds of standards by which student work will be judged. These practices tend to offset the allegations of students that grades are being assigned in arbitrary, capricious ways. Also, being judged primarily on the basis of absolute "merit-based" standards, not by one's relative standing in the group, does much to offset student's feelings that good grades are merely a competitive commodity. Moreover, clarity of grading standards and policies gives much-needed guidance to GSIs who might otherwise have to struggle, unguided and often alone, to create grading schema on their own, much to the frustration of students who often complain bitterly that several quite different grading policies are operating among different GSIs in the same class.

In effect, we have been at work attempting to shift the "motivational freight" that drives achievement from being a threatening visage to a more constructive process by which grades become feedback for personal improvement and self-discovery. Until now this transformation has focused primarily on the *formative* aspects of evaluation, that is, assessment as part of an ongoing diagnostic process by which students receive periodic feedback regarding the quality of their work – assignment-by-assignment, with opportunities for them to improve their subsequent efforts. At any point, this formative process can result in the awarding of grade credits or an actual letter grade. But it need not. Formative feedback also comes in many other forms short of being marks in a grade book. And formative feedback need not be only teacher based, but also can take the form of self-appraisal as well as informal assessments provided by fellow students.

In this chapter, we take up the issues surrounding the transformation of all the formative information accumulated by individual students during the school term, ranging from quizzes to tests and laboratory reports, into a *summative* index of evaluation – that is, the final course grade. It is the rules by which this transformation occurs that stands at the heart of all grading policy.

This chapter is divided into several sections. First, we will provide empirical evidence for the effectiveness of merit-based grading systems in promoting task engagement as well as excellence in subject matter mastery. Second, we will address the ultimate question facing all grading systems: When is a given performance sufficiently meritorious to deserve a grade of A, or a grade of B, and minimally satisfactory for a grade of C? The answer depends on definitions of academic excellence and on the standards by which excellence is measured. Implicit in any definition of excellence are other related questions: Should intangibles such as creativity, academic promise, or student enthusiasm enter into the grading equation that defines excellence? Are some of these factors more important than others in providing the truest picture of the quality of student achievement? And what about the vexing question of how to handle extra-credit requests by students at the last minute? Then, there is the question of how much power should students have, if any, in determining their own final grade. Answers to these questions will have enormous motivational implications for both instructors and students as a course proceeds, and not merely at the end point of final accounting. Third, our advocacy of merit-based evaluations has been challenged on several counts, each of which favors competition as a goad to achievement both in school and beyond. In this final section of the chapter, we will offer rebuttals to these arguments.

## DIFFERENT GRADING / DIFFERENT LEARNING?

So far, the arguments advanced by us regarding preferred grading policies have depended for their validity on the rock-bottom assumption that different grading policies can, in fact, make a difference in the perceived meaning and purpose of grades, for good or ill, and by extension, whether grading policies can enhance or detract from intrinsic-task engagement. This is not a matter of questioning whether or not grades should be given. Grades will always be given in some form. But given by what means? And again, will grading policies make a difference in how well students achieve and how they view themselves as learners, as well as how instructors see their role as mentors?

We have advocated the use of criterion-referenced or merit-based grading from the beginning, yet until now without offering much in the way of empirical justification for our position, except for providing mostly anecdotal evidence. At the same time, we have argued against the practice of relative grading, or grade rationing. Here, too, our arguments have been largely philosophical in nature, directed against those academic and administrative apologists who claim various benefits for relative grading on rational, theoretical, and even ethical grounds such as the assertion that instructors should stand neutral from the process of determining what counts as excellence, simply by letting grades be determined by the rank-ordered performances of all of one's students. What, they argue, could be more fair and less biased? This and other claims have stood indicted in previous chapters. Now is the time to consider in a systematic fashion the real-life experiences of the consumers of various grading policies – that is, the students who are judged by these policies and the reactions of those who administer and enforce them.

As we have repeatedly noted, many students see themselves as being held hostage by grades. Some students fear grades for their potential in defining their worth, and others have come to demean their own integrity, believing that the threat of being graded poorly is the only reason they are motivated to learn. Do some grading policies contribute disproportionately to these negative dynamics, while others tend to offset them? In order to address this question by empirical means, we have identified three qualities against which we believe all grading policies should be assessed regarding their ability to fairly and accurately portray the quality of student accomplishments, while simultaneously encouraging the best academic efforts of students as well as their continued task engagement: (1) strengthening an effort/outcome linking; (2) ensuring feelings of equity; and (3) promoting a positive teaching/learning alliance.

## A GRADE-CHOICE PARADIGM

Over the past several decades, we have assessed the motivational impact of various grading policies and practices against these three criteria (Covington, 1985b; 1998; 2004). In order to provide an empirical basis for these inquiries, we have created a prototypic grading policy that we believe satisfies each of these three criteria. This prototype serves as a benchmark for comparing the motivational impact of various grading policies. We refer to this prototype system as a *grade-choice* arrangement. It embodies those essential features of grading policy that we have advocated from the beginning, most importantly the use of absolute, criterion-referenced standards for evaluating student work and the transparency of grading rules. The rules are straightforward. Students can work for any grade they choose by accumulating grade credits against a predetermined schedule (i.e., so many points for an A, so many for a B, and so on). Simply put, the better the grade that students seek, "the more they must do, and the better they must do it." To be sure, students still must compete, but not against their peers for a limited number of rewards, but rather compete – or better put, *strive* – individually to meet the expectations of instructors regarding what they view as academic excellence in their discipline.

Implicit in this system is the assurance that students will never get a lower grade than that assigned to the number of points earned. Moreover, this arrangement allows students to remain informed about their progress toward the grade they seek over the course of the term. This also means that students can stop accumulating grade credits whenever they want and take a lower grade than they might otherwise have attained if they had kept working. Actually, this option is rarely exercised. Typically, all students strive for top grades, and stopping short is usually not an option. The value of this feature is largely motivational in that it provides students with a choice, even though it may not be exercised. In any event, choice provides a sense of personal control over events, an attribute that is an essential ingredient for sustained task engagement.

## THE RESEARCH PROGRAM

Our overall findings can be easily summarized: under a grade-choice option, students reported more incentives than disincentives for doing their best academically, as well as having more fully enjoyed the experience of learning itself. Conversely, our inquiries of students working under conditions of relative grading elicited largely opposite, mirror-image reactions. These latter informants reported more in the way of drawbacks and obstacles to learning, and fewer benefits. What was particularly striking about the positive reactions of students working under grade-choice policies beyond their mere frequency was their intensity as expressed through high ratings on such statements as "my academic goals seemed clearer and more attainable," "I felt poised ready to learn more," or "I was absorbed in my studies; time passed quickly." Moreover, students were quite clear about the causes of these positive experiences. These explanations are organized around the three criteria just introduced.

### Strengthening an Effort-Outcome Linkage

Students typically described their successes under a grade-choice arrangement as caused largely by their own efforts, and as they frequently pointed out, their efforts were more purposely directed to satisfying known criteria. These criteria were based on criterion-referenced rubrics of the kind discussed in Chapter 7. With clear targets, and knowing the basis on which they would be judged, students said they were willing to spend more time and energy, and in the end believed themselves more deserving of a good grade because, as one informant put it, "I earned it myself." Closely linked to this interpretation of one's successes were statements about being in control of events. These positive expressions depended on the transparency of knowing where one stands in terms of progress measured by accumulating credits toward the final grade to which one aspires. For one student, this means "that you are not [constantly] tortured by grade uncertainty," or as Hafer (2016) recounts a student telling him, "earning credits for effort relieved him of thinking so much about the grade."

Students readily agreed that relative grading policies arouse great energy equal to, and occasionally even surpassing, the amount of effort expended under grade-choice arrangements. But they also pointed out that the quality of the two kinds of effort differs considerably. In the former instance, students said they were driven largely by the fear of the unknown consequences of stopping! They complained of not knowing how much effort to expend, in what ways, or to what ends, due to insufficient feedback. Consider these candid remarks: "I really never understood what it took to get an A, other than outperform my peers." Or, "It makes one put in [more] effort because it is unknown when one should stop studying since one can never know how much others study." But more effort is not necessarily the best effort, since extra effort is likely to be fear-charged. Students told us of awakening late at night and finding, to their dismay, lights burning in neighboring dormitory windows, and then pulling themselves awake to begin studying anew, for fear of being left behind.

For a small minority of respondents, it was argued, competition was a necessary good for high achievement, and that its relative absence created "a lack of incentive to really bear down and put out good work because I was not competing with others." However, by their own admission, on further inquiry, many of these same students acknowledged the costs they pay in the struggle to outperform others, even when they are successful. It is these costs enumerated in earlier chapters that we seek to reduce.

## Ensuring Equity

Grade-choice policies tend to satisfy concerns about equity by giving assurances that all students will have an equal opportunity to do well, grade-wise. This was because students need only aspire to the challenges presented by instructors, not to outperform other students. With these assurances, students tended to see themselves as more in control of their own fate, and came to rely more readily on personal effort and initiative for their successes. In effect, they owned their own successes, a consensus opinion neatly expressed in the sentiments that "now it's up to me to do well." Or, "When you compete with yourself, it pushes you to do better," and "[it] forces me to draw upon my own incentives in achieving my goals for the class."

## Promoting Positive Alliances

Noteworthy was the magnitude of the positive feelings of cooperation expressed by students who worked under grade-choice options. This was owing to the fact that students were no longer in competition with one another for a limited supply of top grades. Some student comments are particularly eloquent on this point: "I felt as though I was part of a community where I could seek and get help without feeling self-conscious and scared." Not surprisingly, a feeling of an alliance among peers was little in evidence for students working under grade-rationing conditions. All students made it clear, however, that no matter what grading policy was in place, friends and roommates in the same class would frequently study together and cooperate in sharing lecture notes. Nonetheless, a general climate of civility was far less likely when competition for grades was the rule. For example, there were occasional reports of asocial acts that underscore the desperation generated by "grade grubbing," such as sabotage in the form of ripping key pages out of assigned library readings to deny other students access to them.

### Reservations and Misgivings

Despite these positive endorsements for grade-choice options, our informants registered several concerns that, ironically enough, stem from the very strengths of this paradigm. These concerns are important not only because of their legitimacy in the minds of students but also because of what they reveal about their vulnerabilities. They also identify some often overlooked difficulties involved in creating any grading policies.

### Owning Failure

First, as just mentioned, a grade-choice arrangement promotes the perception that students own their successes because success is perceived largely as the product of their own efforts. Yet, as one student asked with alarm, "But, what if I fail? Must I own my own failures too?" Accepting personal responsibility for one's learning is not without risk. And the risk can be greater under grade-choice options! The more a grading system favors transparency and rewards personal initiative, the fewer legitimate excuses are available to deflect the implications of failing. This puts additional pressure on students, a fact demonstrated by the results of a thought experiment we conducted in which students agreed by a wide margin that a disappointing grade received under a grade-choice arrangement would be more likely to reflect badly on one's ability than had the failure occurred under a competitive arrangement, once again because the noncompetitive nature of the grade-choice option left less room for creditable, self-serving excuses (Covington, 2014).

We would agree that failure is one of the risks involved in the pursuit of excellence. Academic excellence is the product of calculated risk-taking and of accepting occasional setbacks, not the product of timidity of thought or actions borne out of fear and defensive posturing. The key here is that failure, when it does occur, be accepted as an inevitable, even a beneficial part of the learning process, and not necessarily an indictment of the individual's competency or worth. This seems to be what one informant was expressing when she remarked: "By knowing that I would be graded on what I learned, let[s] me work without looking for an excuse to fail." Nonetheless, despite this hopeful sentiment, the fear of failure is a formidable adversary. This is precisely the whole point of reframing the meaning of grades.

How can learning experiences help students deal successfully with this struggle? Several possibilities have already been mentioned in Chapter 4. One involves assigning tasks for which students have an inherent interest. Recall that when intellectual risks taken in the pursuit of one's interests fail to produce results, the implications go to the natural inevitability of such setbacks, not necessarily to personal shortcomings (Newman, 1990).

### Doing the Minimum

Second, the benefits of clarity prompted some students to wonder why anyone would ever do more than the stated minimums needed for a given grade. Once an acceptable grade is secured in one course, the prudent thing to do, they argued, would be to turn one's attention to other courses in which additional effort might pay off in the form of higher grades. This is a legitimate point. Is knowing with some precision what one must do and how well not counterproductive to the pursuit of any kind of surplus learning beyond minimums? Is simply doing "good enough" the implied de facto goal of a grade-choice arrangement? One part of our answer is that it is often sufficient that students merely achieve the proscribed minimums. Little more than competency or mastery may be all that is required. Yet, we must never equate minimums with mediocrity. We need to remember that sometimes minimums can be highly demanding. Consider the minimal levels of competency needed to pass state licensing examinations to certify physicians, attorneys, and pharmacists. The road to this kind of excellence is best traveled by knowing what is required and how well it must be learned and/or practiced. In these cases, minimums are a goal in themselves.

The other part of our answer is the recognition that typically much more than "good enough" is advisable, if not required. As one faculty member explained it, "Professors need to say, 'This is what I require; anything above that enters into excellence.'" Excellence is that point beyond which no more grade credits of any amount can be offered as inducements. Every grading policy will eventually run out of extrinsic inducements in the form of grade credits. What will take their place to mobilize and sustain the energies and commitment necessary to achieve excellence? The answer is intrinsic inducements – actions that reinforce themselves. A number of these have already been discussed. To mention only a few: the lure of self-improvement; the satisfaction derived from the act of problem solving itself, and the pride knowing that students are worthy of the trust placed in them by their instructors. No grading policies – not even a grade-choice policy – can supply these sustaining rewards, but grading policies can encourage them by creating an environment of fairness, transparency, and trust.

### Feeling Lucky

Third, for all its value, the presence of explicit decision rules for grading can create unintended consequences that reveal, once again, the ever-present preoccupation of students with grades. Our informants overwhelmingly lauded the value of knowing explicitly where they stand, grade-wise, as a course proceeds, which reduces "the torture of grade uncertainty" as was just remarked. Yet, these same students also lamented the loss of the very arbitrary character of those grading practices about which they previously complained bitterly, when it came time for instructors to calculate final grades! Students reasoned that to the extent grading depended on the idiosyncratic judgments of instructors, luck might favor them with a higher grade than would otherwise be possible if calculations were more rigorous and straightforward. Such uncertainty is especially welcome when students find themselves teetering on the cusp of the next highest grade. Clint Eastwood's fabled question as detective Harry Callahan, in the movie, *Dirty Harry* takes on a special urgency in these situations: "Do you feel lucky today?" The policy machinations that create luck, for good or bad, typically occur behind the scenes with little, if any, public disclosure so that the reasons for one's luck, or its lacking, will never be known to students. Yet, some students appear willing to accept such ignorance as a thin substitute for knowing whether or not they have been treated fairly. The fact that students are hoping to fall into the arms of "lady luck" as a last resort serves to underscore the stakes involved.

Under grade-choice options, fairness is up front, and the factors that determine fairness are disclosed from the beginning. Yet, some students characterized this policy as too rigid and inflexible – in effect, "the grade you see is the grade you get." As one informant put it, "Usually [the curve] helps your grade. [It] ... leaves more room for error." But the kinds of errors prized here are generally the result of questionable pedagogy as well as capricious grading policy. From the student perspective, the very mis-begotten flexibility afforded instructors by "grading on a curve," ironically enough, can also operate as a safeguard for students against the most egregious excesses of a system in which standards of grading and test difficulty may vary arbitrarily and widely from one occasion to the next with no explicit pedagogical rationale in sight. For example, when exams prove too difficult in hindsight, then to the great relief of students, instructors may "curve the grades upwards." However, when the reverse is true, and tests prove too easy with student scores piling up disproportio-nately at the top end of the distribution, many students insist that to be "fair," no adjustments should be made in assigning grades. Obviously, fairness is in the eye of the beholder. Actually, the reality is that assign-ments are sometimes ill conceived and tests sometimes too advanced for the current capabilities of students. These missteps in effective instruction and proper test design are not intentional, but they need be corrected – or better yet, if possible, avoided at the level of planning – and certainly not compounded by accepting dubious grading adjustments in the name of flexibility for the sake of quelling complaints.

## SUMMATIVE EXCELLENCE

At this point in the work of seminar participants, we often conduct a thought experiment. We ask them to imagine that they now have created a grading policy of their own that satisfies the requirements for being transparent, and has assured the conditions necessary for grading equity, that is, providing the opportunity for all students to do well so long as they satisfy the prevailing standards for excellence. Now the stage is set for the last step in the summative process of actually giving final letter grades. This process involves two issues. First, we need to ask if progress toward excellence is best reflected simply as the aggregate of students' grade credits equally weighted across all their work, or are some perform-ances more important than others as indicators of excellence, and should be weighted accordingly. This question involves the concept of *grade weighting*.

Second, there is the issue of standard setting. Defining excellence requires that instructors rely on more than the hackney observation of "knowing it [excellence] when one sees it." Instructors must be to able explain on what grounds they justify what they are seeing as excellence, near-excellence, or neither. Addressing this challenge requires the creation of a set of publicly defensible standards to determine, using our grading formula, how much students must do, and how much better they must do it, to deserve a grade of A, or for that matter a B or C?

Let's take up these two issues in turn.

## Grade Weighting

### What Matters Most

Grade weighting involves assigning greater grade credit to one particular task than to others. Grade weighting not only provides cues as to what matters most in terms of course goals, but it also is an effective means for channeling student effort. Typically, the more grade-weighted a task, the more students will expend energy in that direction. Naturally, the reasons for grade weighting will vary from course to course. Consider several examples. As one of our seminar participants explained, "I will award more credit to the development of communication and cooperation skills because of their centrality to an interdisciplinary field such as mine." Another participant, the head of a remedial writing program, indicated that "critical engagement with texts is at the top of my [priorities] and grammar is at the bottom. A student who demonstrates solid textual analysis will not be failed for grammar, while a student who demonstrates competent grammar but includes no textual analysis would fail." Grade weighting can also highlight the operation of critical cognitive skills, especially those that reflect metacognitive levels of knowledge. For example, in describing her rationale for weighting her capstone project, a seminar attendee in physical anthropology put it this way: "The larger, final capstone assignment is worth twice as much as any of the smaller projects taken singly because the capstone task requires combining the skills involved in all these earlier assignments in a higher-order fashion." The same kind of weighting rationale also applies to our psychology instructor who plans to make each successive "fantasy child" crises progressively more valuable grade-wise. It is not that any one of these crises is more "goal rich" than another. Rather, progressively more weight is given to successive tasks because they become more complex and demanding, owing to the requirement that each solution must take into account the constraints and limitations of all prior solutions, not unlike our earlier example of the *Floating Admiral* problem (Chapter 5).

*Providing Incentives*

Grade weighting can also act in the service of perceived fairness, a function that recalls the insistence of students that "a fair day's work deserves a fair day's pay." Nowhere is this sentiment regarding proportionality more strongly held than when it comes to acquiring basic content knowledge such as mastering conventions and notations as well as acquiring computational skills and vocabulary terms. All this can be time-consuming and labor-intensive. First comes memory work and rehearsal, likely via flash-cards, then refining and deepening this initially superficial grasp of the material by students testing one another, or by creating examples of concepts. Then there is the myriad of weekly practice sets, tedious and laborious, but essential for what is to come. For this reason, instructors often do not credit this kind of work at all, arguing that rewards will come when this knowledge is put to work. Nonetheless, because students still see memory work as a thankless task, despite the instructor's novel twist on the notion of "delayed gratification," they continue to argue not only for a "full day's pay" but for "time-and-a-half" as well.

Generally, our seminar participants feel comfortable in awarding some grade credit for such memory work, but not to the extent proportional to the amount of work involved. Rather, the consensus position is to withhold just enough credit to create a moderate penalty if students don't comply, but not give so much credit that it rivals the grade incentives needed to ensure higher-order objectives. A specific example of this policy is offered by the instructor who requires students to turn in work sets in which they put each term or concept to be learned in their own words as well as provide an example of the concept not found in the text. He gives pass/no pass credit for each work set turned in on time, with a pass being worth several grade points, which represent a modest benefit, but not so modest as to be ignored.

*Motivating Students*

Yet another use for grade weighting involves sustaining student morale. As a negative example, we have witnessed grading rules in courses that make it virtually impossible for students to earn more than a final grade of C if they receive a C on each of their first several assignments. Our remedial writing instructor comments once again: "This strikes me as terribly depressing and unfair, especially given that many students do not get into the swing of college writing until halfway through the semester." Such handicapping can be largely avoided, according to one informant, "by giving [early assignments] just enough weight to motivate students to take them [the tasks] seriously, but not so much a part of their [final] grade that it will discourage them if things don't go so well at first." This reasoning seems especially appropriate if assignments are designed as early illustrative examples of what later will be required in more complex forms. The point is that early feedback should not come with a price tag that may penalize a student's resolve to continue learning.

This rationale can be generalized to any series of tasks in which each successive assignment receives increasingly greater grade weighting as tasks become increasingly more demanding of time and ingenuity, with the option that students can "loop back" and rework any prior assignments before proceeding to the next level, and be regraded without penalty for any initially insufficient effort. Such a "second chance" procedure is particularly appropriate for hierarchical course structures in which it is critical to master the material thoroughly at one level of complexity before proceeding to the next level. This procedure is reminiscent of the mastery learning paradigm discussed in Chapter 7. Not only does a mastery procedure ensure a more secure grasp of the material as students proceed; it also offers a "fail safe" incentive for students to persevere in the face of increasing complexities. But why would students not simply blow off the initial effort if they were guaranteed subsequent tries? Actually, in our experience, students are quite diligent the first time around, owing to the fact that not being well prepared initially would represent time lost in having to prepare a second time (Covington, 1985a).

### STANDARD SETTING

We can now take up the task of setting the standards by which all student work will be judged when it comes to final course grades. This process starts by defining the concept of excellence that typically is the benchmark on which grading decisions are made. This is no abstract exercise. By now we are quite familiar with the psychological and practical stakes involved in which grades can define the worth of students as well as constrain or enhance their career choices.

If it is reasonable to assert that the better the grade that students seek, the "more they must do, and the better they must do it," then the underlying question becomes: How much more and better must students perform in order to receive any particular final letter grade? How might we best proceed to address this question? The simplest answer is to tally all the accumulated grade credits, weighted or unweighted, for each student during the term and then rank-order them in a distribution from highest to lowest. We would then establish grade cutoffs and assign a letter grade of A to the top 10% of students. This practice amounts to grade rationing. Or we could assign a letter grade of A to any student whose total scores exceed that 90% cutoff. This latter practice constitutes a merit-based approach to grading. But either way, something is amiss here with these apparently straightforward procedures, because both cutoff formulae represent *nominal* scales. Technically speaking, nominal scales can only establish categorical differences indicating, for example, that students in the A range are not the same as B students. But they cannot represent how much or what kind of a difference. Nor does it help to assume that these formulae possess the characteristics of an *ordinal* scale. Ordinal scales presume equal intervals between all contrasting values. But although it may be that in our example the intervals between the descending grade levels represent 10% decrements, one cannot assume that the differences in intellectual demands between an A grade and a B grade are essentially the same as those between a B and a C. Typically, it takes increasingly more energy and mental application to move up the grade scale, since the "cognitive demand curve" becomes steeper and more difficult to traverse.

The key to establishing a defensible rationale for what makes a given performance worthy of a particular final grade lies in the instructor's expectations or standards for what counts as academic excellence. It is these expectations that should determine grade cutoffs, not simply relying on artificial and dubious differences in percentile decades. Without the stabilizing presence of independent merit-based standards, distortions of the true quality of student work are bound to occur. For example, there is the ever-present temptation to arbitrarily place grade cutoffs wherever there is a break or gap in the rank-ordered distribution of students' total performance scores. Moreover, without absolute standards, even merit-based grading cannot be counted on to avoid the potential for abuse. For example, it may serve equity goals to arbitrarily award a grade of A to all students who achieve, say, 90% or more of the available credits in the course. But what if, on closer inspection, it becomes clear that, on average, students performed better than expected? Assuming this is not the result of an easy test, the cutoff for a grade of A might have been set lower to accommodate a larger pool of worthwhile performances. Then there is the opposite risk. Consider those instructors who may be "blindsided" by an exclusive reliance on preordained percentage cutoffs – even under a merit-based system – when they realize belatedly that those performances above the 90% level may be mediocre at best. In both cases, either overestimating or underestimating the quality of student work creates false impressions regarding levels of competency. The fact that percentage cutoffs alone are inherently arbitrary is real enough in light of the common practice of instructors to curve grade cutoffs up or down once they know the distribution of test scores, a practice that is routinely employed by Professor Jones. In this regard, we have observed cases in which average performances of 40 points out of a possible total of 100 points on a test have been given passing grades to compensate for the presumed difficulty of the test.

## A BENCHMARK NARRATIVE

Standards of excellence are best based on a series of narratives, each spelling out the kinds and qualities of student work associated with a final letter grade, ranging from A to F, or reflecting the distinction between "pass" and "no pass" grades. The construction of these narratives can be thought of as an exercise in the wholistic approach to Primary Trait Analysis (Chapter 7), which is applicable when the attributes of excellence cannot be easily separated as independent variables, and a single index is sought to reflect the merits of the totality of a student's work for an entire term. The advantage of these narratives is that they can take into account intuitive aspects of an instructor's vision of academic excellence above and beyond numerical test scores. This does not mean that these narratives are without tangible performance anchors. Such anchors are represented by a set of specific learning objectives of the kind illustrated in our case studies (Chapter 6, Table 6.2). The extent to which students satisfy these learning objectives represents tangible performance markers. Without these markers, judgments of excellence would remain largely a matter of instructor opinion, even of speculation, absent a firm, commonly agreed-on basis for review and critique.

### Step 10: Creating a Benchmark Narrative

We asked our seminar members to create a benchmark narrative for assigning final grades in their proposed course. An example of one narrative drawn from the psychology case study is presented in Table 8.1.

Now how should we proceed? We favor a two-step process. First, instructors need to assure themselves that numerical grade cutoffs will be in as close an approximation as possible to one's vision of what it means for students' work to be considered excellent. The basis for this calculation is best set up before a course begins by grade-weighting all planned

TABLE 8.1 *Benchmark Behaviors for Final Letter Grades (Psychology 2)*

**A Range: Superior Proficiency**

Performances in the A range indicate that students have learned to analyze real-world situations in psychological terms at a superior level as exemplified by consistently high scores on all learning goals with a particular strength in applying metacognitive, organizing skills around cause/effect modeling and a pervasive past/future perspective. Such problem-solving sensitivities are also reflected in information-driven, plausible reasoning as the basis for crafting advice to parents/guardians. Students in the A range demonstrate complex, curious minds at work. These are students for whom instructors are pleased to write letters of recommendation, who might be welcomed into an instructor's research laboratory as an apprentice, or invited to do independent research of their own under the guidance of an instructor.

**B Range: Adequate Proficiency**

Performances in the B range indicate a record of good work; certainly adequate, if not remarkable. However, despite evidence of overall competency, performances nonetheless fall short of the A range in various ways including the occasional lack of sufficient reasoning to justify one's ideas or conclusions; infrequent but significant failures to adequately interpret the importance of information to an audience of parents; and theory-building not always tested for plausibility, or critical inquires not always followed up. These shortfalls sometimes result in advice offered to parents based on incomplete factual and/or theoretical foundations that is less focused and/or less convincing than the work of students in the A range.

**C Range: Minimal Proficiency**

The benchmark meaning of a letter grade of C represents a range of performances downward from mediocre to the lowest boundaries of competency. The latter reflects the minimum of understanding necessary for students to profit from further instruction in this field. The most noticeable deficits occur in the metacognitive control domain reflecting a mechanical, rote-like application of psychological principles leading to advice for parents that is haphazard and absent of sufficient factual support or logical justification to be convincing. Slow to see underlying problem-solving strategies. This deficit is likely due to a tendency to master concepts only at a rote level, making it difficult to be applied in a flexible and innovative manner. Erratic performances begin to emerge as reflected in several missed deadlines or incomplete assignments.

**D Range: Inadequate Mastery**

Performances in the D range indicate a further deterioration in achieving any of the learning goals. Especially notable are severe deficits in the metacognitive domain reflecting only a dawning recognition of the importance of strategic planning and the value of organizing inquiries. Overall, this condition is insufficient for promotion of students to the next level of instruction without first undergoing substantial remediation, tutoring, or repeating of the course.

**F Range: Unacceptable**

This range of performances reflects an unacceptable level of problem solving across all learning goals. In the typical case, advice is offered with little if any evidence of thought behind it or reasoning to support it, typically leading to flawed, often irrelevant commentary, sometimes bordering on platitudes offered up to parents/guardians without the conviction afforded by sound reasoning and/or compelling evidence. Performances demonstrate little or no consideration for problem-solving principles.

assignments, tests, and exercises to reflect their relative importance in supporting course goals. Thus, the more the number of total grade-weighted credits achieved by students, the more the instructor's definition of excellence will have been honored, and as a consequence, the better the grades students will receive. For example, our case study instructor in psychology plans to weight evidence of metacognitive sophistication to a greater degree than other objectives, given his view of its centrality for achieving excellence in problem solving.

Second, now what about establishing the actual cutting scores that distinguish among letter grades? The criteria for differentiating among grade levels are provided by descriptive narratives of the kind found in Table 8.1 which are composed of a combination of many variables including intangibles, and all linked to tangible test performances regarding the satisfaction of learning objectives.

Consider a practical strategy for establishing these grade cutoffs. Once again our example comes by way of our psychology instructor. To begin, he rank-orders all his students from high to low on the total number of grade-weighted credits each has earned for mastering the learning objectives listed in Table 6.2. Starting at the upper end of this achievement distribution, he selects a sample of students and assesses the quality of their overall work, one student at a time. In each case, he asks himself whether or not the overall quality of problem solving responses to the various childhood crises, does, in fact, reflect his wholistic view of what counts as a grade of A as described in Table 8.1.

Not surprisingly, the performance records of those students at the top of the distribution will likely satisfy his overall intuitive impression of a grade of A. No problem here. These are all solid A students by his wholistic judgment, without reservations. Only one pattern has emerged so far, that of undeniable excellence by his definition, which is anchored to achieving the learning goals. However, as our instructor begins sampling further down the achievement distribution, the test performances in this range begin distributing themselves in uneven ways across assignments, quite unlike the uniform superiority of the very top students. The students at this lower point tend to perform quite well on some learning objectives but somewhat less well on others. Also, wholistic judgments are for various reasons somewhat less flattering than for the top students. Overall, is this record still worthy of a grade of A? Perhaps, but our instructor will likely reserve judgment for the moment as he samples the overall records of students still lower down in the achievement distribution.

Eventually, our instructor reaches a place in the percentage distribution where mastery of the underlying learning goals no longer completely satisfies his expectations for a grade of A, nor do intangible considerations, at least not sufficiently to justify a solid A, but perhaps an A-. In the end, the cutoff between a grade of A and B may settle somewhere in this neighborhood. It is at these transition or "crossover" points in grade cutoffs that deeper subtleties in subjective judgment are likely to come into play, particularly making judgments about individual students who may be on the "cusp" of the next grade level. One promising technique helps justify such decisions, either up or down, and holds considerable appeal because of its transparency. Recall Robert Fried's exercise (Chapter 6) in which he created thumbnail sketches of the behaviors that in his view would differentiate students in the A grade range from those in the B range – above and beyond academic performance per se. For example, students in the A range, Fried argued, are self-starters who take the initiative and demonstrate independence in their thinking. Using such a check list of their own design, instructors can judge if the behavior of a given student who would otherwise receive a grade of B is a closer match to the behavioral descriptions of students in the A range. If so, this student might be given the "benefit of the doubt." Obviously, although subjective judgments are still clearly involved, the essential fairness of this procedure rests on the fact that students will have been put on notice from the beginning of the course as to what counts as evidence for the relative presence or absence of these vital characteristics. But more than merely being an assessment device, these behavioral benchmarks also function as expectations to which students can aspire. Students are far more likely to comply with criteria known to be directly linked to grades.

Because instructors who teach large enrollment courses will likely have little contact with individual students, it is typically a GSI who is in the best position to make these final grading judgments based on weekly contacts with students. Several instructors of our acquaintance give their GSIs the latitude to raise the grade of any student by one-half of a grade, say, from a B to a B+. And if, in the opinion of GSIs, an even higher grade is justified under extraordinary circumstances, then they must make a convincing case to the instructor.

Once having tentatively set the achievement cutoff for a grade of A, our psychology instructor assigns an A to all those students who reach or exceed the cutoff, thus satisfying the merit-based grading policy that we endorse. Our psychology instructor then proceeds to establish the cutoff for a grade of B using the same procedure, and so on.

It will not escape notice that in this example, the standing of students, grade-wise, can be expressed in terms of the percentage of earned grade credits relative to the total possible credits. This use of such percentages is not only legitimate, but also valuable. They avoid the disservice of actually *defining* excellence by applying arbitrary grade quotas on students, as is the case of relative grading practices. Rather, the information conveyed by these percentages *describes* – not *defines*, excellence which is anchored by the professional judgments of instructors, telling students something meaningful about their performances. We can no better underscore the significance of this point than to recall the insightful critique of the student first quoted in Chapter 1: "I hate feeling cheated out of understanding my grade. The curve really does not tell me anything meaningful about my performance. To improve, I need to hear what my score implies in terms of preparation for future exams, and a score relative to other does not give me that kind of feedback."

Obviously, giving grades is not an exact science. Not even carefully reasoned procedures for establishing grade cutoffs of the kinds elaborated here totally eliminate subjectivity in the judgments of instructors, nor are they likely to help avoid arbitrary elements completely. With these cautionary observations in mind, who is to say, and what exactly is their rationale for placing the cutoff between grades of A and B precisely at a given percentile? The answer is not a matter of questioning the basic legitimacy of grading policies to establish the broad rationale for staking out the boundaries between letter grades like the example in Table 8.1. Rather, the issue more often concerns the minutiae or fallout that accompanies *any* grading policy when the fate of an individual student is at stake. This is why sometimes students turn instructor's office hours into debating societies over questions of whether or not they deserve one or two more points on a test that would strengthen their case for a higher grade. These spectacles notwithstanding, in the long run, typically it is not the vagaries of micromanaging grading decisions in the case of individual students that is the issue, so much as it is those arbitrary elements that are built directly into some policies themselves that purport to measure excellence when in fact they actually ration the rewards for excellence through the mechanism of competition.

We are on reasonably firm ground regarding the reasoning presented in this chapter for addressing these policy issues, given all the care that seminar members have taken to define excellence as embodied in specific learning goals in a given course. Moreover, there is also the force of a pedagogical rationale that focuses on the demands of effective problem solving, which in turn are tied to the characteristics of a specific discipline. Also, all the decision-making rules proposed here strive to create transparency and, above all, hopefully can be applied with relative equity and reasonable fairness.

Many complexities abound in the struggle to define summative excellence as is evident by merely glancing at the grade book (or computer file) at the end of the term. It can be a bewildering visage, especially if instructors have postponed a number of critical decisions highlighted in previous chapters. They will likely be confronted by a welter of different student journeys. Some of their students will have shown steady improvement, while others who started well enough will have declined over time. Other students clearly have been consistent but are perhaps only marginal producers. Yet others demonstrate considerable promise but only inconsistently. And then there are all those voids – missed quizzes, forgotten homework assignments, and the failure to attend class regularly. And what about the pleading of students at the very end of the term to make up their prior shortfalls? And, what about acknowledging intangibles such as student dedication and persistence? Are these attributes part of the package that defines excellence?

What does one make of all this when it comes to final grading? Where does excellence reside in this ménage? In this section, we consider possibilities for addressing several of the issues just mentioned: first, dealing with the phenomenon of inconsistent excellence; second, questioning the practice of giving extra-credit at the last minute; and third, considering the legitimacy of rewarding personal attributes such as creative promise.

### INCONSISTENT EXCELLENCE

For all the advantages of injecting the rules of the grading game with a strong dose of certainty and reliability as well as transparency, we nonetheless need to avoid the danger that certainty may create a procrustean straightjacket when it comes to grading, with one formula fitting all these varied student journeys, without the flexibility to accommodate what Robert Fried (2001) refers to as *inconsistent excellence*. By this Fried means those cases where students demonstrate brilliance on one occasion but only mediocrity on another. Fried points to the analogy of the star baseball player who is paid millions despite the fact he fails to do what he is expected to do 7 out of 10 times at bat (a batting average of roughly .300). Yet, ironically, if students bat less than, say, an average of .900 on their assignments, they may risk losing a top grade. And this may be despite the fact that some of their work is equivalent to a "home-run with bases loaded." Of course, consistency of results is absolutely critical in some occupations, especially among surgeons and hopefully stockbrokers. However, in these instances consistency applies to individuals who are already certified as experts. But learning to be an expert is far from a consistent business. Students are not always at their best, nor are they always able to demonstrate their potential promise.

Two reasons are frequently offered by students to account for inconsistent quality. First, they explain that disappointing performances are sometimes due to a mismatch between their capabilities and the demands of the task. Besides serving as a legitimate excuse, such mismatches are often considered to be constructive when students are challenged to visit unexplored realms of potential interests, abilities and talents. T. S. Elliot famously describes the benefits of such discoveries: "No one can become really educated without having pursued some study in which he took no interest. For it is part of education to interest ourselves in subjects for which we have no aptitude." The second explanation for any poor performance is due to overcrowding of one's schedule or the inconveniences of other obligations.

The traditional accommodation made for academic lapses is to let students discard the lowest test score during the term or forgive a missing homework assignment or two when final grades are calculated. To be sure, such practices can provide considerable relief for grade-anxious students, and can even reassure instructors that they have given students the full "benefit of the doubt." However, since these allowances are typically made at the end of the term, hindsight being 20/20, the entire strategy of forgiveness potentially stands unmasked as simply a "numbers game" for maximizing one's grade, a ploy that some students refer to cynically as the "calculus of grading." This is a misplaced emphasis. The focus remains on grading, not on learning. This has the effect of excusing shortcomings or compensating for inconveniences rather than encouraging excellence.

The strategy of disregarding the poorest performances suggests a more interesting parallel procedure, except that students make choices at the beginning of the term, not at the end. At the beginning students are allowed to alter the proportion of the final grade initially assigned to different course assignments as long as the total of grade credit allocations to all tasks equals 100%. For example, students might reduce the grade weighting on an assignment for which they feel less well prepared, thus lowering the stakes involved and hopefully their apprehensions as well, and increase the weightings in other areas of greater self-confidence. The same procedure can be used in the case of personal scheduling problems by altering the grade-weighted importance of assignments accordingly. Of course, this procedure is no guarantee that inconsistencies in the quality of the one's performances would necessarily be smoothed out. But at least the benefits do extend to providing students with some increased sense of personal control over the grading process as well as an opportunity to practice planning for the allocation of one's time and resources in antici- pation of the ebb and flow of future demands. However, having said this, it must be conceded that concerns over maximizing one's grades may also be part of the calculations. Make no mistake, when "push comes to shove," maximizing one's grades is the typical priority.

This priority is wonderfully illustrated by the frequent complaint among students that they don't do well on objective, multiple-choice tests for any number of reasons, each of which may be quite valid. They insist that if they could only have essay tests, they would do far better. One instructor of our acquaintance decided to test this preference. He was not particularly surprised when he found that on giving his students a choice at the beginning of the term of either taking an essay or a multiple-choice final exam, 95% of the class opted for the essay exam. Yet, months later on exam day, when students could once again choose, this percentage was reversed when virtually everyone actually chose to take the objective test! Post-exam exit interviews revealed that the bulk of students felt better prepared to take the multiple-choice test despite feeling generally less adept at this format. But mainly, they felt it might be easier than the essay test!

## EXTRA CREDIT VERSUS EXTRA LEARNING

Decisions about whether or not to allow students extra-credit opportun- ities at the end of the term is one of the most vexing aspects of grading policy. On the positive side, instructors want their students to do well and are often willing to offer some prospects for hope when students find themselves on a borderline, only a point or two below the higher grade, or worse yet, when students find themselves falling increasingly behind as the term progresses. Moreover, allowing extra-credit opportunities some- times seems fair by giving students the benefit of the doubt, when, in retrospect, tests might have been too difficult or the course workload might have been a bit excessive. Also, perhaps there is a temptation among instructors to yield to student pressure so that they themselves also might get the benefit of the doubt when the time comes for students to evaluate their effectiveness as teachers.

On the negative side, allowing students undeserved credit contributes to grade inflation. No instructor wants to cheapen the value of the grades they give, and in the process betray the trust of those students who are already thriving. In this connection, some students who habitually view the world in competitive terms – most likely overstrivers – feel punished by extra-credit opportunities that they argue unfairly compensate otherwise mediocre performers at their expense.

All this can leave instructors in a quandary. Fortunately, however, we believe that the dilemma around giving students an "additional chance" can be resolved by recognizing that the issue is the product of a misplaced emphasis on grades when the focus should be on learning instead. Rarely do instructors or students maintain that extra-credit options actually redress deficiencies in learning. The real purpose is to offset performance deficits. This skews the balance between learning and performance in the wrong direction. This balance can be redressed when extra-credit options are treated as "extra-learning" opportunities. By extra learning we mean any additional activities that go above and beyond otherwise satisfactory scholarship. For example, this might include expanding an otherwise perfectly adequate analysis of Lincoln's Gettysburg Address by appending an additional series of one's own footnotes designed to extract further insights. Going above and beyond minimum requirements could occur at any time during the term and might be rewarded by moving students over a borderline up to the next grade level, thus compensating for any earlier deficiencies or shortfalls that would otherwise compromise a student's final grade.

Several of the seemingly intractable problems associated with usual extra-credit procedures are addressed by this approach besides reemphasizing the goal of learning. Mainly, last-minute pleas for extra-credit opportunities would no longer be justified. Also, because the extra-learning option would be exercised only during the school term, it has less the appearance of being an ad hoc feature, merely tacked on to the course. Moreover, this extra-learning strategy should seem implicitly fair, especially to those students who rightly object to extra credit as essentially an unearned "bailout."

To be sure, student concerns over grades may well convert this extra-learning option into an insurance policy of sorts to offset the possibility of any future shortfalls of credit. Hopefully, the tendency simply to store up credits would give way to more positive reasons for performing. While it is true that students will likely be tempted to perform for extra-grade credits, it is not these tangible inducements that always prevail, especially if the tasks in question have personal relevance. The study described in Chapter 5 concerning voluntary student research projects attests to this point.

REWARDING INTANGIBLES

Few would contend that by themselves, student records of academic achievement – test scores and the like – tell the entire story regarding the educational benefits of learning. Clearly, there are many surplus gains associated with doing well, including profiting from the process of learning itself and experiencing the growth of positive reasons (motives) for learning. These benefits are propelled by various intangible personal characteristics of the learner that include a willingness to cooperate with fellow students, of possessing a determination to persist in one's studies, as well as an inherent enthusiasm that reflects a deep curiosity about the challenges ahead.

The perennial question facing instructors is whether or not to recognize these personal attributes as a legitimate part of the larger reward system when it comes to final grading. But how does one measure these elusive qualities? And even if such measures could be proven reliable, is there not the danger that being a "team player" is merely a commodity, a fungible element of the grading process?

Various perspectives on these issues were revealed through a questionnaire we administered to groups of seminar attendees that assessed the extent to which instructors are inclined to augment grades, and by how much, in light of the personal characteristics of their students. Participants were provided a list of four personal attributes: (1) the talent or future promise shown by students; (2) the degree of academic improvement demonstrated by students over the term; (3) the degree of effort, persistence, or enthusiasm demonstrated by students; and (4) the extent to which students were cooperative team players. A fifth factor was also included: the record of actual classroom performances. Each participant was asked to assign percentages to all five components (not to exceed a total of 100%), reflecting the relative degree to which they believe each component should be factored into a final course grade.

Not surprisingly, there was uniform agreement that academic performance was the single most important component by which excellence should be assessed, with an average of 82% of the final grade allocated to this factor. Every other attribute was also endorsed, but to different degrees. The average contribution for being cooperative was 3% of the total, an average of 2% was assigned for possessing future promise, 5% for improvement over the term, and 8% for effort and enthusiasm.

The appropriateness of rewarding some of the personal characteristics provoked considerable discussion, which revealed the kinds of complications encountered in crediting intangibles, especially concerns around issues of equity and fairness. For example, there was a minority sentiment suggesting that giving credit for evidence of student effort and dedication would, in effect, be "double-counting" in that – as their argument ran – these qualities are already contributing to the learning process otherwise students would not have performed as well as they did. Also, while there was a general endorsement for recognizing academic improvement, a vocal minority of raters wondered why consistently *reliable* producers should not also be credited. Is consistency any less virtuous than improvement? Finally, those who chose not to credit future promise at all – actually a near majority – argued that extraordinary future promise can legitimately be recognized, but not as part of a grade. Rather, it can be rewarded by offering outside avenues of encouragement, such as invitations to work in the instructor's laboratory.

Clearly, attempting to measure these intangibles in valid ways as well as determining their contributions to excellence is a subjective business. But it need not be an arbitrary business. Once again, we can point to techniques of the kind proposed by Robert Fried (Chapter 6) as useful in elevating such decisions above and beyond the arbitrary, and infusing subjectivity with reasoned justification.

## THE MYTHS OF COMPETITION

We first encountered two fundamentally different theories of achievement motivation in Chapter 1. Until recently, researchers have labored under the first of these theories, a drive-theory interpretation that views motivation as an internal force, energy, or impulse that acts as an enabling factor for prompting better performances. The assumption is that teachers can arouse (drive) students to greater effort by offering rewards (invariably extrinsic in nature) that are distributed on a competitive basis. We have expressed dismay at the implications of this position for educational practice in general, and rejected specifically as flawed the assertion that competition is the most effective goad to learning. Despite evidence to the contrary (Kohn, 1993), arguments in favor of competition still persist.

What are these arguments? Are they justified? And do they effectively challenge our advocacy of merit-based evaluation?

There are three related arguments for competition as a necessary condition for an orderly, efficient society. First, there is the assertion that competition engendered by relative grading practices is an effective way to sort people occupationally in order to maximize overall productivity in our society. Second, there is the related argument that competitiveness as a personal attribute is critical to individuals becoming the best they can be. And third, competition among individuals is thought to maximize the performance of each individual competitor. All these arguments have gained momentum owing to the fact that in some quarters objections to competition are viewed as faintly un-American, if not contrary to the laws of nature, or, in any event, are an unavoidable fact of life. In short, then, if the minimizing of competition in schools becomes a widespread policy, what becomes of individual excellence and societal efficiency?

## Competition and Job Sorting

What about the undeniable fact that there must be some orderly way to distribute people proportionally across the available jobs in society, some of which are far more lucrative and attractive than are others? Competitive grading in schools has long been a primary mechanism for assigning talent according to job demands and availability, a realization that has lead David Campbell (1974) to remark bitterly that the whole frantic, irrational scramble to beat others is essential for the kinds of institutions that our schools have become, namely "bargain-basement personnel screening agencies for business and government" (pp. 145–146). If grades calculated in competitive terms are thought to be the best way to allocate individuals in the marketplace, then just how effective is college GPA as a predictor of job success? The evidence is not particularly reassuring for advocates of institutionalized competition. For example, college GPA is essentially unrelated to the quality of subsequent on-the-job ratings by supervisors. Nor is it particularly effective at predicting either personal satisfaction with one's job placement or predicting feelings of general happiness (Spenner, 1985). The reasons for this are not hard to imagine. Those individuals who survive a high-stakes, head-to-head scramble for grades are not always best suited for professional and public service. Students who jostle their way to the top by accumulating a near-perfect GPA are often driven by motives that work against career success. Our self-worth analysis of the overstriver is a case in point. Overstrivers have been characterized as achieving noteworthy success, not necessarily for the sake of personal growth, but as a strongly defended strategy to avoid failure. Little wonder, then, that with a high proportion of such individuals in any graduating sample, college GPA is a relatively poor predictor of various indices of job effectiveness. Basically, it is the underlying reasons for achieving in the first place, not the grades themselves, that count most for sustained occupational success. Obviously, we cannot tolerate incompetence in high places. Yet neither can we afford to promote the kinds of self-doubt and anxiety that, once having driven people to positions of power, then compromises their ability to use that power wisely.

But will not those individuals who are simply more competitive by nature enjoy greater occupational success? Not necessarily. The evidence (e.g., Spence & Helmreich, 1983) suggests that competitiveness is a negative weight in predicting occupational success across a wide range of professions and among various indicators of success. The more that individuals prefer hard work, enjoy mastering new skills, and are cooperative with fellow workers, the more successful they are. By the same token, the personal qualities that employers seek in their workers, when boiled down to the essentials, amount to the willingness to remain competent on the job and cooperative with others.

We submit that the more important attribute for occupational success among individuals as well as for the sake of a productive society at large is competency, not competitiveness, as well as the willingness to upgrade one's skills in the face of continuous change, which means being a life-long learner. It is estimated that the next generation of American workers will change jobs an average of twelve times in their careers – not merely changes within the same family of closely related jobs, but in entirely different job sectors! This kind of change requires schooling in some form into the indefinite future, and a willingness to adapt. Thus, advocates for competitive school climates can only hold out the forlorn hope that by struggling to outperform others, it will be "the others," not "oneself," who are the victims of future economic dislocations. Even if ensuring economic security was the mission of schools, enhancing competitiveness would be the wrong way to go about it, because holding a job rarely depends on outperforming others, but rather on becoming competent. Once competency is attained, the major threats to job security are factors obviously beyond the control of schools, namely dislocations due to job outsourcing, corporate downsizing, displacement by robotics, adverse economic cycles, and occasionally, just plain bad luck. This brings us to the second argument put forward by advocates of competition.

## Survival and Competition

By minimizing academic competition in schools, do we not do an injustice to our graduates who will be unprepared to succeed in a world driven by competitiveness? This question implies that if we elevate cooperation and individual excellence as the higher good, students will be prepared for the wrong kind of world. Is not learning to compete a beneficial exercise for society, especially learning how to lose? Aside from the valid point that schools should teach students how to profit from the lessons of failure, this argument can be faulted on two counts.

First, as noted earlier, far from preparing young people for the rigors of the marketplace, being competitive actually subverts the ability to succeed in *any* world. The inevitable legacy of competition comes in the form of student cynicism and a propensity for sabotage and duplicity as well as compromised effort. These are scarcely the kinds of assets that will serve students well in the future. Second, the world of work as it presently exists is far less competitive than is often assumed. While it may be true that the world economic engine is grounded in competition, it operates largely between countries or regions, among corporations, and within business sectors, but far less frequently among the individuals who make up these larger aggregates (Khana, 2016). The observations of Arthur Combs (1957, p. 265) are particularly persuasive on the point:

> We are impressed by the competitive features of our society and like to think of ourselves as essentially a competitive people. Yet we are thoroughly and completely dependent upon the goodwill and cooperation of millions of our fellow men ... although it is true that we occasionally compete with others, competition is not the rule of life but the exception. Competition makes the news, while cooperation supplies the progress.

It has been estimated that roughly 80% of American workers are compensated through the results of group effort as long as they are competent enough to do their part, and that close to the remaining 20% are paid according to individual productivity – that is, the more one produces, the more one earns, as in the case of salespeople on commission (Covington, 1998). Only the final 1% owe their livelihood to outperforming potential competitors for their job on an ongoing, daily basis, as in the case of competition for positions in the starting lineup of professional football teams or competition among musicians for the first-chair position in the violin section of a symphony orchestra. It is largely the exceptionality of these jobs that captures the public imagination, and in doing so make them appear the rule rather than the rare exception in the world of work. They misrepresent the vast majority of jobs and occupations.

Still, we do not mean to imply that ranking employees for relative competency is irrelevant in the promotion and hiring process. Promotions that depend on being more than merely competent frequently occur in hierarchically structured occupations where there are fewer and fewer job opportunities as one moves up the ladder. Consider the military. Officers on the promotion list at any step in rank typically outnumber the openings at the next higher rank. Consequently, many qualified officers are denied promotion in a given round. In this way, eventually, all officers will rise through the ranks until most will be promoted no further, even though many will be perfectly capable of successfully discharging the duties associated with a higher rank. Much the same description applies to management positions in many business organizations. Such occupational structures are an economic fact of life. We cannot ignore them; but neither should they serve as a pedagogical model for how students are taught and learn. If these competitive realities have any place in schools, it should be in the curriculum as topics for study – say, exploring the economics of supply and demand, with students given the opportunity to explore their personal comfort zones with regard to various working styles and gauging preferred work rewards and sources of personal satisfaction as a prelude to making career choices.

## Promoting Equity

In advocating policies that promote grading equity, we argue for equal opportunity, not for equal performances. Ours is not an equalitarian strategy for treating all students alike – in effect, minimizing individual differences and creating a near uniformity in the hopes of creating a shared sense of dignity. Proponents of this strategy do not always appreciate that bringing the achievement of everyone to a common level will only result in mediocrity and destroy the spirit of individual initiative so critical to great achievements. If anything, a merit-based approach to evaluation fosters diversity of achievement, if for no other reason than the fact that anxiety would no longer exercise the power to "dumb down" all performances to the level of mediocrity. Our point is that by focusing on encouraging competencies, and minimizing competitive pressure to drive this process, far more energy will be released both for the sake of creativity as well as acting as a stimulant for achieving competency. We are under no illusion than the process of occupational sorting will be any easier or less harrowing that it is now as long as 80% of our young people aspire to 20% of the available jobs, the latter being among the most lucrative and attractive. But if keeping those jobs ultimately depends on being competent, and on the reasons one became competent in the first place, then this is all the assurance that schooling can offer.

Nor do we believe that a merit-based approach to evaluation will necessarily reduce the tendency among students to make relative comparisons among themselves, or that feelings of competition will all but disappear. This will not happen. Some students are temperamentally disposed to competitiveness, which amounts to the motivational drive to succeed at all costs. This will not change; the hope is that these reasons for learning can be moderated. Actually, comparisons among learners are inevitable, if not a natural process, and can even prove beneficial. Regarding inevitability, it is known that starting in the earliest years, children seek out information about how well their peers are performing, even when the prevailing evaluations are based on the quality of individual progress (Rosenberg, 1965). The same curiosity is found at the college level (Covington, 2004). We find that students working under merit-based systems still want to know the average score on tests or the average grade on written assignments, even though, once again, this information in no way directly affects the calculus of their own grade. As to potential benefits, such comparisons provide students with moving targets against whose trajectory they can aim to keep pace, a dynamic that recalls the use of the "stalking-horse" in training thoroughbreds for the big race. The slower horse sets the pace early in the practice run against which the contender can judge his progress toward the finish line. The contender is not in competition with the stalking horse, but rather with the stopwatch! Analogously, when absolute standards replace the competitive stopwatch as the universal markers of excellence, students – whether thoroughbred or otherwise – can aid one another toward the finish line.

Happily, we can leave arguments favoring competition on a reassuring note. It is obvious that competitiveness can never be banished entirely. Witness the many students as well as some parents who have an uncanny knack for turning everything into a competitive contest. So if the pursuit of excellence requires the virtual absence of competition, then the chances for reform would seem bleak. Actually, the promotion of intrinsic learning goals does not require the complete elimination of competition. The evidence suggests that as long as there is some effort to promote intrinsic values in schools in the form of the kinds of structural changes we recommend, those behaviors we associate with intrinsic task engagement are not diminished (Ames & Archer, 1987). There is cause for optimism.

## CONCLUSIONS

This time the conclusions are not drawn from a single chapter. This conclusion is different. It draws together all the preceding chapters into two final steps of the Blueprint for Change.

### Step 11: Creating a Course Syllabus

This step provides seminar participants the opportunity to introduce their proposed course to students in a unique manner. Further instructions are found in Appendix A, listed under Step 11.

### Step 12: The Valedictorian Event

This culminating event is for those readers who have worked through all the steps in the Blueprint for Change, either together as seminar participants or in some other more informal arrangement. It is designed to demonstrate just how much you and your colleagues have learned about college course design from a motivational perspective: not just *how* students learn but also *why* they learn – their motives, struggles, and successes – along with the efforts of their instructors and GSIs to establish positive relationships that encourage a love of learning. You will find instructions for this exercise in Appendix A, listed under Step 12.

# 9

# The End of the Beginning

"This is not the end; it is not even the beginning of the end. But, it is, perhaps the end of the beginning."
— Winston Churchill

## INTRODUCTION

We now come to the end of the beginning, a phrase made famous by Winston Churchill that simultaneously conjures up two perspectives: the *beginning*, which implies a threshold that invites a consideration of things yet to come, and where we intend to take our future inquires; and the *end*, which implies the disclosure of a productive past and an opportunity to pause and take stock of what has been accomplished. Among other things, this latter perspective involves the backfilling of details not yet made apparent, but which now in retrospect will be useful for providing a fuller description of our long-range program of research that now stretches back more than four decades (Covington & Beery, 1976), and in particular to acquaint readers with the origins of our graduate seminar that has become the backbone of this book.

## RETROSPECTION

Our graduate seminar is embedded in a larger investigation conducted under the auspices of the Teaching/Learning Project at the University of California, Berkeley. The overall objective of this project is to study both the nature and nurturing of those self-sustaining rewards that promote what we have chosen to call intrinsic task engagement, with particular reference to their relationship with various extrinsic rewards that dominate classroom life, including social recognition, gold stars, and, most importantly, grades.

## Basic Research Phase: The Nature of Task Engagement

Our initial research objective was to investigate the nature of intrinsic motivation, including its developmental antecedents and its personality correlates. All these inquiries have been guided by self-worth considerations, especially as they concern those threats to intrinsic motivation posed by the fear of failure and the implications of failure. To address these dynamics, we initiated inquiries in the context of real-life circumstances. Our primary laboratory has been, and continues to be, the college classroom, where much of the data reported in these pages was generated. By far the most unique feature of this program of research is that it is fully integrated into the ongoing life of college classrooms. Data collection became a continuous, natural part of the course curriculum itself. In these classes, students became candid, committed, and highly involved informants, because our inquiries have been situated in an authentic context of great personal significance for students. Although laboratory research has contributed immeasurably to an understanding of the issues discussed in this book, we believe that we cannot truly understand how students come to appreciate and deeply hold the values of questioning, exploration, and discovery unless the processes involved are also studied in the context of real-life schooling where success and failure carry enormous public promise and penalties, respectively. To date, our total pool of student informants comprises many thousands of undergraduates, more than 120 GSIs, and numerous faculty and staff members. Additionally, several hundred younger students, ranging from the primary grades through high school, have participated in our efforts to track the developmental nature of intrinsic task engagement.

## Implementation Phase: The Nurturing of Task Engagement

As our inquiries regarding the nature of task engagement began to yield significant results, the second phase of our research program, shadowing the first phase, began to take shape in the form of a series of questions concerning implementation: How might these findings be crafted into viable educational programs for the enhancement of intrinsic engagement? Around what principles might such curricula be organized? What would be the most effective delivery system for such programs (e.g., an entire course; supplementary material, etc.)?

The most promising candidate to emerge from these conversations for an overall organizing concept – what we have described elsewhere as the "vital throbbing center" (Covington, 1998) was a problem-focused approach to learning for the reasons articulated throughout this book. But what would a problem-oriented curriculum organized around motivational concerns actually look like? Did it all make sense?

## The Graduate Seminar

Seeking answers to these questions of implementation was the purpose of our graduate seminar, which has now been offered yearly for the past decade. Initially, the seminar served, and continues to serve, as an ongoing study in feasibility in the form of the following challenge to prospective enrollees: "What would an undergraduate course in your field look like that integrated subject-matter mastery with motivational principles designed to enhance a love of learning?"

As you may recall, seminar applicants were expected to be within a year of receiving their Ph.D. from any of the many academic disciplines on the Berkeley campus. Over the years this requirement has lead to ideal cohorts of seminar participants. First, there has been a sense of idealism and openness to the challenges owing to the youthful status of the participants. Second, the diversity of subject matter fields represented ensured the generality of our work and its applicability to all disciplines. Third, because of their advanced status in Ph.D. programs, virtually all applicants had some previous college teaching experience, typically in the role of GSIs, but sometimes even as instructors of record. Thus, responses to the challenge of exploring novel course designs would not occur in a vacuum. The balance was right for innovative thinking: a combination of idealism, openness, and experience.

Our role in the seminar began, and has remained, more that of collegial participants than of formal leaders because we had as much to learn as did our seminar colleagues. The current blueprint for course design evolved over successive offerings of the seminar, as did the curriculum for teaching the seminar found in Appendix A. Also, year-by-year, the course design proposals of seminar participants also became more sophisticated, presently approaching the caliber represented by the three current case studies. Not only were these proposed courses impressive but the processes by which they were created proved highly informative and stimulating for the participants, as revealed in representative testimonials:

> "I feel like I have the resources to speak intelligently about teaching and course design. I also think I can design an awesome class!"

> "This course has been the most challenging course I've taken in graduate school! I learned that a problem-solving approach to teaching is the way to go."

The overall success of the seminar convinced us that courses based on problem-focused, motivationally driven principles are feasible. But feasibility is one thing. What about effectiveness? What assurances could we offer that a problem-focused approach would satisfy the many conditions required by self-worth theory in the service of promoting a vibrant life beyond grades? This question required us to put our proposals to the test under actual classroom conditions. According to self-worth theory, the value attributed to learning depends on the measure of one's worth. Here, then, is the essential research question: Would involving students in a dialogue around self-worth dynamics stimulate self-reflections regarding the measures by which they judge their worth and raise questions about the wisdom of linking one's worth to grades? A challenge as profound as that implied here is unlikely to be adequately met due solely to the presence of a temporary "safe harbor" designed around the benefits of problem-focused learning. Such "breathing space" must afford students opportunities not just for unencumbered learning, but also to be confronted by issues of self-definition, which is a difficult prospect. For example, struggles in favor of valuing learning as a self-defining goal would likely be more difficult for failure-threatened students than for more self-assured students for whom these issues had already been settled in positive ways.

The process of reframing issues of such personal significance begins with a belief that change is possible, an attitude that in turn depends on an understanding of the nature of the problem. This understanding is the potential gift of theories. Not only do theories account for purposeful as well as puzzling, often counterproductive behaviors, but they also imply what those positive purposes should be – goals by another name – and how to achieve them. If this is the true role of theories, then, for starters, we needed to know if students can understand the rationale of a given theory – in this instance, self-worth theory – to accept its message and believe in its benefits. Additionally, are motivation theories perceived as being of personal value to learners? These concerns would be a main focus of our inquiries.

## The Experiment

The next step was to subject this ambitious research agenda to empirical scrutiny. This meant converting one of the proposed courses created in the seminar into an actual regularly scheduled class. We chose to use one of the three case studies featured in the book: the large-enrollment, lower-division psychology course (see Chapter 5 for a description).

On the first day of class the lecturer announced that some changes had been made in the way the course would normally be taught with a goal of increasing student satisfaction with their work and enhancing the joy of learning. The main changes were then described, including reference to the capstone task and a rationale given for the merit-based grading system. Self-worth theory was introduced in the following lecture as a way to think about some of the problems that interfere with student learning, such as the fear of failure, and how the alterations in the structure of the course were designed to offset these negative dynamics. After that, no further reference was made to the theory.

## The Results

Given the complicated nature of our inquiries, the assessment methods were a combination of open-ended, short-answer essays, rating scales, focus groups, and exit interviews. Also, students were free to provide written comments spontaneously at any point. Thus, we built a record of freely occurring thoughts, feelings, and insights that, once set in motion, reverberated through time without prompting by the staff. Also, at the end of the course, students were asked to respond to essay prompts such as, "What was the single most important thing you learned in this course about yourself?"; "What points raised in the course might help you to become the best student you can be?"; "Did self-worth theory change the way you thought about this course and yourself?"

First, consider student observations regarding the value of various structural elements of our problem-focused approach for promoting a sense of intrinsic engagement in their work. The main factor that was thought to be responsible for reduced anxiety over grades was the merit-based grading system. Students' candid remarks explain why this system was a positive presence: "By not having a curve, you create an environment where grading is truly reflective of the time and effort you put into it, which makes learning more intrinsically valuable." And: "It was a relief to know that at least I didn't have to compete with other students for top grades, but only satisfy the instructor's requirements." Efforts to set right the mismatch of faculty and student roles also received high marks: "Matching student and faculty roles is one idea that best increased my confidence. If teachers and students can see each other in the same light, then it provides a better learning environment for everyone." Other students stressed the presence of a community of cooperation among students and a trust in the instructor and GSIs as truly concerned for their welfare.

Now consider the ways that knowledge of self-worth principles might have impacted students. First, there is the basic question of whether or not students simply understood the theory and its rationale. It was clear that students readily understood the concepts involved, and gave the theory high ratings for providing insights into the nature and causes of stress that bedevil students. They often provided relevant lessons to be learned from the theory. And pronouncements that follow from the theory often took the form of dire warnings about the dangers of linking a sense of worth to grades. For example, students frequently cautioned about procrastination, but with a sophisticated appreciation for the dynamics involved, that is, no longer simply dismissing procrastination as a matter of being "lazy," but of being driven by the threat of failure. Students typically seized on different aspects of the theory, sometimes focusing on mere fragments of the message, but in meaningful ways without misrepresenting the theory.

Yet, despite the ability of students to recall the theory, and the appropriateness of the implications drawn from it, many of these student reactions were seemingly offered as an abstract exercise, and fell short of being applied to themselves. We often detected efforts of students to distance themselves personally from the messages by attributing lapses to others, typically acquaintances, especially roommates: "I had a roommate once who really beat up on herself over poor grades."

## TEACHING FROM THE THEORY

Our ultimate interest went beyond confirming that students could reproduce self-worth theory accurately from memory and understand its basic rationale. But did students make personal use of the theory as a catalyst for self-reflection? In order to determine this, we sorted student responses along a continuum of personalization, that is, the extent to which students applied self-worth principles to themselves regarding how best to define a sense of personal worth. At one end of this continuum we placed student responses that were clearly personalized but lacked self-reflection as a purpose. Here self-worth principles served a palliative function of merely putting students at ease, or even of providing a source of relief from the stresses of school: "It helped me understand that I was not the only one concerned with grades." Clearly, feelings of relief are insufficient to sustain long-term personal commitments to change. And when relief becomes feelings of comfort, it can lead to a misreading of the situation. This is likely what happened in those cases where some students concluded, erroneously, as they subsequently discovered to their regret, that the course would be easy, grade-wise.

Then came a second group of students whose reactions were clearly autobiographical, and differed from the first group by revealing a dawning revelation that learning *was* the true goal of schooling: "At first I was shocked. I became very intrigued with the fact of going to classes for its enjoyment rather than anything else!" Arguably, this realization might qualify as a tentative first step on the road to deeper levels of self-reflection regarding one's role as a learner.

Next came a third group of students who accepted self-worth theory as confirmatory of what they already firmly believed. The issue of defining personal worth had already been securely settled for them in favor of valuing learning goals beyond grades, as reflected in their dismissal of grades as a test of worth: "Grades are an inaccurate measure of my worth." And: "They [grades] don't in fact measure my worth as a person, though it would be nice to be gratified by doing well." It was not that these students rejected self-worth principles as irrelevant to their lives, but rather had already embraced them.

Finally came the most compelling instances of personalizing by reason of their depth of expression and intensity. These comments reflected students in the midst of a struggle over self-definition. Obviously, we had aroused considerable doubts regarding the wisdom of linking one's worth predominately to grade goals. Two repeating themes stood out. The first theme concerned revelations regarding the destructive nature of one's past reasons for learning and the realization that their prior successes had been held hostage to strategies that were ultimately self-destructive. Consider the following comments: "The idea of reframing the meaning of grades is significant to me because I was able to recognize my self-sabotage and hope to better cope with my stress from now on." "The [theory] helped me realize the self-defeating nature of defining myself by arbitrarily assigned letter grades." "It [the theory] made me realize how engulfed [I was] feeling worthy only in times of success." "The information is important because I realized that sometimes I am driven by fear." "I felt worthless without the ability to attain exceptional grades."

The second theme involved reports by students of taking positive steps for change, once the destructive nature of their past behavior had been recognized: "I try to achieve these [learning] goals instead of blindly working to avoid failure." "Unlike my previous reaction to adversity, I now look at "failure" in terms of grades as acceptable as long as I enjoy what I am learning and try my best as a student." "The theory has taught me which behaviors and actions trigger the feelings of unworthiness, and as a result I try my best to steer clear of those behaviors." Some students appeared to be on their way to leveraging these insights into a generalized transformation, including affecting relationships not only with one's self but with other students as well as with teachers: "I have actually gained the courage to approach my professors to clarify a point or to ask about other courses they teach. It has improved my interest in my classes."

Taking these data as a whole, it seems clear that our questions regarding a constructive role for applying theory to practical purpose were answered positively, that is, students can understand the rationale behind theories of motivation intended to guide their education; that theories can make both intuitive and practical sense to students, and are potentially capable of being of personal use and value to them.

### FUTURE DIRECTIONS

By reason of their promise, these findings raise a new set of questions that form a growing future research agenda.

First, there is the question of why self-worth theory is an active ingredient in the dynamics just described. In effect, would students respond in similar circumstances to other contemporary theories of motivation in essentially the same ways? It seems important to identify those shared as well as distinct characteristics of various theories that are most likely to affect student self-perceptions as learners. Certain attributes of self-worth theory may offer some clues. When put into practice, self-worth theory offers a readily understood, convincing rationale by which instructors can contribute to the quality of student learning. We suspect that the presence of this ingredient in any theory will promote success. Also, we believe that it is a frank, open discussion of *why* students learn, not just *what* they learn, that ultimately carries the burden of promoting a love of learning. The very act of disclosing the positive goals of self-worth theory, and the means to achieve these goals, appears to activate a sense of security, feelings of trust, and even of sanctuary that is so evident from the reactions of students. Moreover, it may well be that the significant impact of any motivation theory can be attributed not so much to the specifics of its rationale as to the presence of any reasonable argument that gives meaning, direction, and purpose to one's work.

Second, the way the issues of student stress and motivation were introduced in this experiment is not suitable in all teaching situations or for all subject matter fields. Nor is it compatible with all teaching styles. It is for this reason that we will continue exploring various other methods and means by which these messages can be introduced comfortably and effectively by faculty across a wide spectrum of subject matter disciplines and teaching contexts.

Third, the population under study here is clearly quite different from the vast majority of students who pass through the American system of higher education, which limits our ability to generalize from the data. Having said this, it may still be useful to comment on some of the broader social implications of the present findings. For example, it can be asked if self-worth principles apply uniformly across groups from a diversity of social and ethnic backgrounds. Several of our other data sets gathered previously and representing all major ethnic groups among Berkeley undergraduates provide some guidance (Covington, 2001). Some ethnic differences in self-worth linked variables were observed, particularly regarding the extent to which students defined their sense of worth in terms of grades, with Chinese-American students being the most dependent on this index and Hispanic and African Americans least so. However, these ethnic differences were quite modest compared to variations in personality-type variables such as failure avoidance and success-orientated individuals that were largely independent of ethnicity. Overall, this indicates that students in general are subject to the same self-worth dynamics, irrespective of ethnic membership. We anticipate that further research will shed light on other individual differences such as gender and age.

Fourth, and finally, our goal of reducing student vulnerabilities to fear raises the most important question of all, which, perhaps if more accurately characterized, opens teachers to criticisms of naiveté and even of folly. Assuming that courses *can* be created that minimize fear of failure dynamics and, in their place, promote positive reasons for learning, what happens when vulnerable students walk across the hall at the end of the lecture to a different, perhaps less supportive classroom? Don't students simply carry their anxious burdens with them, and find themselves subjected to the fear of failure anytime the situation is no longer designed to offset their vulnerabilities? Might not this occur when instructors are forced by circumstances to tolerate competitive selection, reluctantly so, in the role as "gatekeepers" to prestigious occupations where the number of aspirants far exceeds the openings? Are not our proposals simply a cruel jest that can set students up for defeat and deeper disappointment? Can self-sustaining change of the magnitude we endorse become portable across situations as well as across time? Certainly, the odds against such broad-based, durable changes are considerable. And they lengthen if we attribute change to the wrong or insufficient causes. For example, does the potential for renewed self-confidence lie in a lessening of competitive pressures? Or, rather, does the spark for self-confidence reside in the knowledge that students are being trusted enough by their instructors to undertake significant academic challenges on their own? Perhaps self-sustaining change depends on either one or the other, or both of these factors in combination. Answers to this kind of question will be critical to any attempts to make desirable changes robust and transferable. The success of projecting our motivational message beyond the limits of time and place may well be taken as the ultimate criterion by which one answers the question of whether or not theories of motivation can actually motivate students to higher purpose and greater achievement. What we do know is that profoundly personal choices such as those explored here are unlikely to be made wholesale, all at once, or for all time. Yet, every teacher hopes to leave for their students something in the form of an enduring gift for their futures, perhaps best expressed as "the ability of students to thrive and soar beyond those worlds that may no longer exist."

# A Blueprint for Change

## COURSE OUTLINE AND ASSIGNMENTS

This appendix offers a course outline for using this book as a text for teaching a traditionally organized graduate seminar for the design of new undergraduate college courses as well as the revision of exiting courses based on motivational principles. It can be offered either online or in a real-time classroom setting. This course outline has also been used as the basis for brief faculty and staff workshops as well as satisfying departmental training requirements for new Graduate Student Intructors (GSIs). The book can also be employed on a self-administering schedule by individuals on a reader-by-reader basis under the supervision of staff members. Additionally, the book can serve as a stand-alone reference source for research and theory on the topic of achievement motivation.

The course outline for this graduate seminar features a series of 12 steps organized around book chapters, which on a step-by-step basis leads participants to develop undergraduate college courses. Each step includes one or more workbook-type assignments or exercises. We have found that maximizing the instructional benefits of these activities derive from the opportunity for participants to share their ideas with one another, either by posting their work online or by distributing hard copies before the subsequent class meeting.

The duration of a course is quite flexible, ranging from the assignment of one chapter at a time (with accompanying activities) for each consecutive class meeting to a more streamlined scheduling of assigning several chapters per meeting. For example, brief workshops and abbreviated classes have been successfully accommodated by assigning the first four chapters at the first class meeting, followed thereafter by one chapter per week.

### INTRODUCTORY MEETING/CHAPTER 1

We have had considerable success introducing the course during the first class meeting using either one or both of the two following group activities, both of which are presented in Chapter 1.

1. The presentation of "A Scenario: Afloat But Barely" exercise is an effective way to telegraph the kind of student/instructor motivational dynamics that will be the basis of course design as well as to immediately establish a sense of community among the participants. Follow the instructions given in the textbook as part of the narrative (p. 15).

2. The value of the second activity is that it makes tangible and personal the concept of intrinsic task engagement that otherwise might remain an abstraction:

    "Describe a time or event in your own college experience involving an academic, school-related task of a relatively long duration in which you were fully engaged. Be sure to share what emotions or feelings prevailed; what thoughts were going through your mind; and what were the circumstances. (p. 6)"

    This activity can either be employed as a homework assignment for Chapter 1, with responses posted online (anonymously if preferred), or as an in-class activity for sharing.

    Encourage seminar members to analyze their essays in terms of the four characteristics of intrinsic task engagement mentioned in Chapter 1 (p. 7–10).

### CHAPTER 2

1. What aspects of the reading helped you as a TEACHER (GSI, lecturer, etc.) make sense of STUDENT behaviors, actions, or attitudes that were (are) puzzling, counterproductive, disruptive, or troublesome?

2. How might the ideas presented in Chapter 2 influence or alter the ways you could approach teaching?

### CHAPTER 3

1. As a STUDENT (past or present), what aspects of the reading helped you make sense of TEACHER behaviors, actions, or attitudes that were (are) puzzling, counterproductive, or troublesome?

2. How might the ideas presented in Chapter 3 influence or alter the ways you could approach teaching?

## CHAPTER 4

1. After reading the first four chapters, what one or two things most surprised or sobered you, or confirmed or revealed something about the process of teaching and/or learning?
2. After reading the first four chapters, what might an undergraduate course in your field look like that integrated subject matter mastery with motivational principles designed to enhance a love of learning?

## CHAPTER 5

### Step 1: Envisioning Teachable Problems and Goals

1. Sketch out one or more teachable problems, issues, or controversies central to your subject matter discipline around which a problem-focused course could be organized. Table 5.1 illustrates the kinds of teaching problems we have in mind. Also, you may wish to consult with the three case study examples that have been worked out in some detail (Chapter 5) (p. 121–123).

   Be sure to consult the list of seven problem-solving attributes (Chapter 5) (p. 117–120). Incorporate as many of these characteristics as possible in your proposed capstone problem.

   Also, make a list of several research questions that students, either singly or in groups, could pursue in the course of solving your capstone problem.

   This activity is particularly valuable as the opportunity for individuals to solicit help either from the entire group or from smaller groups for improving or expanding one's ideas.
2. Create a short description (including a title) of a proposed course as it might appear in a course catalog, limited to 100 words. Indicate appropriate student level (e.g., freshman, etc.) and whether it is for majors or non-majors, and where it might fit in a departmental curriculum.
3. A sure-fire trigger for a spirited discussion is for participants to share any shortcomings or limitations they found with a problem-focused approach while working on Step 1. Two potential shortcomings are found in Chapter 5 (p. 124–127). Are there more? What kinds of remedies might seminar participants suggest?

CHAPTER 6

## Step 2: Envisioning Discipline Characteristics

After reviewing Table 6.1 for examples, create a brief statement in broad terms describing your discipline. This mission statement is intended not only to capture the broadest purposes of your discipline but also to set its boundaries – in effect, to stake out the entire subject matter universe in which your capstone task resides. Keeping this target in mind as you proceed is one of the best ways to ensure that your capstone task is representative of major aspects of your field.

## Step 3: Identifying Specific Learning Objectives

What things must students learn in order to become capable problem solvers in your field and, by extension, be able to address your proposed capstone task? Make a list in the form of learning objectives. Follow the format presented in the example of the case study in psychology (Table 6.2). Your list need not be exhaustive, only representative. Answering this question is only the beginning. Keep track of your list of objectives as you go. You will likely revise and expand this list as the broader outline of your course emerges. In this early stage of course development, not all your learning objectives will be immediately apparent.

## Step 4: Necessary Mental Skills and Knowledge

Using the entries in Table 6.3 as inspiration, make up your own list of concepts and principles, research tools, and subject matter knowledge as well as intellectual skills you believe necessary to think like a professional in your field. Again, this list need not be exhaustive – just enough to serve subsequent group discussions.

## Step 5: Categorizing Problem-Solving Components

1. Using your list of entries generated in Step 4, arrange them using the three knowledge domains portrayed in Figure 6.1. Start with meta-cognitive skills. Which of your entries might serve this executive function?

   Next, which of your entries best qualify as procedural knowledge?

Finally, which of your entries might best qualify as content knowledge?

2. As a follow-up to this exercise, you might find it instructive to review your specific learning objectives in Step 3. Some objectives may, for example, require procedural or metacognitive knowledge; others might require content knowledge or – perhaps more often the case – a combination of two or all three knowledge domains. Identifying the connection between learning objectives and the skills on which they depend will help you organize the inherent structure of your emerging curriculum.

## Step 6: Constructing a Causal System

After consulting Chapter 6 for examples, construct a causal system of your own around which your capstone task can be arranged conceptually.

Now that you have cast your capstone task in the form of a causal system, create a visual representation (or metaphor) of your system as the conceptual basis for your capstone task. This is best done, if possible, using butcher paper or giant Post-Its – the larger the better – with colored felt-tip pens. Draw your picture during a group meeting so everyone can share in the fun. Afterwards, share.

1. Did rendering your ideas in an alternative form – drawing rather than verbalizing – cause you to rethink instructional or motivational aspects of your capstone task to improve it or to spotlight unforeseen difficulties in its presentation to students? If so, consult with fellow participants.

2. After reading Chapter 6, prepare the outline of a brief lecture for your prospective students regarding the problem-solving advantages of casting your capstone project in terms of a system analysis. Be sure to challenge them to come up with their own candidates for a system analysis.

## CHAPTER 7

## Step 7: Proposing an Instructional Paradigm

What is the basic problem-solving structure of your capstone task around which your teaching will be organized? Are any of the paradigms described in Chapter 7 suitable? Perhaps your problem-solving structure shares a combination of these paradigms. Or you might have an entirely different paradigm in mind.

### Step 8: Creating a Teaching Assignment

Create a sample teaching assignment intended to promote one or more of your specific learning objectives. Before you start, you may wish to consult the examples proposed by each of the three case study participants in Chapter 7. There are several steps to this assignment.

1. First, briefly describe your teaching assignment as it might appear in a syllabus.
2. Indicate which learning goal(s) your assignment is intended to promote.
3. Indicate some of the key subject-matter concepts needed to complete the assignment successfully.
4. Indicate some of the cognitive skills and strategies needed.
5. Indicate some of the steps/activities needed to prepare students for the assignment.
6. Using the grid in Table 7.1 for reference, locate your assignment on the horizontal timeline of your own design to indicate where in the progression of other teaching assignments this one will fit. Be sure to explain the rationale for this particular location – that is, how does this assignment build on previous learning and how will subsequent learning depend on this assignment. This question represents the essence of the concept of *instructional validity*.

### Step 9: Conducting a Primary Trait Analysis

Create a short list of specific criteria or traits that capture the critical dimensions by which the quality of your students' work on your sample teaching assignment could be evaluated. Before beginning, you may wish to see how the three case study designers approached this same task (Chapter 7).

Next, create a scale for each trait indicating what tangible indicators a rater should look for in student responses that indicate the level or degree of quality on that dimension, ranging from excellent to poor. You are free to divide each scale into as many segments/points on this continuum as suits your purposes. Be sure to give each segment a verbal anchor ("excellent," "satisfactory," etc.).

CHAPTER 8

## Step 10: Creating a Benchmark Narrative

After reviewing Table 8.1, develop a narrative indicating what students must *do* and *how well* in order to deserve a final grade of A in your course. Do the same for a grade of B, and so on. Also, label the overall quality of work at each grade level ("superior," "inadequate," etc.). You may wish to use the traits you identified in Step 9 as dimensions along which the quality of student work will be judged. Also, you are encouraged to consider desirable personal characteristics of students in your analyses ("cooperative," "dedicated," etc.).

## Step 11: Creating a Course Syllabus

Now it is time to introduce the course to your students. Traditionally, this is done through a syllabus that lays out a schedule of events, various deadlines, exam dates, and an obligatory list of course goals. But at this descriptive level, such information does little to telegraph the fundamental rationale of your course, which is embedded in this challenge: "What would an undergraduate course in your discipline look like that integrates motivational principles that could enhance a love of learning?" Students need to know in what ways your course is designed to help reduce student fear of failure, test anxiety, and fear-driven reasons for learning. And, in what ways is your course designed to assist students in defining their worth *more* in terms of valuing learning and *less* in terms of pursuing grades for their own sake. Without your presentation, students are unlikely to recognize, let alone embrace, these provocative and admittedly non-traditional course objectives.

For the sake of disclosure, imagine developing a brief statement (no more than a paragraph or two) – maybe a mini-lecture, concerning these motivational goals, including the rationale for how a problem-focused course can promote a more positive relationship between teachers and learners. Also, consider evaluating student work in terms of absolute, merit-based criteria rather than through the threat of grade rationing, which promotes caring about what one is learning.

### Step 12: The Valedictorian Event

As the final activity – a valedictorian event, so to speak – we suggest conducting a mock job interview for participants. This exercise is meant to simulate the experiences encountered by candidates seeking a college faculty position on their first job hire. Of particular interest to the imagined hiring committee are concerns about recent unrest among students regarding school grading policies and complaints by faculty that students seem more interested in grades than in learning.

The participants should be divided into groups of three. Each member of a group will progressively serve as the "job applicant" who is interviewed by the remaining two members acting in the capacity of a faulty hiring committee. These roles are switched until everyone takes a turn as the job applicant. Set up the exercise at least several days in advance so that everyone knows the procedure.

Each of the three members should come prepared with three or four questions to ask in their capacity as an interviewer. Questions that solicit advice from the job applicant regarding campus concerns over grading policies, faculty discontent with students, and any other motivationally related issues are particularly welcome.

The length of the individual interviews can vary widely, but we have found that 15–20 minutes is optimal. Faculty committees may adjourn at the end of an interview, if they wish, presumably to evaluate the performance of a job applicant. However, in our experience applicants have always been offered the job!

# Guiding the Teaching and Professional Development of Graduate Student Instructors

The effectiveness of student learning in courses that use GSIs is enhanced when faculty provide mentoring and guidance for their GSIs. Effective mentoring can provide GSIs with a clear sense of the relationship of their sections and labs to the goals of the course. Mentoring increases the ability of GSIs to recognize student learning difficulties and to recommend adjustments in the curriculum to accommodate these deficiencies. Also, mentoring enables GSIs to set their own personal teaching goals and, with the assistance of faculty, to work toward achieving these goals and to assess whether these goals have been met.

The GSI Teaching and Resource Center at the University of California, Berkeley has led the way on a national level in developing training programs and materials to aid both faculty and GSIs in making the mentoring process an effective collegial partnership to their mutual benefit and to that of their students. For example, the Center offers seminars and workshops for faculty on how to integrate mentoring goals into any course and addresses topics such as guiding GSIs in the development of grading rubrics and helping GSIs teach according to how students learn.

The materials in this appendix are the product of these workshops along with research conducted by the Center (see Mintz & von Hoene, 2002). By using these materials, faculty can provide a collaborative learning environment for themselves and their GSIs.

The materials include the following items:

1. Checklist for Faculty on Working Well with GSIs
2. Mentoring Plan Form for Faculty
3. Goal-Setting Form for GSIs
4. End-of-Term Self-Assessment Form for Faculty and GSIs.

## CHECKLIST FOR FACULTY ON WORKING WELL WITH GSIs

Working well with GSIs is a systematic checklist of steps for ensuring the best learning environment for students and provides a chronological tutorial for the professional development of GSIs. We recommend that before the school term begins or at the first GSI meeting, instructors not only introduce the syllabus but also share their rationale for the internal pedagogical structure of the course and articulate goals for the mentoring and professional development of their GSIs.

Our research evidence (Mintz & von Hoene, 2002) indicates that providing more consistent and structured mentoring does not require more time or specialized knowledge on the part of faculty; it involves making better use of time, which ultimately decreases the number of problems that can emerge when mentoring of GSIs is inadequate. Faculty who wish to develop their mentoring skills are referred to mentoring statements written by Berkeley faculty who have been awarded the Faculty Award for Outstanding Mentorship of GSIs. These essays describe faculty approaches to mentoring GSIs across the disciplines and can be found at: http://gsi.berkeley.edu/programs-services/award-programs/faculty-mentor-award/faculty-award-recipients/. Recommended readings for GSIs can be found at the end of this appendix.

### MENTORING PLAN FOR FACULTY

Prior to the beginning of the school term, this form can be used to set the framework for a mentoring plan regarding faculty teaching responsibilities for GSIs, and for their professional development. The Berkeley faculty mentoring statements (http://gsi.berkeley.edu/programs-services/award-programs/faculty-mentor-award/faculty-award-recipients/) and the References section at the end of this appendix can assist faculty with this planning. Also available is Berkeley's repository of more than 200 one-page statements on teaching effectiveness by award-winning GSIs from across academic disciplines (http://gsi.berkeley.edu/programs-services/award-programs/teaching-effectiveness/). As a group, these essays have proven particularly effective as a source for innovating teaching ideas as well as offering practical, concrete classroom solutions for a number of obstacles and problems GSIs face in teaching.

## GOAL-SETTING FORM FOR GSIs

Goal setting is important for GSIs both for improving their teaching skills from year to year, and for attending to their professional development. We recommend that at the beginning of the school term, the results of this form be shared with the instructor and among the members of the teaching team, so the entire staff can discover where their goals intersect and discuss how they can be reinforced to mutual advantage.

## END-OF-TERM SELF-ASSESSMENT FORM FOR FACULTY AND GSIs

At the end of the school term, we have found it helpful for both instructors and GSIs to reflect on progress toward reaching their initial goals, with special emphasis on a discussion about the ways members of the team have supported each other. These ideas can take the form of recommendations to be included in future offerings of a course.

## CHECKLIST FOR FACULTY ON WORKING WELL WITH GSIs[1]

**GSI Teaching & Resource Center, University of California, Berkeley**
**http://gsi.berkeley.edu**

### BEFORE THE TERM BEGINS

_____ Review campus and departmental policies on the hiring and mentoring of GSIs. These may include official labor contracts and Faculty Senate policies. Ascertain what your responsibilities are in guiding, observing, and giving feedback to GSIs.

_____ If Letters of Appointment are required on your campus, be aware of the content, and ensure that they have been sent to your GSIs. In addition to pay rate and dates of employment, these letters may specify the responsibilities of the GSI (e.g., grading papers, holding office hours), and may identify you as the formal supervisor.

_____ Familiarize yourself with resources available on campus to assist you in mentoring GSIs, such as materials developed by the GSI Teaching and Resource Center.

_____ Schedule a pre-term meeting with your GSIs.

_____ Complete the form **Mentoring Plan for Faculty** to set goals for your work with GSIs in the coming term.

### PRE-TERM MEETING

_____ Using the **Goal-Setting Form for GSIs**, gather information from GSIs about their previous teaching experience and their learning goals for their students.

_____ Outline your policies regarding attending lectures, turnaround time for grading student work and responding to e-mails, types of activities GSIs should use in sections or labs, and the role of sections and labs in the larger course, whether sections are optional or mandatory, and what part of the grade will be allocated for work done in section. *It is important to have clarity in expectations right from the beginning.* This is particularly true if you have several GSIs. Put these expectations in writing.

_____ Go over the syllabus with the GSIs. Make sure GSIs know how you want them to handle grade disputes, plagiarism, and cheating, and what policies GSIs may establish for their section. Point out dates GSIs should expect to grade midterms, papers, or finals so that they can plan ahead.

_____ Establish a communication plan for consulting with one another and for communicating with students. Have an agreement on what types of e-mail should be copied to one another.

_____ Establish a firm, regular meeting time for the entire term and stick to it. Should you not need to meet, you can always cancel a meeting. Have the GSIs reserve this time for the whole term.

_____ Have GSIs complete and discuss the form, **Goal Setting for GSIs**.

### DURING THE TERM

#### Regular Meetings with GSIs

_____ Meet regularly with your GSIs throughout the term.

_____ Plan a general agenda for the meetings. Effective meetings save time and make for less work.

_____ Plan ahead for upcoming assignments and the work involved for GSIs.

## Communication

\_\_\_\_\_ Respond promptly to e-mail messages from GSIs.

\_\_\_\_\_ Don't override GSI decisions (e.g., grading decisions) without talking to the GSI first.

\_\_\_\_\_ Let GSIs know when you are available to meet one-on-one should that be necessary.

\_\_\_\_\_ If you have meetings with a student, let the student's GSI know. Similarly, GSIs should keep you apprised of significant issues with students (e.g., mental health issues).

\_\_\_\_\_ Maintain a united front in public regarding policy, but be open to discussion in private.

\_\_\_\_\_ Team-taught courses with rotating professors have special challenges. Transitions from one faculty member to the next will create variations in faculty expectations and philosophies. Weekly meetings are especially important in this situation.

## Grading

Without clear policies, grading not only becomes time consuming but can also result in unevenness across sections. Discuss ways to grade efficiently. Coordination among GSIs in grading needs to be emphasized to ensure equity and fairness across sections.

\_\_\_\_\_ Be consistent and establish consistent course-wide norms, rubrics, and protocols for grading to ensure fairness.

\_\_\_\_\_ Make sure GSIs know the policies for grade disputes and regrading requests.

\_\_\_\_\_ Be clear about your expectations for the grading process. Discuss how long GSIs should spend on grading student work, what type of turnaround time is expected, and how detailed GSIs' comments should be on students' papers. Show GSIs sample graded work as models for what you expect.

\_\_\_\_\_ Meet after exams are handed in to establish norms and go over a few papers together using the grading rubric.

\_\_\_\_\_ Consider having GSIs grade in teams or as a group.

\_\_\_\_\_ Meet again after grading (prior to returning papers or exams) to make sure grades line up across sections (or, if they don't, check why that is the case).

\_\_\_\_\_ If GSIs are concerned about how long grading is taking, consider reducing assignments, revisiting the grading rubric, or doing some of the grading yourself, to reduce the burden on GSIs. If departmental resources permit, consider hiring a Reader to assist with grading.

## PROFESSIONAL DEVELOPMENT AND MENTORING

Remember that GSIs are apprentices learning to teach. See your course as a learning experience for the next generation of faculty.

_____ Have GSIs set goals for their development for the term. Revisit these goals periodically with GSIs to see how well goals are being realized.

_____ Invite GSIs to give input to the course syllabus.

_____ "Pull back the curtain" on the art of teaching: what does it take to write a lecture, how do you craft effective assignments, explain the rationale on which you designed the syllabus. Share your notes and outlines used to conduct classes and give lectures.

_____ Have GSIs visit one another's section meetings to experience a variety of teaching approaches and styles.

_____ Visit each GSI's section. Have a discussion afterward with the GSI about what you learned from observing.

_____ Encourage GSIs to contribute to the course in ways that will foster their development and growth. This could mean inviting GSIs to submit questions for exams and helping design assignments or guidelines for a project, having GSIs give a 15-minute review session to the whole class, giving GSIs the opportunity to deliver a lecture (or part of one), especially in large courses. Do remember that you are the Instructor of Record and need to provide oversight and quality control when you allow your GSIs to participate in these ways.

## AT THE END OF THE TERM

At the end of the term, it is important to gather input from GSIs on their experience of the course, both in terms of how the course supported student learning and their own development as GSIs. To this end, the following are recommendations based on input from faculty and GSIs at Berkeley:

_____ Have your GSIs revisit the goal-setting forms they completed at the beginning of the term using the **End-of-Term GSI Self-Assessment** form. Use this as an opportunity to also revisit the mentoring plan you created at the beginning of the term.

_____ Ask GSIs to write out a summary of what worked well in the course, what did not, and what should be changed the next time the course is offered.

_____ Have GSIs write a letter to the next group of GSIs providing insights on how they experienced their work over the term and what advice they would give the next group of GSIs.

_____ Have a colleague gather input from current GSIs as to how you might improve your work with the next cohort of GSIs, and then report back to you.

## MENTORING PLAN FOR FACULTY

**GSI Teaching & Resource Center, UC Berkeley http://gsi.berkeley.edu**

### QUESTIONS PERTAINING TO YOUR MENTORSHIP OF GSIs

1. What professional development goals do you have for the GSIs teaching with you in this course? For example, I would like to assist GSIs in learning how to create and use grading rubrics as a means to foster student learning and create greater transparency.
2. How might you conduct weekly meetings and provide other forms of mentorship to assist your GSIs in meeting those goals?
3. What obstacles or difficulties do you anticipate in working toward these goals with your GSIs?
4. How can you know if your GSIs have achieved those goals or are making progress toward them?
5. In what ways can a consultant from the teaching resource center or other faculty members be of assistance to you in meeting these goals?

### QUESTIONS PERTAINING TO YOUR DEVELOPMENT AS A GSI MENTOR AND AS AN INSTRUCTOR

1. What topics about teaching or in mentoring GSIs would you like to know more about?
2. What goals would you like to set for yourself as a GSI mentor over the course of the term? For example, I would like to hone my skills in doing classroom observations of GSIs.

3. What goals would you like to set for yourself as a teacher for the term? For example, I would like to integrate group work into the teaching of my large lecture class.

## GOAL-SETTING FORM FOR GSIs

**GSI Teaching & Resource Center, UC Berkeley http://gsi.berkeley.edu**

### QUESTIONS FOR GSIs PERTAINING TO STUDENT LEARNING

1. What are your learning goals for students in this course?
   For example, I want students to be able to be able to propose solutions to problems outlined in case studies; or I want students to develop writing skills required of a professional in this field.
2. How might you teach section to promote these goals?
3. What are the most pressing questions you have or what obstacles or difficulties do you anticipate in working toward these goals?
4. How can you know when your students have achieved these goals or are making progress toward them?
5. In what ways might the faculty member in charge and other GSIs be of assistance to you in meeting these goals?

### QUESTIONS PERTAINING TO YOU AS A GSI

1. What topics or issues about teaching would you like to know more about? How can you as a GSI obtain information about these topics? What resources can you seek out?
2. What goals would you like to set for yourself as a teacher over the course of this term?
   Example: Over the course of the term, I would like to learn some specific ways to get students to do the reading before coming to section, or I would like to learn how to pose more effective questions.
4. How might the faculty member and/or other GSIs help you reach these goals?
5. How can the weekly staff meetings be most useful for your professional development as an instructor?

### BACKGROUND INFORMATION

1. How many terms have you taught as a GSI at Berkeley? _____
2. Did you have teaching experience prior to coming to Berkeley? If so, what level, and how many years? YES / NO
   Level_____ Number of Years_____
3. Did you have discussion sections as an undergraduate? YES / NO

### END-OF-TERM SELF-ASSESSMENT FORM FOR FACULTY AND GSIs

**GSI Teaching & Resource Center, UC Berkeley http://gsi.berkeley.edu**

1. What goals did you set for yourself at the beginning of the term?
2. What steps did you take during the term to try to meet those goals?
3. How successful were you in accomplishing those goals?
4. What obstacles did you encounter in pursuing these goals?
5. What goals would you set for yourself the next time you teach?
6. What specific steps will you take to move toward those goals the next time you teach?

### TEACHING AND LEARNING IN HIGHER EDUCATION

### SELECTED BIBLIOGRAPHY

The following texts have proven useful to faculty and GSIs in developing their teaching skills both in the context of pedagogy seminars and in the teaching of large courses. These references can also be of use to faculty in guiding the professional development of GSIs.

Ambrose, S. (2010). *How learning works: Seven research-based principles for smart teaching.* San Francisco: Jossey-Bass.

Bain, K. (2004). *What the best college teachers do.* Cambridge, MA: Harvard University Press.

Barkley, E. Cross, K. P., & Major, C. H. (2005). *Collaborative learning techniques: A handbook for college faculty.* San Francisco: Jossey-Bass.

Bean, J. C. (2001). *Engaging ideas: The professor's guide to integrating writing, critical thinking, and active learning in the classroom.* San Francisco: Jossey-Bass.

Bligh, D. A. (2000). *What's the use of lectures?* San Francisco: Jossey-Bass.

Brookfield, S., & Preskill, S. (2005). *Discussion as a way of teaching.* San Francisco: Jossey-Bass.

Davis, B. G. (2009). *Tools for teaching.* San Francisco: Jossey-Bass.

Fink, L. D. (2003). *Creating significant learning experiences: An integrated approach to designing college courses.* New York: Routledge.

Grunert, J. (1997). *The course syllabus: A learning-centered approach.* Bolton, MA: Anker Publishing.

GSI Teaching & Resource Center (2015). *Teaching guide for GSIs.* University of California, Berkeley. Retrieved March 9, 2017 from http://gsi.berkeley.edu/.

—— (2016a). *Faculty mentoring statements.* University of California, Berkeley. Retrieved March 9, 2017 from http://gsi.berkeley.edu/programs-services/award-programs/faculty-mentor-award/faculty-award-recipients/.

—— (2016b). *Teaching effectiveness award essays.* University of California, Berkeley. Retrieved March 9, 2017 from http://gsi.berkeley.edu/programs-services/award-programs/teaching-effectiveness/.

—— (2016c). *Teaching with GSIs.* University of California, Berkeley. Retrieved March 9, 2017 from http://gsi.berkeley.edu/faculty-departments/teaching-with-gsis/.

Hedengren, B. F. (2004). *A TA's guide to teaching writing in all disciplines.* Boston, MA: Bedford/St. Martin's.

Johnson, W. B. (2007). *On being a mentor: A guide for higher education faculty.* Mahwah, NJ: Lawrence Earlbaum.

Johnson, D., Johnson, R., & Smith, K. (1991). *Cooperative learning: increasing College faculty instructional productivity.* ASHE-ERIC Higher Education Report, No. 4.

Lave, J., & Wenger, E. (1991). *Situated learning: Legitimate peripheral participation.* Cambridge: Cambridge University Press.

Meyers, C., & Jones, T. (1993). *Promoting active learning: Strategies for the college classroom.* San Francisco: Jossey-Bass.

Millis, B., & Cottell. P. (1998). *Cooperative learning for higher education faculty.* Phoenix, AZ: Oryx Press.

Mintz, J., & von Hoene, L. (2002). Research on faculty as teaching mentors: Lessons learned from a study of participants in UC Berkeley's seminar for faculty who teach with graduate student instructors. *To Improve the Academy,* 20, 77–93.

National Research Council (2000). *How people learn: Brain, mind, experience, and school: Expanded edition.* Washington, DC: National Academy Press.

Nilson, L. (2003). *Teaching at its best.* San Francisco: Anker.

Palloff, R. M., & Pratt, K. (1999). *Building learning communities in cyberspace.* San Francisco: Jossey-Bass.

Prégent, R. (1994). *Charting your course: How to prepare to teach more effectively.* Madison, WI: Magna Publications.

Prosser, M., & Trigwell, K. (1999). *Understanding learning and teaching.* Buckingham: SRHE and Open University Press.

Ramsden, P. (2003) *Learning to teach in higher education* (2nd ed.). New York: RoutledgeFalmer.

Stanley, C. A., & Porter, M. E. (2002). *Engaging large classes: Strategies for college faculty.* San Francisco: Anker/Jossey-Bass.

Svinicki, M. D. (2004). *Learning and motivation in the postsecondary classroom.* Boston, MA: Anker.

Toohey, S. (1999). *Designing courses for higher education.* Buckingham: SRHE and Open University Press.

Walvoord, B., & Anderson, V. J. (1998). *Effective grading: A tool for learning and assessment.* San Francisco: Jossey-Bass.

Weimer, M. (2002). *Learner-centered teaching.* San Francisco: Jossey-Bass.

# Notes

### CHAPTER 1

1 Graduate student instructors (GSIs), or teaching assistants, are graduate students who typically teach discussion and lab sections in large-enrollment undergraduate courses under the supervision of faculty. They are also responsible for grading, recordkeeping, and holding office hours. With the oversight and mentoring of faculty, GSIs are apprentices preparing for future careers in college teaching and research.

### CHAPTER 5

1 A literature search counts some 5,000 references pertaining to problem-based learning (Education Resources Information Center, https://eric.ed.gov). The growing visibility and impact of problem-based learning is due to its theoretical merits as well as its classroom effectiveness (Baldi, 2014; Weimer, 2002).

### APPENDIX B

1 This checklist has been developed with input from faculty and GSIs who have taken part in the annual seminar for faculty, *Teaching with GSIs,* offered by UC Berkeley's GSI Teaching & Resource Center since 1993.

# References

Abt, C. C. (1986) *Serious games.* New York: Lanham.

Adelson, B. (1981). Problem solving and the development of abstract categories in programming languages. *Memory and Cognition,* 9, 422–423.

Ambrose, S. (2010). *How learning works: Seven research-based principles for smart teaching.* San Francisco: Wiley.

Ames, C., and Archer, J. (1987). Mothers' beliefs about the role of ability and effort in school learning. *Journal of Educational Psychology,* 79, 409–414.

Atkinson, J. W. (1957). Motivational determinants of risk-taking behavior. *Psychological Review,* 64, 359–372.

Barr, R. B., and Tagg, J. (1995). From teaching to learning: A new paradigm for undergraduate education. *Change* (November–December), 13–25.

Baldi, V. (2014). The effects of a problem based learning approach on students' attitude levels: A meta-analysis. *Educational Research and Reviews,* 9(9), 272–276.

Beery, R. G. (1975). Fear of failure in the student experience. *Personnel and Guidance Journal,* 54, 190–203.

Birney, R. C., Burdick, H., & Teevan, R. C. (1969). *Fear of failure.* New York: Van Nostrand.

Black, P., & William, D. (2009). Developing the theory of formative assessment. *Educational Assessment Evaluation and Accountability,* 21, 5–31.

Bloom, B. (1956). *Taxonomy of educational objectives handbook.* New York: David Mckay Co.

Born, D. G., & Zlutnick, S. (1972). Personalized instruction. *Educational Technology,* 12, 30–34.

Born, D. G., Gledhill, S. N., & Davis, M. L. (1972). Examination performance in lecture-discussion and personalized instruction courses. *Journal of Applied Behavior Analysis,* 5, 33–43.

Boyer, E. (1998). *Reinventing undergraduate education: A blueprint for America's research universities.* New York: State University of New York of Stony Brook.

Bransford, J. D., Nitsch, K. E., & Franks, J. J. (1977). The facilitation of knowing. In R. C. Anderson, R. J. Spiro, & W. E. Montague (Eds.), *Schooling and the acquisition of knowledge.* Hillsdale, NJ: Erlbaum.

Brown, A. L., & Campione, J. C. (1990). Communities of learning and thinking, or a context by any other name. *Contributions to Human Development [Special Issue]*, 21, 108–126.

Burns, R. (1978). *Models of instructional organization: A case book on mastery learning and outcome-based education.* San Francisco: Far West Laboratory for Educational Research and Development.

Butler, D., & Winne, P. H. (1995). Feedback and self-regulated learning: A theoretical synthesis. *Review of Education Research*, 65, 245–281.

Butler, R., & Nisan, M. (1986) Effects of no feedback, task-related comments, and grade on intrinsic instruction and performance. *Journal of Educational Psychology*, 78, 210–216.

Campbell, D. N. (1974, October). On being number one: Competition in education. *Phi Delta Kappan*, 143–146.

Carver, C. S., & Scheier, M. F. (1986). Functional and dysfunctional responses to anxiety: The interaction between expectancies and self-focused attention. In R. Schwrzer (Ed.), *Self-related cognitions in anxiety and motivation.* (pp. 111–141). Hillsdale, NJ: Erlbaum.

Chase, W. C., & Simon, H. A. (1973). Perception in chess. *Cognitive Psychology*, 4, 55–81.

Christie, A. (1931). *The floating admiral.* New York: Doubleday, Doran Co.

Churchill, W. S. (1923). *The world crisis* (Vol. 1, Part 1). New York: Scribner's Sons.

Clement, J. (1982). *Analogical reasoning patterns in expert problem solving: Proceedings of the Fourth Annual Conference of the Cognitive Science Society.* Ann Arbor: University of Michigan Press.

Combs, A. W. (1957). *The myth of competition: Childhood education.* Washington, DC: Association for Childhood Education International.

Condry, J. D., & Chambers, J. (1978). Intrinsic motivation and the process of learning. In M. R. Lepper & D. Greene (Eds.), *The hidden costs of rewards: New perspectives on the psychology of human motivation* (pp. 61–84). Hillsdale, NJ: Lawrence Erlbaum Associates, Inc.

Corno, L. (1993). The best laid plans: Modern conceptions of volition and educational research. *Educational Research*, 22, 14–22.

Covington, M. V. (1985a). The effects of multiple-testing opportunities on rote and conceptual learning and retention. *Human Learning*, 4, 57–72.

Covington, M. V. (1985b). Text anxiety: Causes and effects over time. In H. M. van der Ploeg, R. Schwarzer, & C. D. Spielberger (Eds.), *Advances in test anxiety research* (Vol. 4, pp. 55–68). Hillsdale, NJ: Erlbaum.

Covington, M. V. (1998). *The will to learn: A guide for motivating young people.* New York: Cambridge University Press.

Covington M. V. (1999). Caring about learning: The nature and nurturing of subject-matter appreciation. *Educational Psychologist*, 34, 127–136.

Covington, M. V. (2000a). Goal theory, motivation, and school achievement: An integrative review. *Annual Review of Psychology*, 51, 171–200.

Covington, M. V. (2000b). Intrinsic versus extrinsic motivation in schools: A reconciliation. *Current Directions in Psychological Science*, 9, 22–25.

Covington, M. V. (2001). *Making the grade: A self-worth perspective on motivation and school reform.* New York: Cambridge University Press.

Covington, M. V. (2002). Rewards and intrinsic motivation: A needs-based, developmental perspective. In T. Urdan & F. Pajares (Eds.), *Motivation of adolescents* (pp. 169–192). New York: Academic Press.

Covington, M. V. (2004). Self-worth theory goes to college, or do our motivation theories motivate? In D. M. McInerney & S. Van Etten (Eds.), *Big theories revisited* (pp. 91–114). Greenwich, CT: Information Age Publishing.

Covington, M. V. (2005). Foreword. In A. J. Elliot & C. S. Dweck (Eds.), *Handbook of competence and motivation* (pp. xi–xii). New York: Guilford Press.

Covington, M. V. (2006). How can optimal self-esteem be facilitated in children and adolescents by parents and teachers? In M. H. Kernis (Ed.), *Self esteem: Issues and answers* (pp. 125–141). New York: Psychology Press.

Covington, M. V. (2009). Self-worth theory: Retrospective and prospects. In A. Wigfield & K. Wentzel (Eds.), *Handbook of motivation at school* (pp. 141–170). New York: Erlbaum.

Covington, M. V. (2014). Creativity reconsidered. Unpublished manuscript. Department of Psychology, University of California, Berkeley.

Covington, M. V., & Beery, R. G. (1976). *Self-worth and school learning.* New York: Holt, Rinehart & Winston.

Covington, M. V., & Dray, E. (1976). The developmental course of achievement motivation: A need-based approach. In A. Wigfield & J. S. Eccles (Eds.), *Development of achievement motivation* (pp. 33–56). New York: Academic Press.

Covington, M. V., & Elliot, A. J. (Eds.) (2001). *Special issue of* Educational Psychological Review. New York: Plenum Press.

Covington, M. V., & Mueller, K. (2000). Intrinsic versus extrinsic motivation: An approach/avoidance reformulation. In M. V. Covington & A. J. Elliot (Eds.), *Special issue of educational psychology review* (pp. 111–130). New York: Plenum Press.

Covington, M. V., & Omelich, C. L. (1979). Effort: The double-edged sword in school achievement. *Journal of Educational Psychology, 71,* 169–182.

Covington, M. V., & Omelich, C. L. (1981). As failures mount: Affective and cognitive consequences of ability demotion in the classroom. *Journal of Educational Psychology, 73,* 799–808.

Covington, M. V., & Omelich, C. L. (1982). Achievement anxiety, performance, and behavioral instruction: A cost/benefits analysis. In R. Schwarzer, H. M. van der Ploeg, & C. D. Spielberger (Eds.), *Advances in text anxiety research* (Vol. 1, pp. 139–154). New York: Erlbaum.

Covington, M. V., & Omelich, C. L. (1987a). "I knew it cold before the exam:" A test of the anxiety-blockage hypothesis. *Journal of Educational Psychology, 77,* 446–459.

Covington, M. V., & Omelich, C. L. (1987b). Item difficulty and test performance among high-anxious and low-anxious students. In R. Schwarzer, H. M. van der Ploeg, & C. D. Spielberger (Eds.), *Advances in test anxiety research* (Vol. 5, pp. 127–135). Hillsdale, NJ. Erlbaum.

Covington, M. V., & Omelich, C. L. (1988). Achievement dynamics: The interaction of motives, cognitions and emotions overtime. *Anxiety Journal, 1,* 165–183.

Covington, M. V., & Omelich, C. L. (1990). The second time around: Coping with repeated failures. Unpublished manuscript, Department of Psychology, University of California, Berkeley.

Covington, M. V., Spratt, M. F., & Omelich, C. L. (1990). Is effort enough, or does diligence count too? Student and teacher reactions to effort stability in failure. *Journal of Educational Psychology, 72*, 717–729.

Covington, M. V., & Wiedenaupt, S. (1997). Turning work into play: The nature and nurturing of intrinsic task engagement. In R. Perry & J. C. Smart (Eds.), *Effective teaching in higher education: Research and practice* (Special ed., pp. 101–114). New York: Agathon Press.

Cox, R. (2009). *The college fear factor: How students and professors misunderstand one another.* Cambridge, MA: Harvard University Press.

Culler, R. E., & Holahan, C. J. (1980). Text anxiety and academic performance: The effects of study-related behaviors. *Journal of Educational Psychology, 72*, 16–20.

Deci, E. L. (1975). *Intrinsic motivation.* New York: Plenum.

Diener, C. T., & Dweck, C. S. (1978). An analysis of learned helplessness: Continuous changes in performance, strategy and achievement cognitions following failure. *Journal of Personality and Social Psychology, 36*, 451–462.

Diener, C. T., & Dweck, C. S. (1980). An analysis of learned helplessness II: The processing of success. *Journal of Personality and Social Psychology, 39*, 940–952.

Dillon, J. T. (1982). Problem finding and solving. *Journal of Creative Behavior, 16*, 97–111.

Dweck, C. S., & Bempechat, J. (1983). Children's theories of intelligence: Consequences for learning. In S. G. Paris, G. M. Olson, & H. M. Stevensen (Eds.), *Learning and motivation in the classroom* (pp. 239–256). Hillsdale, NJ: Erlbaum.

Elliot, A. J., & Dweck, C. S. (2005). *Handbook of competence and motivation.* New York: Guilford Press.

Ellis, A., & Kraus, W. J. (1977). *Overcoming procrastination.* New York: Institute of Rational Living.

Feldman, K. A. (1976). The superior college teacher from the student's view. *Research in Higher Education, 5*, 243–288.

Fogg, P. (2004). Hello ... I must be going. *The Chronicle of Higher Education, 50* (41), A10.

Freeman, S., Eddy, S. L., McDonough, M., Smith, M. K., Okoroafor, N., Jordt, H., & Wenderoth, M. P. (2014). Active learning increases student performance in science, engineering, and mathematics. *Proceedings of the National Academy of Sciences USA, 111*, 8410–8415.

Fried, R. (2001). *The passionate learner: How teachers and parents can help children reclaim the joy of discovery.* Boston: Beacon Press.

Getzels, J. W. (1975). Problem-finding and the inventiveness of solutions. *Journal of creative behavior, 9*, 12–18.

Glick, M. L., & Holyoak, K. (1983). Schema induction and analogical transfer. *Cognitive Psychology, 15*, 1–38.

Goldsmith, T. E., & Johnson, P. J. (1989). A structural assessment of classroom learning. In R. W. Schvaneveldt (Ed.), *Pathfinder associative networks: Studies in knowledge organization* (pp. 231–254). Norwood, NJ: Ablex.

Gough, G. H. (1966). Graduation from high school as predicted from the California Psychological Inventory. *Psychology in the Schools*, 3, 208–216.

Gough, G. H. (1968). College attendance among high-aptitude students as predicted from the California Psychological Inventory. *Journal of Counseling Psychology*, 15, 269–278.

Hafer, G. (2016). Unexpected benefits of grading effort and habit. faculty focus: Higher Ed teaching strategies from Magna Publications, March 7.

Harari, O., & Covington, M. V. (1981). Reactions to achievement behavior from a teacher and student perspective: A developmental analysis. *American Educational Research Journal*, 18, 15–28.

Hativa, N. (1998). Lack of clarity in university teaching: A case study. *Higher Education*, 36(3), 353–381.

Hativa, N., & Birenbaum, M. (2000). Who prefers what? Disciplinary differences in students' approaches to teaching and learning styles. *Research in Higher Education*, 4(2), 209–236.

Heider, F. (1958). *The psychology of interpersonal relations*. New York: Wiley.

Hill, K. T. (1980). Motivation, evaluation, and educational testing policy. In L. J. Fyans (Ed.), *Achievement motivation: Recent trends in theory and research* (pp. 34–95). New York: Springer.

Hill, K. T. (1984). Debilitating motivation and educational testing policy: A major problem, possible solutions, and policy applications. In R. Ames & C. Ames (Eds.), *Research on motivation in education: Student motivation* (pp. 245–274). New York: Academic Press.

Hunt, E. (1994). Problem solving. In R. J. Sternberg (Ed.), *Thinking and problem solving* (pp. 215–232). San Diego, CA: Academic Press.

Karp, D., & Yoels, W. (1976). The college classroom: Some observations on the meaning of student participation. *Sociology and Social Research*, 60, 421–439.

Khanna, P. (2016). A new map for America. *The New York Times*, April 25.

Kohn, A. (1993). *Punished by rewards*. New York: Houghton Mifflin.

Kuh, G. (2008). *High-impact educational practices: What they are, who has access to them, and why they matter*. Washington, DC: American Association of Colleges and Universities.

Kuhl, J., & Blankenship, V. (1979). Behavioral change in a constant environment: Shift to more difficult tasks with constant probability of success. *Journal of Personality and Social Psychology*, 37, 551–563.

Kulik, J. A., Kulik, C. C., & Cohen, P. A. (1979). A meta-analysis of outcome studies of Kellar's personalized system of instruction. *American Psychologist*, 34, 307–318.

Larkin, J. J., McDermott, J., Simon, D. P., & Simom, H. A. (1980). Modes of competency in solving physics problems. *Cognitive Science*, 4, 317–345.

Lepper, M. R., Greene, D., & Nisbett, R. E. (1973). Undermining children's intrinsic interest with extrinsic rewards: A test of the "overjustification" hypothesis. *Journal of Personality and Social Psychology*, 28, 129–137.

Lloyd-Jones, R. (1977). The politics of research into the teaching of composition. *College Composition and Communication*, 28, 218–222.

Locke, E. A., & Latham, G. P. (1984). *Goal setting: A motivational technique that works!* Englewood Cliffs, NJ: Prentice-Hall.

Manchester, W. (1983). *The last lion: Winston Spencer Churchill*. Boston, MA: Little, Brown.

Marshall, H. H. (1988). Work or learning: Implications of classroom metaphors. *Educational Researcher, 9*, 9–16.

Maslach, C. (2015). Personal communication.

McClelland, D. C. (1961). *The achieving society*. Princeton, NJ: Van Nostrand.

McClure, J. R., Sonak, B., & Suen, H. K.(1999). Conceptual map assessment of classroom learning: Reliability, validity, and logistical practicality. *Journal of Research in Science Teaching, 36*, 475–492.

McTighe, J. & Wiggins, G. (2013) *Essential questions: Opening doors to student understanding*. Alexandria, VA: Association for Supervision and Curriculum Development.

Merriam Webster (2011). *Webster's American English Dictionary. New Edition*. Springfield, MA: Federal Street Press.

Merrow, J. (2005). The undergraduate experience: Survival of the fittest. *The New York Times*, April 24.

Merton, R. K. (1949). *Social theory and social structure*. Glencoe, IL: Free Press.

Naveh-Benjamin, M. (1985). A comparison of training programs intended for different types of test-anxious students. Paper presented at symposium on information processing and motivation, American Psychological Association, Los Angeles.

Newell, A., & Simon, H. A. (1972). *Human problem solving*. Englewood Cliffs, NJ: Prentice-Hall.

Newman, R. S. (1990). Children's help-seeking in the classroom: The role of motivational factors and attitudes. *Journal of Educational Psychology, 82*, 71–80.

Newman, R. S., & Goldin, L. (1990). Children's reluctance to seek help with schoolwork. *Journal of Educational Psychology, 82*, 92–100.

Nilson, L. (2007). *The graphic syllabus and the outcomes: Communicating your course*. San Francisco: Wiley.

Norem, J. K., & Cantor, N. (1986). Defensive pessimism: Harnessing anxiety as motivation. *Journal of Personality and Social Psychology, 51*, 1208–1217.

Omelich, C. L. (1974). Attribution and achievement in the classroom: The self-fulfilling prophecy. Paper presented at the meeting of the California Personnel and Guidance Association, San Francisco.

Palmer, P. (1998). *The courage to teach: Exploring the inner landscape of teacher's life*. San Francisco: Jossey-Bass.

Perry, R. P. (1981). *Educational seduction: Some implications for teaching evaluation and improvement (Rep. No. 7)*. Vancouver, British Columbia, Canada: University of British Columbia, Center for Improving Teaching and Evaluation.

Perry. R. P., & Dickens, W. J. (1984) Perceived control in the college classroom: Response-outcome contingency training and instructor expressiveness effects on student achievement and causal attributions. *Journal of Educational Psychology, 76*, 966–981.

Renninger, K. A, Hidi, S. A., & Krapp, A. (1992). *The role of interest in learning and development in learning a task*. Hillsdale, NJ: Lawrence Erlbaum Associates.

Rocklin, T., & O'Donnell, A. M. (1986). Self-adapted testing: A performance-improving variant of computerized adaptive testing. Paper presented as a poster at the annual meeting of the American Psychological Association, Washington, DC.

Rosenberg, J. (1965). *Society and the adolescent self-image*. Princeton, NJ: Princeton University Press.

Rothblum, E. D., Solomon, L. J., & Murakami, J. (1986). Affective, cognitive and behavioral differences between high and low procrastinators. *Journal of Counseling Psychology, 33*, 387–394.

Ryan, R. M., & Deci, E. L. (2000). Self-determination theory and the facilitation of intrinsic motivation, social development, and well-being. *American Psychologist, 55*, 68–78.

Sarason, I. G., & Potter, E. H. (1983). Self-monitoring: Cognitive processes and performance. Technical Report prepared for Office of Naval Research, December 12.

Schlesinger, A. (2008). *The politics of hope*. Princeton, NJ: Princeton University Press.

Schoenfeld, A. H. (1985). *Mathematical problem solving*. New York: Academic Press.

Simon, H. A. (1973). The structure of ill-structured problems. *Artificial Intelligence, 4*, 181–202.

Simon, H. A. (1980). Problem solving and education. In D. T. Tuma & F. Reif (Eds.), *Problem solving and education: Issues in teaching and research*. Hillsdale, NJ: Erlbaum.

Smith, T. W., Snyder, C. R., and Handelsman, M. M. (1982). On the self-serving function of an academic wooden leg: Test anxiety as a self-handicapping strategy. *Journal of Personality and Social Psychology, 42*, 314–321.

Snyder, C. R. (1984). Excuses, excuses: They sometimes actually work to relieve the burden of blame. *Psychology Today, 18*, 50–55.

Speilberger, C. D. (1972). Anxiety as an emotional state. In C. D. Speilberger (Ed.), *Anxiety: Current trends in theory and research* (Vol. 1, pp. 23–49). New York: Academic Press.

Speilberger, C. D. (1985). Personal communication.

Spence, J. T., & Helmreich, R. L. (1983). Achievement-related motives and behaviors. In J. T. Spence (Ed.), *Achievement and achievement motives*. (pp. 7–74). San Francisco: Freeman.

Spenner, K. I. (1985). The upgrading and downgrading of occupations: Issues, evidence, and implications for education. *Review of Educational Research, 55*, 125–154.

Steinberg, E. (1989). Cognition and learner control: A literature review, 1977–1988. *Journal of Computer-Based Instruction, 16*(4), 117–121.

Stevens, E. (1988). Tinkering with teaching. *Review of Higher Education, 12*(4), 63–78.

Stevenson, J. A. (1921). *The project method of teaching*. New York: MacMillan.

Thompson, T. (1993). Characteristics of self-worth protection in achievement behavior. *British Journal of Educational Psychology, 63*, 469–488.

Tompkins, J. (1990). Pedagogy of the distressed. *College English, 52*, 653–660.

Wallace, D. W., & Mintzes, J. J. (1990). The conceptual map as a research tool: Exploring conceptual change in biology. *Journal of Research in Science Teaching*, 27, 1033–1052.

Walvoord, B. E., & Anderson, V. J. (1998). *Effective grading: A tool for learning and assessment.* San Francisco: Jossey-Bass.

Weimer, M. (2002). *Learner-centered teaching: Five key changes to practice.* San Francisco: Jossey-Bass.

Weiss, D. J. (1983). *New horizons in testing: Latent trait test theory and computerized adaptive testing.* New York: Academic Press.

Whitehead, A. N. (1929). *The aims of education.* New York: New American Library.

Wine, J. D. (1980). Cognitive-attentional theory of test anxiety. In I. G. Sarason (Ed.), *Test anxiety: Theory, research, and applications* (pp. 349–385). Hillsdale, NJ: Erlbaum.

Zeidner, M., & Matthews, G. (2005). Evaluation anxiety: Current theory and research. In A. J. Elliot & C. S. Dweck (Eds.), *Handbook of competence and motivation* (pp. 141–163). New York: Guilford.

# Index